BERLITZ®

Chinese

PHRASE BOOK
& DICTIONARY

D0672634

Easy to use features

- Handy thematic colour coding
- Quick Reference Section—opposite page
- Tipping Guide—inside back cover
- Quick reply panels throughout

How best to use this phrase book

● We suggest that you start with the **Guide to pronunciation** (pp. 8-10), then go on to **Some basic expressions** (pp. 11-16). This gives you not only a minimum vocabulary, but also helps you get used to pronouncing the language.

● Consult the **Contents** pages (3-5) for the section you need. In each chapter you'll find travel facts, hints and useful information. Simple phrases are followed by a list of words applicable to the situation.

● Separate, detailed contents lists are included at the beginning of the extensive **Eating out** and **Shopping guide** sections (Menus, p. 40, Shops and services, p. 97).

● If you want to find out how to say something in Chinese, your fastest look-up is via the **Dictionary** section (pp. 166-190). This not only gives you the word, but is also cross-referenced to its use in a phrase on a specific page.

● If you want to learn more about constructing sentences, check the **Basic grammar** (pp. 160-163).

● Note the **colour margins** are indexed in Chinese and English to help both listener and speaker. And, in addition, there is also an **index in Chinese** for the use of your listener.

● Throughout the book, this symbol ☞ suggests phrases your listener might use to answer you. If you still can't understand, hand the phrase book to the Chinese-speaker to encourage pointing to an appropriate answer.

Library of Congress Catalog Card No. 87-70573

Revised edition—7th printing 1995   Printed in Switzerland

Contents

4

Acknowledgments
We are particularly grateful to Hu Xiaoming, Sun Daqing and Paddy Jackson for their help in the preparation of this book.

THE LANGUAGE

汉语简介

Chinese characters

Several thousand years ago, while still in the Stone Age, China had already developed good pictorial techniques. Though the designs used in this era in a certain way constituted the dawn of writing, they were virtually limited to representation of men, animals and objects; feelings and other abstract ideas could not as yet be expressed in this manner.

The ancient hunting and gathering societies gradually gave way to more sophisticated agricultural ways of life, with a settled, rather than a nomadic mode of existence. Little by little, clans and tribes coalesced into something more like small states. Human relations were expanded and languages merged. By this stage, it would have been quite clear to those in the know that the human figure in the drawing shown below was meant to represent "man" in general. Art was put to the service of language, giving rise to an ideographic system of writing in which drawings were progressively reduced to their basic elements.

(Stag and hunter)

stag   bow*   man

	stag	bow*	man	
2100 B.C.				
221 B.C.				
today	鹿	弓	又	人

* and action by hand

In 1890, bones and tortoise shells bearing engraved characters dating back to the *Shāng* dynasty (around 1600-1066 B.C.) were discovered in Henan Province. Altogether, around 3,500 ideograms from this period have been identified, though only 1,500 of them are in a sufficient state of preservation to be accurately interpreted.

The *Zhōu* (1066-256 B.C.) replaced the *Shāng*, taking over their culture, technology and writing. During the period of ascendancy of the Eastern *Zhōu*, the country split into a number of political units with various writing systems. In 221 B.C., the *Qín* dynasty united the country, at the same time standardizing the system of writing in the *zhuàn* style.

Since their primitive beginnings, Chinese characters have changed considerably, principally in the first half of their history. Though their strictly representational nature has largely disappeared, the original underlying structure remains. Today, about 50,000 ideograms exist, of which 5,000 or so are in common use.

The various dialects of Chinese, spoken by 94% of the population, are known collectively as *hàn-yǔ*. Though a number of these dialects are mutually unintelligible, Chinese from all parts of the country communicate verbally in *pǔ tōng huà*, a kind of *lingua franca*. The written language is everywhere the same, and is understood by all.

After 1949, the Chinese government set up a committee for the reform of Chinese writing. This committee has succeeded in simplifying a large number of characters in everyday use, either by going back to an original form of the ideograms or by reducing the number of strokes involved. In 1958, the National People's Assembly also approved a rational system for the transcription of Chinese characters into the Latin alphabet, called *pinyin* — the transcription you will find in this book. Traditionally, Chinese was written in columns and read from top to bottom, and right to left. Nowadays, however, the policy is to write horizontally from left to right.

PRONUNCIATION

语音

Guide to pronunciation

If you follow carefully the indications supplied below, you will have no difficulty in reading the transliterations in such a way as to make yourself understood. In addition, listening to the native speakers in China and constant practice will help you to improve your accent. (This book also contains the Chinese script. If, despite your efforts, your listener does not seem to understand you, show him or her the book and indicate what you want to say.)

Chinese is composed less of vowels and consonants than of syllables. The transliteration used in this book is based on the official Chinese phonetic system *(pīn-yīn)*. A transliteration is a representation of the sounds of the language in the Latin (our) alphabet, as opposed to traditional Chinese characters. It can be read quite easily once a few rules have been mastered. Still, any attempt of this kind is open to criticism, for some of the sounds of the Chinese tongue cannot be exactly reproduced by the letters of the English alphabet.

For ease of reading and pronunciation, we have broken down multisyllabic Chinese words by inserting hyphens in the *pīn-yīn* transliteration. For example, *zhōngguó* (China) becomes *zhōng-guó*.

Tones

Every syllable in Chinese has a definite tone, and therefore tones are as important as vowels and consonants in forming syllables. The difference in tone is the deciding factor in the meaning of words. For example, *mài* with falling tone means "sell" and *mǎi* with falling-rising tone means "buy".

There are four basic tones in Mandarin Chinese:

- 1st tone (high level): is spoken high and the voice neither rises nor falls

- 2nd tone (rising): starts with the voice lower but ends up as high as in the first tone

- 3rd tone (falling-rising): starts with the voice lower than the second tone, dips and then rises in a rather drawn-out way

- 4th tone (falling): the voice falls from high to low

Every syllable is pronounced on one of these four tones, except when it is unstressed. In this case, the tone distinctions disappear, and the unstressed syllable is pronounced light and short. In speech, when two 3rd tones follow one another, the first automatically becomes 2nd tone.

Vowels

Letter **Approximate pronunciation**

like **a** in c**a**r (but with no **r**-sound)

like **e** in h**e**r (but with no **r**-sound)

1) like **ee** in b**ee**
2) after **c, s, z, ch, sh, zh, r**, like **e** in h**e**r (with no **r**-sound)

like **aw** in s**aw**

like **oo** in sp**oo**n

similar to German **ü** or **u** in French "l**u**ne"; round your lips and try to say **ee**

语音

Though Chinese syllables most often end with a straigh
vowel, they may also end in a diphthong or a vowel and a
consonant. A few of these letter combinations are no
pronounced exactly as one would expect, notably the fol
lowing:

ou as in **soul**   **ian** like **yen**   **ui** like **way**

In compound vowels (diphthongs and triphthongs) the pro
nunciation starts from one vowel and "glides" to or to
wards another vowel; e.g. **i, ia, iao.**

Consonants

These are pronounced approximately as in English, with the
following exceptions:

c	like **ts** in i**ts**, followed by a strong puff of breath
ch	like **ch** in **ch**urch, but with the tip of the tongue turned up an back to touch the roof of the mouth
g	always as in **g**ive
h	like **ch** in Scottish lo**ch**
j	like **j** in **j**eer (strongly fronted: pronounced as near to the fror of the mouth as possible)
q	similar to **ch** in **ch**eap
r	like English **r**, but with the tip of the tongue turned up an back to touch the roof of the mouth, so that it sounds some thing like the **s** in plea**s**ure
s	like **s** in **s**it
sh	like **sh** in **sh**oe, but with the tip of the tongue turned up an back to touch the roof of the mouth
x	like **sh** in **sh**eep (strongly fronted), but with lips widely spread
y	like **y** in **y**ard
z	like **ds** in li**ds**
zh	like **j** in **j**ug, but with the tip of the tongue turned up and bac to touch the roof of the mouth

The three consonants **k, p** and **t** should be pronounced with
a strong puff of breath.

Some basic expressions

Correct/Is.*	对/是。	duì/shì
Incorrect/Is not.*	不对/不是。	bú duì/bú shì
Please.	请。	qǐng
Thank you.	谢谢。	xiè-xie
Thank you very much.	十分感谢。	shí-fēn gǎn-xiè
That's all right/ You're welcome.	不客气。	bú kè-qi

Greetings 问候

Good morning/ Good afternoon/ Good evening.	你好。	nǐ hǎo**
Good night.	晚安。	wǎn-ān
Goodbye.	再见。	zài-jiàn
See you soon.	回头见。	huí-tóu-jiàn
This is Mr. …	这是…先生。	zhè shì … xiān-sheng
This is Mrs. …	这是…夫人。	zhè shì … fū-rén
This is Miss…	这是…小姐。	zhè shì … xiǎo-jie
How do you do? (Pleased to meet you.)	你好，很高兴能认识你。	nǐ-hǎo hěn gāo-xìng néng rèn-shi ni
How are you?	你好吗？	nǐ hǎo ma
Very well, thank you.	很好，谢谢。	hěn hǎo xiè-xie
And you?	你呢？	nǐ ne
Fine.	很好。	hěn hǎo
How's life?	怎么样，忙吗？	zěn-me yàng máng ma
Not bad/So so.	还可以。	hái kě-yǐ

---

* The Chinese do not say "yes" and "no", instead they repeat the verb. E.g. Do you speak Chinese? I speak. or I don't speak. You may also answer with the words "correct" or "incorrect".

** The nǐ form is the general word for "you". The special polite form nín should be used when talking to an older person, a business partner, or anyone else to whom special respect is due.

I beg your pardon?/ Sorry!	对不起。	duì-bu-qǐ
Excuse me. (May I get past?)	对不起。	duì-bu-qǐ
Excuse me. (Can you tell me…?)	请问…	qǐng wèn

Questions 问话

Where?	哪儿？	nǎr
Where is there …?	哪儿有…？	nǎr yǒu
Where is…?	…在哪儿？	…zài nǎr
Where are…?	…在哪儿？	…zài nǎr
Where can I buy/ get…?	我在哪儿能买/找到…？	wǒ zài nǎr néng mǎi/ zhǎo dào
When? (time)	几点？	jǐ diǎn
When? (date)	几号？	jǐ hào
When does … open?	…几点开门？	…jǐ diǎn kāi mén
When does … close?	…几点关门？	…jǐ diǎn guān mén
How?	怎么？	zěn-me
How far?	多远？	duō yuǎn
How long?	多长时间？	duō cháng shí-jiān
How much? (money)	多少钱？	duō-shao qián
How much/ How many?	多少/多少个？	duō-shao/duō-shao ge
How much does this cost?	这要多少钱？	zhè yào duō-shao qián
Who?	谁？	shéi
Why?	为什么？	wèi shén-me
Which?	哪个？	nǎ ge
What?	什么？	shén-me
What do you call this?	这叫什么？	zhè jiào shén-me
What do you call that?	那叫什么？	nà jiào shén-me
What does this mean?	这是什么意思？	zhè shì shén-me yì-si
What does that mean?	那是什么意思？	nà shì shén-me yì-si

Do you speak...? 你会说…？

Do you speak English?	你会说英语吗？	nǐ huì shuō yīng-yǔ ma
Does anyone here speak English?	这儿谁会说英语？	zhèr shéi huì shuō yīng-yǔ
Do you speak...?	你会说…吗？	nǐ huì shuō ... ma
French	法语	fǎ-yǔ
German	德语	dé-yǔ
Spanish	西班牙语	xī-bān-yá-yǔ
I don't speak Chinese.	我不会说汉语。	wǒ bú huì shuō hàn-yǔ
I only speak a little Chinese.	我只会说一点儿汉语。	wǒ zhǐ huì shuō yì-diǎnr hàn-yǔ
Could you speak more slowly?	请说慢点儿。	qǐng shuō màn dianr
Could you repeat that?	请再说一遍。	qǐng zài shuō yí-biàn
Please write it down.	请写下来。	qǐng xiě xià lai
Can you translate this for me?	请把这个翻译出来。	qǐng bǎ zhèi-ge fān-yì chū lai
Please point to the ... in the book.	请在这本书里找出这个…	qǐng zài zhè běn shū li zhǎo chū zhèi-ge
word/phrase	词/短语	cí/duǎn-yǔ
Please point to the sentence in the book.	请在这本书里找出这句话。	qǐng zài zhè běn shū li zhǎo chū zhè jù huà
Just a moment.	请等一下。	qǐng děng yí-xià
I'll see if I can find it in this book.	看我能否在这本书里找到。	kàn wǒ néng fǒu zài zhè běn shū li zhǎo dào
I understand.	我懂了。	wǒ dǒng le
I don't understand.	我不懂。	wǒ bù dǒng

Can/May...? 能…吗？

Can I...?	我能…吗？	wǒ néng ... ma
Can we...?	我们能…吗？	wǒ-men néng ... ma
Can I/we have...?	能给我/我们…吗？	néng gěi wǒ/ wǒ-men ... ma

Can you show me...?	你能让我看看…吗？	nǐ néng ràng wǒ kàn-kan ... ma
Can you tell me...?	你能告诉我…吗？	nǐ néng gào-su wǒ ... ma
Can you help me, please?	你能帮助我吗？	nǐ néng bāng-zhù wǒ ma
Can you direct me to...?	去…怎么走？	qù ... zěn-me zǒu

Wanting 需要

I'd like (to have)...	我想（要）…	wǒ xiǎng (yào)
We'd like (to have)...	我们想（要）…	wǒ-men xiǎng (yào)
Please give me...	请给我…	qǐng gěi wǒ
Give it to me, please.	请把这个给我。	qǐng bǎ zhè-ge gěi wǒ
Please bring me...	请给我拿…	qǐng gěi wǒ ná
Show me...	让我看看…	ràng wǒ kàn-kan
I'm looking for...	我找…	wǒ zhǎo
I'm hungry.	我饿了。	wǒ è le
I'm thirsty.	我渴了。	wǒ kě le
I'd like something to eat.	我想吃点什么。	wǒ xiǎng chī diǎn shén-me
I'd like something to drink.	我想喝点什么。	wǒ xiǎng hē diǎn shén-me
I'm tired.	我累了。	wǒ lèi le
I'm lost.	我迷路了。	wǒ mí-lù le
It's important.	这很重要。	zhè hěn zhòng-yào
It's urgent.	这很紧急。	zhè hěn jǐn-jí

It is/There is... 这是/有…

It is...	这是…	zhè shì
Is it...?	这是…吗？	zhè shì ... ma
It isn't...	这不是…	zhè bú shì
There is/There are...	有…	yǒu
Is there/Are there...?	有…吗？	yǒu ... ma

| There isn't/
There aren't… | 没有… | méi yǒu |
| There isn't any/
There aren't any. | 没有。 | méi yǒu |

It's… 这…

big/small	大/小	dà/xiǎo
quick/slow	快/慢	kuài/màn
early/late	早/晚	zǎo/wǎn
cheap/expensive	便宜/贵	pián-yi/guì
near/far	近/远	jìn/yuǎn
hot/cold	热/冷	rè/lěng
full/empty	满/空	mǎn/kōng
easy/difficult	容易/难	róng-yi/nán
heavy/light	重/轻	zhòng/qīng
open/shut	开/关	kāi/guān
right/wrong	对/错	duì/cuò
old/new	旧/新	jiù/xīn
old/young	年老/年轻	nián-lǎo/nián-qīng
beautiful/ugly	好看/难看	hǎo-kàn/nán-kàn
good/bad	好/坏	hǎo/huài
better/worse	好些/更坏了	hǎo xiē/gèng huài le
long/short	长/短	cháng/duǎn
free (vacant)/ occupied	没人/有人	méi rén/yǒu rén
here/there	这儿/那儿	zhèr/nàr

Quantities 数量

a little/a lot	一点儿/很多	yì-diǎnr/hěn duō
some	一些	yì-xiē
few/a few	很少/有几个	hěn-shǎo/yǒu jǐ-ge
much/many	很多/很多	hěn duō/hěn duō
more/less	多些/少些	duō xiē/shǎo xiē
more than/less than	超过/不到	chāo-guò/bú dào
enough/too	足够/太	zú-gòu/tài

SOME BASIC EXPRESSIONS

一些基本语汇

A few more useful words 一些常用词汇

at	在	zài
on	在…上	zài … shàng
in	在…里	zài … li
to	向	xiàng
from	从	cóng
for	为了	wèi-le
with*	有	yǒu
with (person)	跟…一起	gēn … yì-qǐ
without	没有	méi-yǒu
before (place)	在…前面	zài … qián-miàn
before (time)	前	qián
after	后	hòu
through	经过	jīng-guò
towards	向	xiàng
until	直到	zhí-dào
during	在…的时候	zài … de shí-hou
next to	在…旁边儿	zài … páng-biānr
near	在…附近	zài … fù-jìn
behind	在…后面	zài … hòu-miàn
between	在…中间	zài … zhōng-jiān
since	从	cóng
above	在…上	zài … shàng
below	在…下	zài … xià
under	在…下面	zài … xià-miàn
inside	里边儿	lǐ-bianr
outside	外边儿	wài-bianr
upstairs	楼上	lóu-shàng
downstairs	楼下	lóu-xià
and	和	hé
or	还是	hái-shì
but	但是	dàn-shì
not	不	bù
never	从来没有	cóng-lái méi-yǒu
very	很	hěn
too (also)	也	yě
yet	还没有	hái méi-yǒu
soon	很快就	hěn kuài jiù
now	现在	xiàn-zài
then	然后	rán-hòu
perhaps	也许	yě-xǔ
only	只	zhǐ

* If you want to use the word "with" followed by an object, i.e. room with a view, cup with a handle, then you must say 有 *yǒu*. If you are talking about people, i.e. with my sister, with a friend, you must use a different construction 跟…一起 *gēn … yì-qǐ*.

Arrival

检验护照
jiǎn-yàn hù-zhào
PASSPORT CONTROL

Here's my...	这是我的…	zhè shì wǒ-de
passport	护照	hù-zhào
vaccination certificate	预防注射证	yù-fáng-zhù-shè-zhèng
visa	签证	qiān-zhèng
I'll be staying...	我将停留…	wǒ jiāng tíng-liú
a few days	几天	jǐ tiān
a week	一星期	yì xīng-qī
a month	一个月	yí-ge yuè
I don't know yet.	还不一定。	hái bù yí-dìng
I'm here on holiday.	我来这里渡假。	wǒ lái zhè-lǐ dù-jià
I'm here on business.	我因工作来这里。	wǒ yīn gōng-zuò lái zhè-lǐ
I'm a student.	我是学生。	wǒ shì xué-sheng
I'm here with a group.	我是团体来的。	wǒ shì tuán-tǐ lái de

海关
hǎi-guān
CUSTOMS

Before arriving you will have filled out a baggage-declaration form listing any watches, jewellery, cameras or electronic gadgets in your possession. When you leave China at the end of your stay, you may be asked to prove that you are taking with you all the items on the list.

In general, it is forbidden to carry into the People's Republic of China the following: arms and explosives, radio transmitting equipment, Chinese currency, material deemed morally or ideologically subversive, and habit-forming drugs.

The duty-free allowance for tourists entering China consists of two bottles of alcoholic beverages (neither exceeding ¾ litre), 400 cigarettes, food, clothing and medicine for personal use, and any quantity of foreign currency.

To change money back on departure you must show your exchange receipts.

I have nothing to declare.	我没有要报关的东西。	wǒ méi-yǒu yào bào-guān de dōng-xi
I have…	我带了…	wǒ dài le
…packets of cigarettes	…包香烟	…bāo xiāng-yān
a bottle of whisky	一瓶威士忌	yì-píng wēi-shì-jì
Here's my camera.	这是我的照相机。	zhè shì wǒ de zhào-xiāng-jī
I've brought … rolls of film with me.	我带了…卷胶卷。	wǒ dài le … juǎn jiāo-juǎn
It's not professional equipment.	这不是专业器材。	zhè bú shì zhuān-yè qì-cái
Here are my valuables.	这些是我的贵重品。	zhè xiē shì wǒ de guì-zhòng-pǐn
It's (not) gold.	这（不）是金的。	zhè (bú) shì jīn de
It's a gift.	这是送人的礼物。	zhè shì sòng rén de lǐ-wù
It has no commercial value.	这不是要出售的。	zhè bú shì yào chū-shòu de
It's for my personal use/It's not new.	这是我的私人用品/这不是新的。	zhè shì wǒ de sī-rén yòng-pǐn /zhè bú shì xīn de

---

你们的向导在出口等着你们。	Your guide is waiting for you at the exit.
这件东西应该上税。	You'll have to pay duty on this.
请到那边的办公室去付。	Please pay at the office over there.
你还有别的行李吗？	Do you have any more luggage?

Baggage 行李

You carry your own luggage to the customs checkpoint. At
large airports you will find luggage trolleys. Although there
are no porters, the coach driver of your tour group will help
in carrying and loading up the luggage.

Please take my...	请搬我的…	qǐng bān wǒ de
travelling bag	旅行袋	lǚ-xíng-dài
luggage	行李	xíng-li
suitcase	箱子	xiāng-zi
That's mine.	这是我的。	zhè shì wǒ de
There's one piece missing.	少了一件。	shǎo le yí-jiàn
Where are the luggage trolleys (carts)?	哪儿有手推车？	nǎr yǒu shǒu-tuī-chē
Where is the left-luggage office (baggage check)?	行李寄存处在哪儿？	xíng-li jì-cún-chù zài nǎr

Changing money 兑换外汇

Foreign currency and traveller's cheques can be exchanged
or cashed only at authorized exchange offices (there is one
at every major airport). Most hotel exchange counters stay
open until 7 p.m., or even later. Any money still in your
hands when you leave China will be changed back at the
same rate as when you entered.

Where can I change money?	在哪儿能兑换外汇？	zài nǎr néng duì-huàn wài-huì
What's the exchange rate?	兑换率是多少？	duì-huàn-lǜ shì duō-shao

外汇兑换处
wài-huì duì-huàn-chù
CURRENCY EXCHANGE OFFICE

BANK — CURRENCY, see page 129

到达

I want to change some ...	我想用…兑换。	wǒ xiǎng yòng ... duì-huàn
traveller's cheques (checks)	旅行支票	lǚ-xíng-zhī-piào
U.S. dollars	美元	měi-yuán
pounds	英磅	yīng-bàng
Here's my currency declaration form.	这是我的外汇申报单。	zhè shì wǒ de wài-huì shēn-bào-dān

Where is ...? …在哪儿？

Where is the ...?	…在哪儿？	... zài nǎr
duty-free shop	免税商店	miǎn-shuì shāng-diàn
information office	问询处	wèn-xùn-chù
newsstand	售报亭	shòu-bào-tíng
restaurant	餐厅	cān-tīng
taxi booking-office	出租汽车站	chū-zū-qì-chē-zhàn
ticket office	售票处	shòu-piào-chù
How do I get to ...?	去…怎么走？	qù ... zěn-me zǒu
Is there a(n) ... into town?	有去城里的…吗？	yǒu qù chéng-lǐ de ... ma
airport bus	机场班车	jī-chǎng bān-chē
bus	公共汽车	gōng-gòng qì-chē
Where can I get a taxi?	哪儿有出租汽车？	nǎr yǒu chū-zū qì-chē
Where can I hire (rent) a car?*	哪儿能租到包车？	nǎr néng zū dào bāo-chē

Hotel reservation 预订房间

Could you reserve a room for me at a hotel?	可以给我在旅馆订一间房间吗？	kě-yǐ gěi wǒ zài lǚ-guǎn dìng yì-jiān fáng-jiān ma
a single room	单人房间	dān-rén fáng-jiān
a double room	双人房间	shuāng-rén fáng-jiān
not too expensive	要便宜些的	yào pián-yi xiē de
Is there a student hostel nearby?	附近有专门接待学生的旅馆吗？	fù-jìn yǒu zhuān-mén jiē-dài xué-sheng de lǚ-guǎn ma
Could you reserve a bed for me?	可以给我订一张床位吗？	kě-yǐ gěi wǒ dìng yì-zhāng chuáng-wèi ma

---

* Self-drive cars cannot be hired in China (see page 22).

HOTEL/ACCOMMODATION, see page 23

到达

| Where is the hotel? | 这家旅馆在哪儿？ | zhè jiā lǚ-guǎn zài nǎr |
| Do you have a street map? | 你有交通图吗？ | nǐ yǒu jiāo-tōng-tú ma |

Taxi 出租汽车

Many airports and railway stations have special counters at which you can book a taxi. Occasionally they may be hailed on the street; there are no taxi ranks. The easiest way to get a taxi is through your hotel receptionist. All Friendship Stores have a transport officer who will order a taxi for you, and tell the driver where you need to go.

If you're out sightseeing on your own for a few hours, it's wise to take a taxi and keep it waiting for you between stops — a relatively inexpensive investment in convenience. When travelling independently ask someone to write down your destination in Chinese on a piece of paper; drivers rarely speak anything other than Chinese.

Taxis are not metered, but drivers are universally trustworthy and honest. They usually insist on giving receipts; tips should not be offered.

Where can I get a taxi?	哪儿有出租汽车？	nǎr yǒu chū-zū-qì-chē
Can you call me a taxi, please?	能给我叫辆出租汽车吗？	néng gěi wǒ jiào liàng chū-zū-qì-chē ma
Do you know this place?	你认识这个地方吗？	nǐ rèn-shi zhè-ge dì-fang ma
What's the fare to …?	到…的车费是多少？	dào … de chē-fèi shì duō-shao
How long does it take to get to …?	到…要多少时间？	dào … yào duō-shao shí-jiān
Take me to …	请送我去…	qǐng sòng wǒ qù
this address	地址上写的地方	dì-zhǐ shàng xiě de dì-fang
the airport	飞机场	fēi-jī-chǎng
the … Hotel	…旅馆	… lǚ-guǎn
the railway station	火车站	huǒ-chē-zhàn
the town centre	市中心	shì-zhōng-xīn

到达

Back to the hotel, please.	请开回旅馆。	qǐng kāi huí lǚ-guǎn
I'm in a hurry.	我很急。	wǒ hěn jí
Go straight ahead.	一直走。	yì-zhí zǒu
Turn ... at the next corner.	在前边的路口向…拐。	zài qián-bian de lù-kǒu xiàng ... guǎi
left/right	左/右	zuǒ/yòu
Could you drive more slowly?	请开慢点儿。	qǐng kāi màn diǎnr
Please stop here.	请停一下。	qǐng tíng yí xià
Could you help me carry my luggage?	可以帮我提行李吗？	kě-yǐ bāng wǒ tí xíng-li ma
Could you wait for me?	请等我。	qǐng děng wǒ
Can you come back and pick me up at ... o'clock?	能在…点回来接我吗？	néng zài ... diǎn huí lái jiē wǒ ma

Car hire (rental) 租包车

Self-drive cars cannot be hired in China, but chauffeur-driven cars are readily available. If you don't want to hire a car for the whole day, it's often possible to arrange for a taxi by the hour plus mileage.

I'd like to hire (rent) a car.	我想租一辆包车。	wǒ xiǎng zū yí-liàng bāo-chē
I'll be alone.	我一个人。	wǒ yí-ge rén
There will be ... of us.	我们…个人。	wǒ-mén ... ge rén
I'd like it for ...	我想用…	wǒ xiǎng yòng
a day/a week	一天/一星期	yì-tiān/yì xīng-qī
What's the charge per day/per week?	一天/一星期多少钱？	yì tiān/yì xīng-qī duō-shao qián
Do you charge ...?	是按…计价吗？	shì àn ... jì-jià ma
by the hour	时间	shí-jiān
according to mileage	里程	lǐ-chéng
What's the deposit?	押金多少？	yā-jīn duō-shao

TELLING THE TIME, see page 155

Hotel

Whether you are going to China on your own or as part of a group, your hotel accommodation will probably be reserved in advance by the China International Travel Service (CITS). At present, only a few Chinese hotels accept individual reservations, but this will change as computers come into wider use.

Hotels (旅馆 – lǚ-guǎn) in China range from first class to grimly spartan. The newest hotels, often built with foreign cooperation and expertise, bear the closest resemblance to their counterparts in Europe and America. More adventurous travellers may prefer the charm of old-fashioned establishments in interesting or scenic locations.

In general, hotels in small or remote towns offer few comforts. Air conditioning is a relatively new feature in China; radios and telephones are usually provided, and ever more hotels are now equipped with small refrigerators and television sets.

In almost every room you'll find cups and a large thermos of hot water for making tea. A small container of tea is often provided as well. The separate carafe of "drinking water" may not always be trusted; *never* drink water from the tap.

Large hotels now have post offices, exchange offices, bars, swimming pools, bookshops, hairdressers, theatres (with shows staged especially for foreign visitors) and Chinese massage parlours.

If staying in a larger hotel you will find a service desk on each floor. The floor monitor will probably speak a little English and be able to handle small problems that may crop up during your stay. The desk also sells cigarettes, snacks, drinks and postcards.

旅馆

Checking in — Reception 住宿-接待

The phrases below can be used either in the hotel or at the CITS office if they are organizing your accommodation.

My name is …	我叫…	wǒ jiào
I have a reservation.	我预订了。	wǒ yù-dìng le
Here's the confirmation.	这是订单。	zhè shì dìng-dān
I don't have a reservation.	我没预订。	wǒ méi yù-dìng
Do you have any vacancies?	你这儿有空房间吗?	nǐ zhèr yǒu kōng fáng-jiān ma
I'd like a …	我想要一间…	wǒ xiǎng-yào yì-jiān
single room	单人房间	dān-rén fáng-jiān
double room	双人房间	shuāng-rén fáng-jiān
with twin beds	有两张单人床的	yǒu liǎng zhāng dān-rén-chuáng de
with a double bed	有一张双人床的	yǒu yì-zhāng shuāng-rén-chuáng de
room with a bath	有澡盆的房间	yǒu zǎo-pén de fáng-jiān
room with a shower	有淋浴的房间	yǒu lín-yù de fáng-jiān
We'd like a room …	我们想要一个…房间。	wǒ-men xiǎng-yào yí-ge … fáng-jiān
with a balcony	有阳台的	yǒu yáng-tái de
with a view	窗外风景好看的	chuāng wài fēng-jǐng hǎo-kàn de
at the front	临街的	lín-jiē de
at the back	在后面的	zài hòu-miàn de
facing the sea	朝着海的	cháo zhe hǎi de
It must be quiet.	要安静的。	yào ān-jìng de
Is there (a) …?	有…吗?	yǒu … ma
air conditioning	空调	kōng-tiáo
heating	暖气	nuǎn-qì
hot water	热水	rè-shuǐ
laundry service	洗衣服务	xǐ-yī fú-wù
private toilet	私人厕所	sī-rén cè-suǒ
room service	清扫整理服务	qīng-sǎo zhěng-lǐ fú-wù
running water	自来水	zì-lái-shuǐ
Could you put … in the room?	可以在房间里加…吗?	kě-yǐ zài fáng-jiān li jiā … ma

CHECKING OUT, see page 32

旅馆

| an extra bed | 一张床 | yì-zhāng chuáng |
| a cot | 一张小床 | yì-zhāng xiǎo-chuáng |

How much? 多少钱？

Meals are not normally included in the price if you aren't part of a tour group. If you eat in the hotel dining room you should pay at the end of each meal.

What's the price …?	…多少钱？	… duō-shao qián
per night	一夜	yí-yè
per week	一星期	yì xīng-qī
Does that include …?	这包括…吗？	zhè bāo-kuò … ma
breakfast	早饭	zǎo-fàn
meals	伙食费	huǒ-shí fèi
Is there any reduction for children?	儿童有减价吗？	ér-tóng yǒu jiǎn-jià ma
Do you charge for the baby?	这儿婴儿也要付钱吗？	zhèr yīng-ér yě yào fù qián ma
That's too expensive for me.	对我来说这太贵了。	duì wǒ lái shuō zhè tài guì le
Don't you have anything cheaper?	有便宜些的吗？	yǒu pián-yi xiē de ma

How long? 多长时间？

I'll be staying …	我打算住…	wǒ dǎ-suan zhù
We'll be staying …	我们打算住…	wǒ-men dǎ-suan zhù
overnight only	一夜	yí-yè
a few days	几天	jǐ tiān
a week (at least)	（最少）一星期	(zuì shǎo) yì xīng-qī
I don't know yet.	还不一定。	hái bù yí-dìng

Decision 决定

May I see the room?	我可以看看房间吗？	wǒ kě-yǐ kàn-kan fáng-jiān ma
No, I don't like it.	我不喜欢这间。	wǒ bù xǐ-huan zhè-jiān
It's too …	这里太…	zhè-li tài
cold/hot	冷/热	lěng/rè
dark/small/noisy	暗/小/吵	àn/xiǎo/chǎo

NUMBERS, see page 149

旅馆

I asked for a room with a bath.	我要的是一个有澡盆的房间。	wǒ yào de shì yí-ge yǒu zǎo-pén de fáng-jiān
Do you have anything …?	你这儿有…的吗？	nǐ zhèr yǒu … de ma
better/bigger	好些/大些	hǎo xiē/dà xiē
cheaper/quieter	便宜些/安静些	pián-yi xiē/ān-jìng xiē
higher up/lower down	楼层高些/楼层低些	lóu-céng gāo xiē/lóu-céng dī xiē
Do you have a room with a better view?	你这儿有窗外风景更好些的房间吗？	nǐ zhèr yǒu chuāng wài fēng-jǐng gèng hǎo xiē de fáng-jiān ma
That's fine.	这间很好。	zhè jiān hěn hǎo
I'll take it.	我要了。	wǒ yào le

Registration 住宿登记

Upon arrival at a hotel you will be asked to fill in a registration form (住宿登记表 zhù-sù dēng-jì-biǎo).

姓/名	Name/First name
家庭住址/街道/门牌号	Home address/Street/Number
国籍/职业	Nationality/Profession
出生年月日/籍贯	Date/Place of birth
从…来/到…去	Coming from …/Going to …
护照号码	Passport number
地点/日期	Place/Date
签名	Signature

| What does this mean? | 这是什么意思？ | zhè shì shén-me yì-si |

我可以看看你的护照吗？	May I see your passport?
请你填写这份住宿登记表。	Please fill in this registration form.
请在此签名。	Sign here, please.
你打算住多长时间？	How long will you be staying?

What's my room number?	我的房间号是多少？	wǒ de fáng-jiān-hào shì duō-shao
Will you have our luggage sent up?	请把我们的行李送到房间里。	qǐng bǎ wǒ-men de xíng-li sòng dào fáng-jiān li
I'd like to leave this in your safe.	我想把这个寄存在你们的保险箱里。	wǒ xiǎng bǎ zhè-ge jì-cún zài nǐ-men de bǎo-xiǎn-xiāng li

Hotel staff 旅馆工作人员

bank clerk	银行职员	yín-háng zhí-yuán
cashier	出纳员	chū-nà-yuán
floor supervisor	楼层负责人	lóu-céng fù-zé-rén
lift attendant	电梯服务员	diàn-tī fú-wù-yuán
maid/room attendant	客房服务员	kè-fáng fú-wù-yuán
person in charge (manager)	经理	jīng-lǐ
porter	行李员	xíng-li-yuán
postal clerk	邮局职员	yóu-jú zhí-yuán
receptionist	接待员	jiē-dài-yuán
switchboard operator	接线员	jiē-xiàn-yuán

There is just one form of address you need to know for anybody you meet in the service sector in China (porters, waiters etc ...): 服务员 *fú-wù-yuán,* for both men and women.

General requirements 一般要求

The key, please.	请给我钥匙。	qǐng gěi wǒ yào-shi
Room 1-2-3.	一二三号房间。	123 hào fáng-jiān
Will you wake me at ..., please?	请…叫醒我。	qǐng ... jiào-xǐng wǒ
Is there a bath room on this floor?	这楼层有浴室吗？	zhè lóu-céng yǒu yù-shì ma
How does the shower work?	这个淋浴怎么用？	zhè-ge lín-yù zěn-me yòng
Where's the socket (outlet) for the shaver?	接电动剃须刀的插座在哪儿？	jiē diàn-dòng tì-xū-dāo de chā-zuò zài nǎr

TELLING THE TIME, see page 155

旅馆

28

HOTEL

What's the voltage here?	电压是多少？	diàn-yā shì duō-shao
Can you lend me an adaptor?	能借我一个多路插座吗？	néng jiè wǒ yí-ge duō lù chā-zuò ma
Can we have breakfast in our room?	我们可以在房间里用早饭吗？	wǒ-men kě-yǐ zài fáng-jiān li yòng zǎo-fàn ma
Would you serve … in our room, please?	请你把…送到我的房间里来。	qǐng nǐ bǎ … sòng dào wǒ de fáng-jiān li lái
breakfast	早饭	zǎo-fàn
lunch	午饭	wǔ-fàn
dinner	晚饭	wǎn-fàn
I don't want to be disturbed.	请不要打扰我。	qǐng bú-yào dǎ-rǎo wǒ
Can you find me a …?	请帮我找…。	qǐng bāng wǒ zhǎo
babysitter	一位临时保姆	yí-wèi lín-shí bǎo-mǔ
secretary	一位秘书	yí-wèi mì-shū
typewriter	一架打字机	yí-jià dǎ-zì-jī
May I have a/an/ some …?	请给我…	qǐng gěi wǒ
ashtray	一个烟灰缸	yí-ge yān-huī-gāng
bath towel	一块浴巾	yí-kuài yù-jīn
boiled water	一些开水	yì-xiē kāi-shuǐ
extra blanket	一条毯子	yì-tiáo tǎn-zi
electric fan	一架电扇	yí-jià diàn-shàn
envelopes	几个信封	jǐ ge xìn-fēng
hangers	几个挂钩	jǐ ge guà-gōu
hot-water bottle	一个暖水袋	yí-ge nuǎn-shuǐ-dài
ice cubes	一些冰块	yì-xiē bīng-kuài
mosquito net	一顶蚊帐	yì-dǐng wén-zhàng
needle and thread	一些针和线	yì-xiē zhēn hé xiàn
extra pillow	加一个枕头	jiā yí-ge zhěn-tou
reading lamp	一盏台灯	yì-zhǎn tái-dēng
soap	一块肥皂	yí-kuài féi-zào
writing paper	几张信纸	jǐ zhāng xìn-zhǐ
Where's the …?	…在哪儿？	… zài nǎr
bathroom	浴室	yù-shì
dining room	餐厅	cān-tīng
emergency exit	太平门	tài-píng-mén
hairdresser's	理发室	lǐ-fà-shì
lift (elevator)	电梯	diàn-tī
Where are the toilets?	厕所在哪儿？	cè-suǒ zài nǎr

旅馆

FOR VOLTAGE, see page 119

Telephone — Post (mail) 打电话-邮寄

Can you get me Beijing 123 4567?	请接北京一二三—四五六七？	qǐng jiē běi-jīng 123-4567
Do you have any stamps?	你这儿卖邮票吗？	nǐ zhèr mài yóu-piào ma
Would you post (mail) this for me?	请帮我寄出这封信。	qǐng bāng wǒ jì-chū zhè-fēng xìn
Are there any letters for me?	有我的信吗？	yǒu wǒ de xìn ma
Are there any messages for me?	有给我的留言吗？	yǒu gěi wǒ de liú-yán ma
What is my telephone bill?	我的电话费一共多少？	wǒ de diàn-huà-fèi yí-gòng duō-shao

Difficulties 出毛病了

The ... doesn't work.	…坏了。	... huài le
air conditioner	空调	kōng-tiáo
electric fan	电扇	diàn-shàn
heating	暖气	nuǎn-qì
light	电灯	diàn-dēng
toilet	厕所	cè-suǒ
radio	收音机	shōu-yīn-jī
television	电视机	diàn-shì-jī
The tap (faucet) is dripping.	水龙头关不紧。	shuǐ-lóng-tóu guān-bu-jǐn
There's no hot water.	没有热水。	méi-yǒu rè-shuǐ
The washbasin is blocked.	水池子的下水道堵了。	shuǐ-chí-zi de xià-shuǐ-dào dǔ le
The window is jammed.	窗户卡住了。	chuāng-hu qiǎ-zhù le
The curtains are stuck.	窗帘儿拉不动。	chuāng-liánr lā-bu-dòng
The bulb is burned out.	灯泡儿烧坏了。	dēng-pàor shāo huài le
The mosquito net on my window is torn.	沙窗破了。	shā-chuāng pò le
My room hasn't been prepared.	我的房间还没有整理。	wǒ de fáng-jiān hái méi-yǒu zhěng-lǐ

POST OFFICE AND TELEPHONE, see page 134

旅馆

There are some insects in my room.	我的房间有虫子。	wǒ de fáng-jiān yǒu chóng-zi
The ... is broken.	…坏了。	... huài le
blind	百叶窗	bǎi-yè-chuāng
bulb	灯泡	dēng-pào
lamp	电灯	diàn-dēng
plug	插头	chā-tóu
switch	开关	kāi-guān
Can you get it repaired?	你能找人把它修理好吗？	nǐ néng zhǎo rén bǎ tā xiū-lǐ hǎo ma

Laundry — Dry cleaner's 洗衣店-干洗店

Hotels process laundry and dry-cleaning quickly and efficiently. Most hotels provide their guests with laundry bags; if you're in a hurry, deliver the filled bag to the service desk on your floor; otherwise it will be picked up when the room is cleaned. Laundry is usually returned within 24 hours, but dry-cleaning may take an extra day in all but the largest hotels.

I want these clothes ...	请把这些衣服…	qǐng bǎ zhè-xiē yī-fu
cleaned	弄干净	nòng gān-jìng
ironed/pressed	熨好	yùn hǎo
washed	洗干净	xǐ gān-jìng
When will they be ready?	什么时候能洗好？	shén-me shí-hou néng xǐ hǎo
I need them ...	我…需要。	wǒ ... xū-yào
today	今天	jīn-tiān
tonight	今晚	jīn-wǎn
tomorrow	明天	míng-tiān
before Friday	星期五以前	xīng-qī-wǔ yǐ-qián
I want them as soon as possible.	请尽早给我洗好。	qǐng jìn-zǎo gěi wǒ xǐ hǎo
Can you ... this?	你能…这个吗？	nǐ néng ... zhè-ge ma
mend/stitch	补/缝	bǔ/féng
Can you sew on this button?	请帮我把这个钮扣缝上好吗？	qǐng bāng wǒ bǎ zhè-ge niǔ-kòu féng-shang hǎo ma
Can you get this stain out?	请帮我把这个污点去掉好吗？	qǐng bāng wǒ bǎ zhè-ge wū-diǎn qù-diào hǎo ma

Is my laundry ready?	我的衣服洗好了吗？	wǒ de yī-fu xǐ hǎo le ma
This isn't mine.	这不是我的。	zhè bú shì wǒ de
There's one piece missing.	少了一件。	shǎo le yí-jiàn
There's a hole in this.	这件衣服上有一个洞。	zhè-jiàn yī-fu shàng yǒu yí-ge dòng

Hairdresser's — Barber's 理发店

The larger hotels usually have a hairdresser and a barber shop. The service is good and extremely cheap by Western standards. The treatment may include a head and neck massage, which is most relaxing. Tipping is not allowed.

Is there a ... in the hotel?	这个旅馆里有…吗？	zhè-ge lǚ-guǎn li yǒu ... ma
barber/hairdresser	理发室	lǐ-fà-shì
beauty salon	美容室	měi-róng-shì
Can I make an appointment for ...?	请给我约个…的时间。	qǐng gěi wǒ yuē ge ... de shí-jiān
Please give me a head and neck massage.	请给我按摩一下头部和脖子。	qǐng gěi wǒ àn-mó yí xià tóu-bù he bó-zi
I'd like a haircut, please.	我想剪发。	wǒ xiǎng jiǎn fà
blow dry	把头发吹干定型	bǎ tóu-fa chuī gān dìng-xíng
colour rinse	着色洗发	zhuó sè xǐ fà
dye	染发	rǎn fà
face pack	绞脸	jiǎo liǎn
perm(anent)	烫发	tàng fà
shampoo and set	洗头和做发	xǐ tóu hé zuò fà
I'd like a shampoo for	我想用一种适用于…的洗发剂。	wǒ xiǎng yòng yì-zhǒng shì yòng yú ... de xǐ-fà-jì
normal hair	普通头发	pǔ-tōng tóu-fa
dry hair	很干的头发	hěn gān de tóu-fa
greasy (oily) hair	出油的头发	chū yóu de tóu-fa
Don't cut it too short.	不要剪得太短。	bú yào jiǎn de tài duǎn
A little more off the ...	…再剪短一点。	... zài jiǎn duǎn yì-diǎn
back	后头的	hòu tóu de
neck	脖子上的	bó-zi shàng de

DAYS OF THE WEEK, see page 153

旅馆

sides	两侧的	liǎng cè de
top	头顶上的	tóu-dǐng shàng de
Would you trim my ..., please?	请给我修剪一下我的…？	qǐng gěi wǒ xiū jiǎn yí-xià wǒ de
beard	下胡子	xià hú-zi
moustache	上胡子	shàng hú-zi
sideboards (side-burns)	两侧的胡子	liǎng cè de hú-zi
I'd like a shave.	我想要刮脸。	wǒ xiǎng-yào guā liǎn
I'd like a ...	我想要…	wǒ xiǎng yào
manicure	修手指甲	xiū shǒu zhǐ-jia
pedicure	修脚指甲	xiū jiǎo zhǐ-jia

Checking out 结帐离开

May I have my bill, please?	我想要结帐。	wǒ xiǎng-yào jié-zhàng
I'm leaving early in the morning. Please have my bill ready.	我明天早上要很早离开。请先开好帐单。	wǒ míng-tiān zǎo-shang yào hěn zǎo lí kāi. qǐng xiān kāi hǎo zhàng-dān
I'll be checking out around noon.	我想在中午办理结帐离开手续。	wǒ xiǎng zài zhōng-wǔ bàn-lǐ jié-zhàng lí-kāi shǒu-xù
I must leave at once.	我必须马上走。	wǒ bì-xū mǎ-shàng zǒu
Can I pay by credit card?	我可以用信用卡付钱吗？	wǒ kě-yǐ yòng xìn-yòng-kǎ fù qián ma
I think there's a mistake in the bill.	这个帐单好象有错吧。	zhè-ge zhàng-dān hǎo-xiàng yǒu cuò ba
Can you get me a taxi?	请给我叫辆出租汽车好吗？	qǐng gěi wǒ jiào liàng chū-zū qì-chē hǎo ma
Would you have our luggage sent down?	请把行李帮我拿下来可以吗？	qǐng bǎ xíng-li bāng wǒ ná-xia-lai kě-yǐ ma
Here's the forwarding address.	这是通讯地址。	zhè shì tōng-xùn dì-zhǐ
You have my home address.	你有我家的地址了。	nǐ yǒu wǒ jiā de dì-zhǐ le
It's been a very enjoyable stay.	这次住得很愉快。	zhè cì zhù de hěn yú-kuài

Note: Tipping is not customary in the People's Republic, and can only cause embarrassment.

Eating out

Chinese cuisine, long known and highly appreciated throughout the world by lovers of good food, is gaining an ever broader following. Chinese restaurants continue to spring up and flourish in the towns and cities of Europe and America, affording a mouth-watering insight into the gastronomic riches of the "Middle Kingdom".

The Western visitor may be astonished at the variety, flavour and finesse of the products of Chinese culinary art. It is the culmination of age-old traditions, extending over thousands of years of the world's longest continuous civilization. Cooking techniques have been modified and adapted from one century to the next across the many troubled epochs of China's existence.

In the north, rice is not the staple, and wheat-, corn-, and millet-based dishes are the rule. As a result of long, harsh winters, Northerners have become very skilled in the preparation of dried and pickled foods. The general emphasis is on strongly-flavoured dishes, but Beijing is the exception due to the Imperial influence. This can still be seen in the more complex and spectacular dishes like Peking Duck.

In the western inland provinces of Sichuan and Hunan, food is spicy and hot, with red chillis, Sichuan peppercorns and ginger as principal ingredients. While the East, with its long coastline, excels in the preparation of fish and seafood. The food of Guangdong (Canton) province is probably the best known in the West, with its sweet and sour dishes and exotic delicacies. In this region, visitors will have the pleasure of trying snake, turtle or even dog. Here the emphasis is on the preservation of natural colour and taste, so cooking methods are swift, and avoid using heavy flavourings.

上饭馆儿

At your hotel you'll have no trouble ordering a special meal. All you need to do is indicate the number of dishes you'd like, the number of diners there will be, and the hour.

If you're planning to dine out at a top restaurant, be sure to reserve a table in advance. Comfortably esconced in an armchair, you'll have time for a cup of tea before the meal if you wish. On the round table in front of you, there will be, not the cutlery you are used to, but a pair of chopsticks (see p.36 for how to use them) and a spoon. There will also be a small plate and, to your left, a gravy boat and bowl. Beside each place setting are three glasses, a big one for the beer, a wine glass and a smaller glass for spirits. A word of advice: take care not to over-indulge in the first few dishes; save your appetite so that you are fully able to savour and appreciate all the items on the menu.

Banquets 宴会

During your stay in China you may be invited to a formal dinner or banquet. Here is a brief guide to etiquette on such occasions.

After welcoming you, your host will invite you to be seated at a low table where the ice will be broken over tea and conversation. After about a quarter of an hour you will move to your place at the customary large round table. The host usually sits facing the entrance, and the guests are seated to his right and left.

You will notice an extra pair of chopsticks on the table. These are for the use of the host, who will serve the guests seated to his right and left with them, thereby giving the signal that the meal may begin.

Toasts regularly punctuate a formal Chinese dinner or banquet, but it is considered bad form to drink before the host has first proposed a toast to his guests' health. He will raise his glass shortly after the dinner begins, and the guest of honour is expected to reply to this opening toast either straight away or when the next dish is served. Though the Chinese generally drink very little, especially in the presence of foreigners (it is considered undignified to show signs of inebriety to those one doesn't know), they do sip the fiery *máo-tái* (53% alcohol) before, during and after the meal. Moderation is advised. Your hosts will not be offended if you prefer to toast in wine, beer, fruit juice or even mineral water. Always raise your glass when a toast is proposed.

If you don't feel like a particular dish, just leave it, and it will soon be removed from the table. But it would be considered polite to try a mouthful in any case.

Fruit marks the end of the meal. The Western custom of rounding off dinner with coffee, cigars and brandy is unknown in China, and the party will break up quite quickly at 9 or 10 p.m. at the latest.

Courses 上菜顺序

A formal Chinese meal normally follows this pattern: first some highly seasoned cold hors-d'oeuvre such as crab-meat, chicken salad, shark's fin or pork- or shrimp-balls are served. The bowl in front of you is then filled with rice. Next come the "star" dishes, likely to include chicken, duck, pigeon (squab), fish, pork, etc. You help yourself directly from the dishes using chopsticks and can dip your food in the sauces provided (soya, ginger and other spices) to enhance its flavour.

Cheese is virtually unknown in China.

Dessert as such is rarely included in a Chinese meal, though a pie, sweet soup or other sweet dish — walnut purée, for example — is often served between two savoury dishes.

Don't be surprised if the person in charge of the restaurant invites his guests to take the remaining fruit, pies or cigarettes home with them. It's quite customary.

上饭馆儿

Chopsticks 筷子

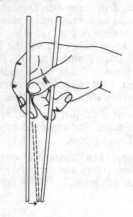

How to use chopsticks can be briefly explained as follows: you hold the upper stick between your thumb and first two fingers, while holding the lower stick stationary with the third, or third and fourth finger. Hold them about one third of the way down their length. Contrary to our own customs, in China you are expected to bring the bowl up to your mouth when eating.

Mealtimes 用餐时间

Meals in China are taken considerably earlier than in the West. Breakfast (*zǎo-fàn*) is usually served between 6.30 and 9 a.m., while lunch (*wǔ-fàn*) can start as early as 10.30 a.m. and goes on until 1.30 p.m. Dinner (*wǎn-fàn*) is served between 4.30 and 7.30 or 8 p.m., and banquets tend to finish by 9.30 p.m.

Hungry? 饿吗？

I'm hungry/I'm thirsty.	我饿了/我渴了。	wǒ è le/wǒ kě le
Can you recommend a good restaurant?	你能介绍一家好的饭馆吗？	nǐ néng jiè-shào yì-jiā hǎo de fàn-guǎn ma

If you want to be sure of getting a table in a well-known restaurant, it is better to book in advance.

I'd like to reserve a table for 4.	我想预订一张桌子，四个人。	wǒ xiǎng yù-dìng yì-zhāng zhuō-zi sì-ge rén
We'll come at 7.	我们七点来。	wǒ-men qī-diǎn lái
Could we have a table ...?	能给我们定一张···的桌子吗？	néng gěi wǒ-men dìng yì-zhāng ... de zhuō-zi ma
in the corner	在屋角	zài wū-jiǎo
by the window	靠窗户	kào chuāng-hu
outside	在室外	zài shì wài
in a non-smoking area	在禁止吸烟的地方	zài jìn-zhǐ xī-yān de dì-fang
in a private room	在单间里	zài dān-jiān li

Ordering 点菜

Although you can't normally get a set menu, a good way of having a cheap meal with plenty of variety is to join a table where there is a set price per diner. The restaurant waits until the table is full (around 8 people), and then puts between 5 and 8 dishes in the centre of the table, which everybody shares.

Waiter/Waitress!	服务员！	fú-wù-yuán
May I have the menu, please?	能给我看看菜单吗？	néng gěi wǒ kàn-kan cài-dān ma
Do you have local dishes?	你们这儿有地方风味菜吗？	nǐ-men zhèr yǒu dì-fāng fēng-wèi cài ma
Is there a set-price table?	你们这儿有包桌吗？	nǐ-men zhèr yǒu bāo-zhuō ma
What do you recommend?	你能介绍些什么菜吗？	nǐ néng jiè-shào xiē shén-me cài ma
I'd like ...	我想要···	wǒ xiǎng-yào
Could we have a/an ..., please?	请给我们···	qǐng gěi wǒ-men
ashtray	一个烟灰缸	yí-ge yān-huī-gāng
cup	一个茶杯	yí-ge chá-bēi
fork	一把叉子	yì-bǎ chā-zi
glass	一个杯子	yí-ge bēi-zi
knife	一把刀子	yì-bǎ dāo-zi
napkin (serviette)	一条餐巾	yì-tiáo cān-jīn
plate	一个盘子	yí-ge pán-zi
spoon	一把勺子	yì-bǎ sháo-zi

May I have some …?	能给我些…吗？	néng gěi wǒ xiē … ma
bread	面包	miàn-bāo
butter	黄油	huáng-yóu
green tea	绿茶	lǜ-chá
jasmine tea	茉莉花茶	mò-lì huā-chá
lemon	柠檬	níng-méng
pepper	胡椒	hú-jiāo
salt	盐	yán
seasoning	调料	tiáo-liào
soy sauce	酱油	jiàng-yóu
sugar	糖	táng
toothpicks	牙签	yá-qiān
vinegar	醋	cù

Some useful expressions for dieters and special requirements:

I am on a special diet.	我必须遵守特别的食谱。	wǒ bì-xū zūn-shǒu tè-bié de shí-pǔ
I mustn't eat food containing …	我不能吃含有…的食物。	wǒ bù néng chī hán-yǒu … de shí-wù
fat/flour	脂肪/面粉	zhī-fáng/miàn-fěn
monosodium glutamate	味精	wèi-jīng
salt/sugar	盐/糖	yán/táng
I can't eat spicy food.	我不能吃味厚的食物。	wǒ bù néng chī wèi-hòu de shí-wù
Do you have … for diabetics?	你这儿有给糖尿病人吃的…吗？	nǐ zhèr yǒu gěi táng-niào bìng-rén chī de … ma
fruit juice	果汁	guǒ-zhī
a special menu	特别的食物	tè-bié de shí-wù
Do you have vegetarian dishes?	你这儿有素菜吗？	nǐ zhèr yǒu sù-cài ma

And …

I'd like some more.	我还想要。	wǒ hái xiǎng-yào
Can I have more …, please?	请再给我些…？	qǐng zài gěi wǒ xiē
Just a small portion.	就要一点儿。	jiù yào yì-diǎnr
Nothing more, thanks.	不要了，谢谢。	bú yào le. xiè-xie
Where are the toilets?	厕所在哪儿？	cè-suǒ zài nǎr

Breakfast 早饭

Chinese breakfasts don't differ substantially from any other meal of the day. A typical breakfast might consist of some tea cakes, a plate of meat and vegetables, pickles, a kind of doughnut, rice porridge, bean-curd gruel and maybe a fish-flavoured omelet. Most tourist hotels will serve both Western and Chinese breakfasts.

I'd like a … breakfast, please.	我想吃…早饭。	wǒ xiǎng chī … zǎo-fàn
Chinese	中式	zhōng-shì
Western	西式	xī-shì
I'll have a/an/ some …	我要…	wǒ yào …
bacon and eggs	咸肉和鸡蛋	xián-ròu hé jī-dàn
boiled egg	煮鸡蛋	zhǔ jī-dàn
soft/hard	嫩的/老的	nèn-de/lǎo-de
eggs	鸡蛋	jī-dàn
fried eggs	煎鸡蛋	jiān jī-dàn
scrambled eggs	炒鸡蛋	chǎo jī-dàn
fruit juice	果汁	guǒ-zhī
grapefruit juice	西柚汁	xī-yòu-zhī
orange juice	桔子汁	jú-zi-zhī
ham and eggs	火腿和鸡蛋	huǒ-tuǐ hé jī-dàn
jam	果酱	guǒ-jiàng
marmalade	桔子酱	jú-zi-jiàng
toast	烤面包片	kǎo miàn-bāo piàn
yoghurt	酸奶	suān-nǎi
May I have some …?	能给我些…吗。	néng gěi wǒ xiē … ma
(hot) chocolate	（热）巧克力	(rè) qiǎo-kē-lì
coffee	…咖啡	… kā-fēi
decaffeinated	不带咖啡因的	bú dài kā-fēi-yīn de
black/with milk	纯的/加牛奶的	chún de/jiā niú-nǎi de
honey	蜂蜜	fēng-mì
milk	牛奶	niú-nǎi
cold/hot	冷/热	lěng/rè
pepper	胡椒	hú-jiāo
rolls (bread)	小圆面包	xiǎo yuán miàn-bāo
salt	盐	yán
tea	…茶	… chá
with milk	加牛奶的	jiā niú-nǎi de
with lemon	加柠檬的	jiā níng-méng de
(hot) water	（热）水	(rè) shuǐ

What's on the menu? 菜单上有什么？

Most restaurants display their menus just inside the door, and some, particularly those that cater to tourists, also have English translations alongside. In places where restaurateurs have experience of foreign visitors, a set menu may be on offer, but if not, you can tell the waiter how much you would like to spend, and he will be able to suggest an appropriate menu for you.

Under the headings below you'll find lists of dishes that might be offered on a Chinese menu, with their English equivalent. You can simply show the book to the waiter. If you want some fruit, for instance, let *him* point to what's available on the list. Use pages 36 and 37 for ordering in general.

Cooking methods 烹调方法

If you go to China expecting to find food prepared according to Western methods, then you will probably be disappointed. You will see very few chops, steaks and chips, unless you eat in a Western restaurant. However, if you approach this ancient and fascinating cuisine with an open mind you are unlikely to come away dissatisfied.

One very important aspect of Chinese cookery is the preparation time. This will usually be longer than the actual cooking time. Most food will be chopped to a uniform size so that no one element takes any longer to cook than any other. Another important aspect is the visual one; the finished dish should satisfy the eye as well as the stomach.

The chopping of the food is in itself an art, and each food will be chopped, sliced, diced, minced or shredded differently, according to its shape, size and texture. The point of this is not only decorative but practical, to present the largest surface area for swift cooking and absorption of spices.

barbecued	炭火烤	tàn-huǒ-kǎo
blanched (vegetables)	焯	chāo
braised	干烧	gān-shāo
crystal cooked*	白斩	bái-zhǎn
deep-fried	焦炸	jiāo-zhá
fried	炸	zhá
marinaded	腌	yān
red-braised (red-cooked)**	红烧	hóng-shāo
steamed	清蒸	qīng-zhēng
stir-fried	爆炒	bào-chǎo

---

* Meat cooked in boiling stock for a short length of time (1-3 minutes), then taken off the heat and left to continue cooking in the cooling stock.

* Food cooked for a long time in a dark liquid, like soy sauce, giving the food a reddish-brown appearance.

EATING OUT

Starter (appetizers) 凉菜拼盘儿

Nibbling while sipping an aperitif is not customary in China. However, a good meal always includes a wide variety of hors d'oeuvres. Here is a selection of what you are likely to come across.

I'd like a starter.	我想要一个拼盘儿	wǒ xiǎng-yào yí-ge pīn-pánr
What do you recommend?	你能介绍些什么凉菜吗？	nǐ néng jiè-shào xiē shén-me liáng-cài ma

酱鸡	jiàng jī	chicken in soy sauce
盐水鸡	yán-shuǐ jī	salted chicken
拌鸭掌	bàn yā-zhǎng	ducks' feet
盐水鸭	yán-shuǐ yā	salted duck
糟鸭片	zāo yā-piàn	duck slices in wine
叉烧肉	chā-shāo ròu	pork barbecue
陈皮牛肉	chén-pí niú-ròu	beef with dried orange peel
酱牛肉	jiàng niú-ròu	beef in soy sauce
盐水虾	yán-shuǐ xiā	salted prawns
干贝松翠丝	gān-bèi sōng-cuì sī	shredded scallop with spring onion
田鸡腿	tián-jī tuǐ	frogs legs
炸花生米	zhá huā-shēng-mǐ	fried peanuts
酸辣泡菜	suān-là pào-cài	sour and hot pickles

炸鱼仔 (zhá yú-zǐ)	Five small fish, such as sardines or herrings, that have been slowly simmered in a mixture of garlic, onions, soy sauce, vinegar, ginger and tangerine or lemon peel.
茶鸡蛋 (chá jī-dàn)	Tea eggs. Hard-boiled eggs that have been marinaded overnight in a tea and cane-sugar marinade.
牛肉干 (niú-ròu-gān)	Spiced, salted beef (jerky). The beef is oven-dried and eaten at any time of day with beer or tea.
鸡珍肝 (jī-zhēn-gān)	Giblets in soy sauce, boiled together with aniseed, soy sauce and cinnamon sticks. The Chinese are very fond of giblets which were formerly considered only a rich man's food.
炸铁雀 (zhá tiě-què)	Marinaded sparrow, fried until crunchy.

上饭馆儿

Eggs 蛋类

The Chinese invest a great deal of imagination in egg pre-parations. Probably the best known dish is "thousand-year eggs" (松花蛋 *sōng-huā-dàn*): duck eggs buried in lime for 60 days, with a resulting cheese-like taste. Apart from serving eggs hard-boiled, they are also stir-fried or steamed.

Steamed eggs (鸡蛋羹 *jī-dàn-gēng*) look rather like a wobbly egg custard and go well with rice. The basic mixture can also be combined with "extras" like chopped or minced meat, flaked fish or vegetables. This mixture of beaten eggs, stock and seasonings is steamed, with or without the extras. And the finished article is garnished with spring onions or chives.

If steamed eggs sound a little exotic, then it's worth trying stir-fried eggs — the nearest thing to an omelet. The eggs are beaten with seasoning and thrown into a very hot pan. Just before the eggs set, a dash of rice wine is added, giving the "omelet" a very special flavour. This recipe can be combined with a variety of other ingredients like seafood, fish or vegetables.

爆腌鸡蛋 (bào-yān jī-dàn)	Soya eggs. Shelled hard-boiled eggs simmered in soy sauce. Served cold in quarters.
芙蓉虾仁儿 (fú-róng xiā-rénr)	Stir-fried eggs with prawns. Prawns are stir-fried and set aside. Eggs are mixed with sesame oil, rice wine, soy sauce and stock. The egg mixture is stir-fried and the prawns are added at the last moment.
芙蓉蛋 (fú-róng dàn)	Egg yolks mixed with monosodium glutamate and salt. Milk is added to the whites which are then beaten until stiff. The flesh of a crab is crumbled and added to the yolk mixture. This preparation is then fried and served sprinkled with coriander and accompanied by the egg whites which have also been fried.
芙蓉牡蛎 (fú-róng mǔ-lì)	Eggs with oysters. The flesh of oysters is mixed with spring onions and soy sauce. Eggs and soy sprouts are added, and the mixture is shaped into little cakes.

Soup 汤类

Soup is not served at the beginning of a meal. Instead it accompanies the main course or it can be served separately at a banquet to cleanse the palate between courses. There are two basic types of soup: clear and thicker ones. The latter often constitute a meal in themselves.

What do you recommend?	你能介绍些什么汤吗？	nǐ néng jiè-shào xiē shén-me tāng ma
蟹肉汤	xiè-ròu tāng	crab soup
扇贝汤	shàn-bèi tāng	scallop soup
鸡汤	jī-tāng	chicken soup
鸡蛋汤	jī-dàn tāng	egg drop soup
猪脚汤	zhū-jiǎo tāng	pig's trotter (feet) soup
豆腐腰花汤	dòu-fu yāo-huā tāng	kidney and beancurd soup
榨菜汤	zhà-cài tāng	hot pickled mustard tuber soup
白菜汤	bái-cài tāng	cabbage soup
黄瓜汤	huáng-guā tāng	cucumber soup
芦笋汤	lú-sǔn tāng	asparagus soup
酸辣汤	suān-là tāng	hot and sour soup
鸡汤面	jī tāng-miàn	chicken noodle soup
长寿汤面	cháng-shòu tāng-miàn	long-life noodle soup
莲蓬豌豆	lián-peng wān-dòu	pea and lotus-seed soup
竹笋汤	zhú-sǔn tāng	bamboo shoot soup
鱼肚汤	yú-dǔ tāng	fish maw soup
云片鸽蛋	yún-piàn gē-dàn	pigeon's egg soup
西红柿鸡蛋汤	xī-hóng-shì jī-dàn tāng	tomato and egg soup
什锦火锅	shí-jǐn huǒ-guō	Chinese hot pot

燕窝汤
(yàn-wō tāng)
Bird's nest soup (renowned for its delicate taste). The nests of a certain type of small swift are collected, then boiled. It's the mucus from the bird's salivary glands that flavours the soup.

鱼翅汤
(yú-chì tāng)
Shark's fin soup. This rare and famous soup is prepared with shark's fin, shredded chicken and crabmeat or pork in chicken stock.

馄饨
(hún-tun)
Wuntun soup. Savoury dumplings are wrapped in wafer-thin wuntun wrappers and served in a rich broth.

Fish and seafood 鱼和海鲜

The Chinese eat their fish as fresh as possible, and also like to serve it whole rather than filleted as they believe this way it retains its natural juices better. For the same reason fish and seafood are steamed and quick-braised or stir-fried.

I'd like a fish dish.	我想要一个鱼。	wǒ xiǎng-yào yí-ge yú
What kinds of seafood do you serve?	你们这儿都有些什么海鲜？	nǐ-men zhèr dōu yǒu xiē shén-me hǎi-xiān
What do you recommend?	你能介绍些什么鱼类菜吗？	nǐ néng jiè-shào xiē shén-me yú-lèi cài ma

鲍鱼	bào-yú	abalone
鳊鱼	biān-yú	bream
大黄鱼	dà huáng-yú	large yellow croaker
大马哈鱼	dà mǎ-hā-yú	dog salmon
带鱼	dài-yú	hairtail
真鲷	zhēn-diāo	porgy
鳜鱼	guì-yú	mandarin fish
鳇鱼	huáng-yú	sturgeon
鲫鱼	jì-yú	crucian carp
鲤鱼	lǐ-yú	carp
鲢鱼	lián-yú	silver carp
鲈鱼	lú-yú	perch
鳗鱼	mán-yú	eel
鮸鱼	miǎn-yú	slate cod croaker
墨斗鱼	mò-dǒu-yú	cuttlefish
鲇鱼	nián-yú	catfish
鲆鱼	píng-yú	flounder
鲭鱼	qīng-yú	mackerel
鳝鱼	shàn-yú	yellow eel
鲥鱼	shí-yú	reeves shad
鳎鱼	tǎ-yú	sole
武昌鱼	wǔ-chāng yú	blunt snout bream
鱿鱼	yóu-yú	squid
对虾	duì-xiā	prawns
龙虾	lóng-xiā	lobster
虾	xiā	shrimp
螃蟹	páng-xiè	crab
蚝	háo	oyster
扇贝	shàn-bèi	scallop

带子炒什锦 (dài-zi chǎo shí-jǐn)	Marinated scallops, gratineed and served with a distinctive sauce. Garnished with cucumber, celery, carrots and ham.

核桃虾
(hé-tao xiā)

Prawns with nuts (a delicious recipe from the Guangzhou region): the prawns are prepared in a mixture of cashew nuts, peanuts, peppers, ginger and spring onions.

蘑菇鱼片
(mó-gu yú-piàn)

Fillet of fish with mushrooms: chunks of fish served with flavoured mushrooms, bamboo shoots and ginger.

蒜味鱼
(suàn-wèi yú)

Fried fish with garlic. The fish is fried whole in oil for 4 to 6 minutes. Generally served with a garlic, soy and sugar sauce.

咖喱鱼
(gā-lí yú)

Curried fish. Browned in oil for 3 to 4 minutes and served together with carrots, chillies, peppers, cabbage etc …

熏鱼
(xūn yú)

Smoked fish, accompanied by a seasoning consisting of tea, cane-sugar and a spirit; it will have previously been marinaded for half an hour in a soy-based marinade.

清蒸鱼
(qīng-zhēng yú)

Steamed black sea bream. Bream stuffed with onions and ginger, seasoned with sugar, vinegar and soy sauce, and garnished with sliced mushroom caps and bamboo shoots.

炒龙虾
(chǎo lóng-xiā)

Guangzhou-style lobster. This dish is accompanied by black beans mixed with finely-chopped pork sprinkled with garlic.

蟹肉豆腐
(xiè-ròu dòu-fu)

Fresh crabmeat mixed with soy paste, seasoned with black pepper and sprinkled with finely-chopped spring onion.

鲜贝腰花
(xiān bèi yāo-huā)

Scallops served on the half-shell with pork kidneys fried and glazed in rice wine, seasoned with ginger and spring onions.

虾饺儿
(xiā-jiǎor)

Prawn pouches. Prawns sealed into tiny omelets and steamed, then doused with a soy and chicken-stock sauce.

鱼丸子
(yú-wán-zi)

Fishballs with broccoli. Poached fishballs served with florets of broccoli in a light sauce.

干烧鲤鱼
(gān-shāo lǐ-yú)

Carp in hot sauce. Fried carp with spring onions and garlic served in a hot sauce flavoured with chilli bean sauce, yellow bean sauce, rice wine and soy sauce.

Meat 肉类

When the Chinese talk about meat they are usually referring to pork. This is the most popularly-used meat in Chinese cookery, contrasted with veal which is almost unknown in China. You will come across beef and lamb but these are also rather rare.

I'd like some …	我想要些…	wǒ xiǎng-yào xiē
beef	牛肉	niú-ròu
mutton	羊肉	yáng-ròu
pork	猪肉	zhū-ròu

Pork dishes 猪肉菜肴

狮子头 (shī-zi-tóu)	"Lion's head" meatballs, a favourite dish of the Chinese. Made of chopped pork, shrimp, ginger, egg, soy sauce and wine, mixed together and formed into balls. These are then browned in oil.
卤猪脚 (lǔ zhū-jiǎo)	Steamed pig's trotters (feet). Cut into pieces, the trotters are served after having simmered three to four hours. They're deliciously enhanced with ginger and aniseed.
古老肉 (gǔ-lǎo ròu)	Sweet and sour pork. Chunks of pork are dipped into egg yolk and then deep fried. The pork is then mixed with pineapple, sweet pepper, carrots and spring onion, and dressed with a spicy sauce.
白云猪手 (bái-yún zhū-shǒu)	Marinaded pig's trotters (feet), served chilled after being marinaded the night before in sugar, salt and vinegar. A delicious aspic, made from the cooking broth, celery, ham and coriander, generally garnishes the platter on which the trotters are served.
回锅肉 (huí-guō ròu)	Sichuan-style pork. The pork is cut into chunks which are browned in oil. They're served with garlic, chilli paste, soy sauce and cubes of bean curd.
猪肉炖豆腐 (zhū-ròu dùn dòu-fu)	Braised pork with bean curd. Stir-fried minced pork braised together with yellow bean sauce, soy sauce, rice wine, chilli bean sauce, spring onion and bean curd.
宫爆肉丁 (gōng-bào ròu-dīng)	Stir-fried cubed pork with fried peanuts.

Beef dishes 牛肉菜肴

卤水牛肉
(lǔ-shuǐ niú-ròu)

Beef with four spices. This dish is considered by the Chinese as one that can be eaten anytime, anywhere, and is usually served chilled or as a snack. It keeps a long time and its taste only improves. Chunks of meat are placed in a marinade of salt, aniseed, powdered ginger, candied sugar and soy sauce. Then chicken thighs, hard-boiled eggs and a slice of liver are added. It all marinades overnight.

芦笋牛肉
(lú-sǔn niú-ròu)

Jade beef. Thinly-sliced beef accompanied by sautéed asparagus.

洋葱牛肉
(yáng-cōng niú-ròu)

Beef with onions. Finely-sliced beef in a soy-sauce marinade.

西片炒牛肉
(xī-piàn chǎo niú-ròu)

Beef with celery. Finely-sliced beef is marinaded in soy sauce, vinegar and egg white. The celery is cut into julienne strips which are blanched. The dish is served with a spicy sauce.

牛肉丸子
(niú-ròu wán-zi)

Meatballs. They're served as a first course. Fillets of fish are minced, then mixed with beef, spring onion and a seasoning of soy sauce and ginger.

干边牛肉丝
(gān biān niú-ròu-sī)

Slowly fried shredded beef with sesame seeds.

Lamb dishes 羊肉菜肴

涮羊肉
(shuàn yáng-ròu)

Mongolian hot pot. Each diner gets a plate of thinly-sliced lamb, fresh spinach and Chinese cabbage leaves, small pieces of which are dipped into a communal pot of stock with garlic, ginger, spring onions and coriander. The cooked morsels are then dipped in a sauce. At the end transparent noodles are thrown into the stock which is drunk as a soup.

烧羊肉
(shāo yáng-ròu)

Beijing braised lamb. Cubes of lamb are first blanched then stir-fried with onions, ginger and spring onions. They are then braised in stock, rice wine, sesame paste, soy sauce and cinnamon.

葱爆羊肉
(cōng bào yáng-ròu)

Stir-fried slices of mutton with spring onion.

Game and poultry 野味及禽类

Chicken almost rivals pork in its popularity and versatility.
You'll also find duck and game. As the flavour of game is
rather strong, it is usually served stewed or used as a base
for soups.

I'd like some game.	我想吃点儿野味。	wǒ xiǎng chī diǎnr yě-wèi
What poultry dishes do you serve?	你们有什么禽类菜肴？	nǐ-men yǒu shén-mo qín-lèi cài-yáo
鹌鹑	ān-chún	quail
雏鸽	chú gē	squab
雏鸭	chú yā	duckling
鹅	é	goose
鸽子	gē-zi	pigeon
火鸡	huǒ-jī	turkey
鸡	jī	chicken
鸡胸脯	jī xiōng-pú	chicken breast
麻雀	má-què	sparrow
烧鸡	shāo-jī	braised chicken
鸭子	yā-zi	duck
野鸡	yě-jī	pheasant
野猪	yě-zhū	wild boar

烤鸭
(kǎo yā)
Glazed duck. This succulent dish, a Beijing speciality, is renowned the world over. A young crammed duck is coated with a salt-malt-sugar syrup, hung up for a few hours, and then half-filled with water. It is cooked for about 40 minutes. As it roasts on the outside, it is boiled on the inside. The duck is served with a sauce made from sesame oil, sugar, stock and chives.

四川香酥鸭
(sìchuān xiāng-sū yā)
Crispy Sichuan duck. A duck is stuffed with ginger and spring onions, steamed and then deep fried.

五香鸽子
(wǔ-xiāng gē-zi)
Five-spice braised pigeons. Pigeons are braised in a sauce of soy sauce, five spice powder, rice wine and sugar. After cooking, the pigeons are cooled and served cold.

冬笋鹌鹑
(dōng-shǔn ān-chún)
Stir-fried quails. Marinaded quail stir fried with spring onions and bamboo shoots, and coated with a sauce flavoured with chicken stock and oyster sauce.

Chicken dishes 鸡类菜肴

I'd like a chicken dish.	我想要一个鸡做的菜。	wǒ xiǎng-yào yí-ge jī zuò de cài
酱鸡	jiàng-jī	chicken with soy sauce
花菇鸡	huā-gū jī	with wild rice-stems
辣鸡	là jī	with several spices
芝麻鸡	zhī-ma jī	with sesame seeds
青椒鸡丁	qīng-jiāo jī-dīng	with sweet peppers
菠萝鸡	bō-luó jī	with pineapple
莲子鸡	lián-zǐ jī	with lotus seeds
炸酱鸡	zhá jiàng-jī	sautéed chicken Sichuan-style
熏鸡	xūn-jī	smoked chicken
咖喱鸡	gā-lí jī	curried chicken
双冬鸡	shuāng dōng jī	Empress chicken
棒棒鸡	bàng-bàng jī	Sichuan-style cold chicken
辣凤爪	là fèng-zhuǎ	spiced chicken feet
甜酸鸡	tián-suān jī	sweet and sour chicken

炸子鸡
(zhá zǐ-jī)

Deep-fried chicken. Chicken legs are marinaded in a soy, wine and pepper mixture. They're then dusted with flour, fried in oil and garnished with chopped shallots.

核桃炸鸡片
(hé-tao zhá jī-piàn)

Deep-fried chicken with walnuts. Chicken breasts are cut into little pieces and seasoned with wine and condiments. The chicken portions are dipped in beaten egg whites, rolled in chopped walnuts and deep-fried.

香酥鸡
(xiāng-sū jī)

Crispy chicken. Simmered chicken halves, glazed and deep-fried.

炒鸡肝
(chǎo jī-gān)

Chicken livers with ginger. Marinaded livers are fried in a sauce of ginger, soy sauce, rice wine, rice vinegar and sesame oil. This dish can be eaten hot or cold.

宫爆鸡丁
(gōng-bào jī-dīng)

Spicy chicken with peanuts. Cubed chicken and peanuts are stir-fried with chillies and then simmered for a short time in rice wine, soy sauce and stock.

Vegetables 蔬菜

Vegetables are certainly tops in China where vegetarianism is widespread. Some vegetables are served cold but they are normally cooked first and then allowed to cool. There is no direct equivalent to the Western salad.

What vegetables do you recommend?	你能介绍些什么蔬菜吗？	nǐ néng jiè-shào xiē shén-me shū-cài ma
白菜	bái-cài	Chinese cabbage
油菜	yóu-cài	rape
菠菜	bō-cài	spinach
芹菜	qín-cài	celery
韭菜	jiǔ-cài	Chinese leeks
菜花	cài-huā	cauliflower
葱	cōng	spring onions
蒜	suàn	garlic
姜	jiāng	ginger
蒜薹	suàn-tái	garlic stems
柿子椒	shì-zi-jiāo	sweet pepper
辣椒	là-jiāo	pimento
茄子	qié-zi	aubergine (eggplant)
西红柿	xī-hóng-shì	tomatoes
豆芽儿	dòu-yár	bean sprouts
竹笋	zhú-sǔn	bamboo shoots
芦笋	lú-sǔn	asparagus
藕	ǒu	lotus root
蘑菇	mó-gu	mushrooms
西葫芦	xī-hú-lu	summer squash
白萝卜	bái luó-bo	radish (white)
小萝卜	xiǎo luó-bo	radish (red)
冬瓜	dōng-guā	wax gourd
南瓜	nán-guā	pumpkin
黄瓜	huáng-guā	cucumber
小黄瓜	xiǎo huáng-guā	gherkins
苦瓜	kǔ-guā	bitter gourd
芥菜	jiè-cài	mustard plant
甜玉米	tián yù-mǐ	corn
扁豆	biǎn-dòu	French (green) beans
豌豆	wān-dòu	peas
蚕豆	cán-dòu	broad beans
土豆	tǔ-dòu	potatoes
米	mǐ	rice
豆腐	dòu-fu	bean curd
花茎甘蓝	huā-jìng gān-lán	broccoli
青葱	qīng-cōng	shallots
红豆	hóng-dòu	aduki beans

Vegetable dishes 蔬菜类

炒什锦蔬菜 (chǎo shí-jǐn shū-cài)	Mixed vegetables. A selection of vegetables stir-fried and then braised in soy sauce, salt and sugar.
烧茄子 (shāo qié-zi)	Braised aubergines. Deep-fried sliced aubergine with spring onions and mushrooms in a sauce of ginger, garlic, soy sauce, rice wine and chilli sauce — with a sprinkle of Sichuan pepper.
炒甘蓝 (chǎo gān-lán)	Stir-fried broccoli with ginger. Blanched broccoli florets are stir-fried with shredded ginger in sesame oil.
炒冬笋 (chǎo dōng-sǔn)	Stir-fried bamboo shoots. Sliced bamboo shoots fried in soy sauce with a little rice wine, stock and sugar.
芙蓉菜花 (fú-róng cài-huā)	Steamed cauliflower in an egg-white sauce. Cauliflower florets fried in stock and soy sauce, coated in egg-white sauce, and steamed.
甜酸新菜 (tián-suān xīn-cài)	Sweet and sour cabbage. Shredded cabbage stir fried with carrots and served in a sweet and sour sauce.

Bean curd 豆腐类

Although bean curd has been known in the east for many thousands of years it has only recently made its debut in the west. Many people dismiss it as tasteless, but it is, in fact, a very versatile food, and delicious when imaginatively prepared.

Bean curd is made from yellow soya beans that have been ground and cooked, then pressed into a mould. It is a valuable source of protein that contains no cholesterol, and is much cheaper than steak.

Its texture is similar to that of blancmange and it is used in chunks, perhaps marinaded and stir-fried, or as a base for soups and sauces.

炸豆腐 (zhá dòu-fu)	Fried bean curd. Cakes of bean curd are fried until golden and then served in a sauce of soy sauce, chilli oil, rice wine and coriander.

Spices and seasonings 作调和调料

The aim of the Chinese chef is to design a menu in which the sensations of sight, smell and taste are in perfect harmony. To this end he will use a wide range of seasonings, many of which were originally used for their medicinal properties.

葱	cōng	spring onion
丁香	dīng-xiāng	cloves
干蘑菇	gān mó-gu	dried mushrooms
桂皮	guì-pí	cinnamon
姜	jiāng	ginger
酱油	jiàng-yóu	soy sauce
辣椒	là-jiāo	chillies
蒜	suàn	garlic
味精	wèi-jīng	monosodium glutamate
香菜	xiāng-cài	coriander
小茴香	xiǎo huí-xiāng	fennel seeds

大料 (dà-liào) Chinese aniseed (star anise). The fruit of a Chinese evergreen that opens up into a star shape and contains one very pungent seed, faintly reminiscent of aniseed.

陈皮 (chén-pí) Citrus peel. Dried lemon, orange or even tangerine peel which imparts a strong citrus flavour.

蚝油 (háo-yóu) Oyster sauce. Oyster concentrate in soy sauce.

黄酱 (huáng-jiàng) Yellow bean sauce. An aromatic sauce of yellow beans fermented with flour and salt.

辣酱油 (là jiàng-yóu) Chilli bean sauce. A hot and spicy sauce made from chillies and soya beans.

五香粉 (wǔ-xiāng fěn) Five-spice powder. A mixture of aniseed, fennel, cinnamon, cloves and Sichuan pepper.

虾酱 (xiā-jiàng) Shrimp sauce. A very savoury golden sauce.

香油 (xiāng-yóu) Sesame oil. A pungent oil made from toasted sesame seeds.

芝麻酱 (zhī-ma jiàng) Sesame paste. Sesame seeds ground into a creamy paste.

Rice 饭类

China is far and away the world's foremost producer of rice, the staple of two-thirds of the country's population. It is considered such a precious foodstuff that the Chinese would never leave even a few grains at the bottom of their bowl.

Rice growing occupies a major share of Chinese agriculture and demands important irrigational and hoeing-up care. After soaking the rice grain 24 hours in water, the rice is sown broadcast in a region of good earth, and takes root in three to four days. Then the plant is trimmed back when it reaches about a foot in height. As soon as the grain is planted, water is slowly let into the paddy and remains until the rice buds. Irrigation is then regulated to permit the maturing of the shaft. The harvest takes place, depending on the region, anywhere from four to five months after the seeding, which allows a new seeding and hence two crops annually.

Here are some dishes found in China which use a rice base:

炒饭 (chǎo fàn)	Fried rice. Gammon, pork and chicken are diced, then mixed with rice, peas, marinaded shrimp and an omelet cut into thin strips, served with soy sauce. This dish is usually prepared ahead of time, and reheated before serving.
珍珠肉丸 (zhēn-zhū ròu-wán)	"Pearl meatballs". Made of prawns, spring onions, pork, eggs, and spices, mixed together and covered with sticky rice, steamed and served lukewarm.
菠菜花生炒饭 (bō-cài huā-shēng chǎo fàn)	Jade rice. This dish is accompanied by chopped spinach, diced ham and finely chopped garlic.
江米粥 (jiāng-mǐ zhōu)	Sticky rice. Boiled rice porridge often eaten for breakfast.
米粉肉 (mí-fěn-ròu)	Steamed pork in ground rice. Marinaded cubed pork steamed, and served mixed with heated ground rice.

Noodles 面条及粉丝菜肴

The best known of Chinese noodles (which, together with rice, are staples in the Chinese diet) are *fěn-sī*, also called Chinese vermicelli or cellophane noodles. *Fěn-sī* are made from mung bean starch. Noodles are also made from wheat and rice flour. They absorb the aroma of the seasoning and spices cooked with them perfectly.

The Chinese are very fond of ravioli which they eat steamed, boiled, lightly fried or in soup.

蚂蚁上树 (mǎ-yǐ shàng shù)	"Ants climbing the tree". Braised *fěn-sī* coated with grains of fried minced meat.
凉拌粉丝 (liáng-bàn fěn-sī)	Noodle salad. An "Imperial sauce" made of soy sauce, spring onion, slivers of ginger, sesame oil, lemon juice and pimento paste which accompanies the noodles as a garnish to chicken, ham, soy sprouts, peas and bamboo shoots.
粉丝炒羊肉 (fěn-sī chǎo yáng-ròu)	Lamb with *fěn-sī*. 2-inch lengths of *fěn-sī* served with turnips, lamb, ginger, leeks and a seasoning of soy sauce, alcohol and candied sugar.
菊花芙蓉块 (jú-huā fú-róng kuài)	"Chrysanthemum flowers". Finely chopped prawns mixed with egg white and pork fat. Square patties are formed and covered with sliced *fěn-sī*. This is served with spring carrots and some pimento sauce.
猪肉炒面 (zhū-ròu chǎo miàn)	Pork with noodles. Egg noodles are served with pork cut into strips, cabbage, carrots, celery and chicken broth.
什锦炒面 (shí-jǐn chǎo miàn)	Chow mein. Boiled egg noodles, fried and then combined with shredded meat and chopped vegetables.
阳春面 (yáng-chūn miàn)	A light chicken broth Shanghai-style, with vegetables and noodles.
鸡丝面 (jī-sī miàn)	Shredded chicken with noodles in stock.

Fruit 水果

Thanks to its geographical location, extending from the Siberian steppes in the north to tropical jungles in the south, China has an incomparable range of fruits to offer. If you can, try an Ice Mountain fruit salad. It is a simple but effective arrangement of a variety of fresh fruit, peeled and sliced, and served on a bed of crushed ice.

Do you have any fruit?	你们这儿有水果吗？	nǐ-men zhèr yǒu shuǐ-guǒ ma
I'd like a (fresh) fruit salad.	我想要一个（鲜）什锦水果。	wǒ xiǎng-yào yí-ge (xiān) shí-jǐn shuǐ-guǒ

荸荠	bí-qi	water chestnuts
槟榔	bīng-lang	areca nuts, betel nuts
菠萝	bō-luó	pineapple
（干）橄榄	(gān) gǎn-lǎn	(dried) olives
甘蔗	gān-zhe	sugar cane
桔子	jú-zi	tangerine
核桃	hé-tao	walnuts
柑子	gān-zi	orange
梨	lí	pear
栗子	lì-zi	chestnuts
李子	lǐ-zi	plum
荔枝	lì-zhī	lychees
莲子	lián-zǐ	lotus seeds
龙眼	lóng-yǎn	longan
芒果	máng-guǒ	mango
梅子	méi-zi	prune
木莓	mù-méi	raspberries
柠檬	níng-méng	lemon
枇杷	pí-pa	loquat
苹果	píng-guǒ	apple
葡萄	pú-táo	grapes
桑葚儿	sāng-rènr	mulberries
石榴	shí-liú	pomegranate
柿子	shì-zi	persimmon
桃子	táo-zi	peach
甜瓜	tián-guā	sweet melon
无花果	wú-huā-guǒ	figs
西瓜	xī-guā	watermelon
香蕉	xiāng-jiāo	banana
杏	xìng	apricot
草莓	cǎo-méi	strawberry
椰子	yē-zi	coconut
樱桃	yīng-táo	cherries
枣	zǎo	Chinese dates

Dessert 糕点甜食

Desserts are rarely served in China except at banquets, where they come as very sweet, minor dishes interposed between savouries. If you enjoy something sweet between meals, try some caramel walnuts or chunks of banana in toffee.

If you are invited to dinner in a Chinese home, you will probably be offered seasonal fruit such as oranges, kumquats, longans, cherries or lychees.

I'd like a dessert, please.	我想要一个甜食。	wǒ xiǎng-yào yí-ge tián-shí
What do you recommend?	你能介绍些什么甜食吗？	nǐ néng jiè-shào xiē shén-me tián-shí ma
Something light, please.	要清口点儿的。	yào qīng-kǒu diǎnr de
Just a small portion, please.	就要一点儿。	jiù yào yì-diǎnr
Nothing more, thanks.	不要了，谢谢。	bú yào le. xiè-xie

冰镇果羹	bīng-zhèn guǒ-gēng	fruit jelly
菠萝醪糟	bō-luó láo-zāo	pineapples marinaded in rice wine
什锦瓜瓶	shí-jǐn guā-píng	water melon with fruit
西米桔羹	xī-mǐ jú-gēng	hot orange cakes
拔丝苹果	bá-sī píng-guǒ	caramelized apple
八宝饭	bā-bǎo-fàn	rice cake with eight treasures
杏仁儿酥	xìng-rénr sū	almond biscuits (cookies)
杏仁儿豆腐	xìng-rénr dòu-fu	almond flavoured custard
芝麻糊	zhī-ma hú	sesame cream
杏仁儿糊	xìng-rénr hú	almond cream
花生糊	huā-shēng hú	peanut cream
千层糕	qiān-céng gāo	thousand layer cake
甜蛋羹	tián dàn-gēng	egg custard
冰糖蒸梨	bīng-táng zhēng lí	steamed pears
莲子羹	lián-zǐ gēng	lotus root custard
枣泥饼	zǎo-ní bǐng	date paste pancakes
栗子羹	lì-zi-gēn	chestnuts in jelly
元宵	yuán-xiāo	sweet rice dumplings

Drinks 酒类

As a general rule, the Chinese take neither aperitifs before a meal nor spirits after it. The powerful *máo-tái*, a wheat-and-sugarcane-based spirit, is widely drunk at banquets and when toasts are proposed. The uninitiated should beware of its punch. You will also come across *shào-xīng*, a red rice-wine served hot in tiny cups. Regional wines are generally rather sweet, and the white wines are often reminiscent of certain resinated wines encountered in southern Europe. The inexpensive local sparkling wines tend to be very sweet.

Beer is very similar to Western brews. The most popular brand comes from the city of Qingdao and is known by that city's old-style transliterated name, Tsingtao.

China imports alcohol for its foreign residents, and home-brewed whisky, gin and brandy are also available. In certain regions, spirits are produced in which snakes, lizards and stag's antlers have been steeped. These brews are credited with special, often medical, properties.

I don't drink alcohol.	我不喝酒。	wǒ bù hē jiǔ
I'd like a *máo-tái*	我想要一小杯茅台。	wǒ xiǎng-yào yì xiǎo bēi máo-tái
aperitif	开胃酒	kāi-wèi-jiǔ
brandy	白兰地	bái-lán-dì
gin	金酒	jīn-jiǔ
gin and tonic	金酒和奎宁水	jīn-jiǔ hé kuí-níng-shuǐ
sherry	雪利酒	xuě-lì jiǔ
vermouth	味美思	wèi-měi-sī
vodka	伏特加	fú-tè-jiā
whisky	威士忌	wēi-shì-jì
neat (straight)	纯的	chún de
on the rocks	加冰块	jiā bīng-kuài

> 干杯！
> gān-bēi
> YOUR HEALTH!/ CHEERS!

Do you have ... beer?	你这儿有…啤酒吗？	nǐ zhèr yǒu ... pí-jiǔ ma
bottled	瓶装的	píng-zhuāng de
draught	散装的	sǎn-zhuāng de
imported	进口的	jìn-kǒu de
light/dark	清爽型/黑	qīng-shuǎng xíng/hēi
I'd like (a) ...	我想要…	wǒ xiǎng-yào
half a bottle	半瓶	bàn píng
half a glass	半杯	bàn bēi
litre	一升	yì-shēng
Bring me another ..., please.	请再拿…来。	qǐng zài ná ... lái
glass/bottle	一杯/一瓶	yì bēi/yì píng
I'd like a bottle of wine.	我想要一瓶葡萄酒。	wǒ xiǎng-yào yì-píng pú-táo-jiǔ
What's the name of this wine?	这是什么葡萄酒？	zhè shì shén-me pú-táo-jiǔ
Where does this wine come from?	这葡萄酒是哪儿出产的？	zhè pú-táo-jiǔ shì nǎr chū-chǎn de

red	红	hóng
dry white/sweet white	干白/甜白	gān bái/tián bái
sparkling	带气的	dài qì de

Tea 茶

The Chinese drink tea all day long. The history of tea-drinking in China goes back to the year 2737 B.C. and the reign of Shen Nong. This emperor treated some of his ailments with herbal remedies. One of these was tea, which is now claimed to contain 300 chemical constituents, many of them of acknowledged medical value. In A.D. 730, in the Tang dynasty, Lu Yu wrote a "Book of Tea" in which he described the cultivation of the shrub and how to prepare an infusion from its leaves. The beverage was exported to Japan in the thirteenth century and was known in England by the seventeenth. Today, as many as 250 varieties can be distinguished. The Chinese obtain the delicious aroma of their tea by leaving it in the proximity of aromatic plants for some time.

Chinese tea is taken without sugar or milk. Among the varieties available are black (fermented) tea, fragrant green tea, tea scented with jasmine or magnolia, or blends of flowers, and slightly fermented oolong tea.

Every national minority has its own special way of making tea. The Tibetans, for instance, boil it in a pot with salt. Special occasions, such as a visit by a long-absent friend, are celebrated by adding yak's milk to the tea which is served with great ceremony. Mongolian herdsmen of the northern steppes and deserts boil tea leaves together with cow's or goat's milk and add salt. The Moslem Huis welcome their guests with hot tea served in covered cups to which brown sugar and dates are added to bring good luck.

I'd like some ...	我想要一杯…	wǒ xiǎng-yào yì-bēi
tea	茶	chá
green tea	绿茶	lù-chá
jasmine tea	茉莉花茶	mò-lì huā-chá
oolong tea	乌龙茶	wū-lóng chá

Nonalcoholic drinks 饮料

apple juice	苹果汁	píng-guǒ zhī
(hot) chocolate	（热）巧克力	(rè) qiǎo-kè-lì
coffee	咖啡	kā-fēi
black	纯的	chún de
with cream	加奶油的	jiā nǎi-yóu de
with milk	加牛奶的	jiā niú-nǎi de
decaffeinated	不带咖啡因的	bú dài kā-fēi-yīn de
fruit juice	果汁	guǒ-zhī
grapefruit juice	西柚汁	xī-yòu-zhī
iced tea	冰茶	bīng-chá
lemon juice	柠檬汁	níng-méng zhī
lemonade	柠檬汽水	níng-méng qì-shuǐ
milk	牛奶	niú-nǎi
mineral water	矿泉水	kuàng-quán-shuǐ
fizzy	带汽的	dài qì de
still	不带汽的	bú dài qì de
orange juice	桔子汁	jú-zi-zhī
orangeade	桔子汽水	jú-zi qì-shuǐ
tomato juice	西红柿汁	xī-hóng-shì-zhī
tonic water	奎宁水	kuí-níng shuǐ

Complaints 有意见

There is a plate/ glass missing.	少一个盘子/杯子。	shǎo yí-ge pán-zi/ bēi-zi
I have no knife/ fork/spoon.	我没有刀子/叉子/ 勺子。	wǒ méi yǒu dāo-zi/ chā-zi/sháo-zi
I have no chopsticks.	我没有筷子。	wǒ méi yǒu kuài-zi
That's not what I ordered.	这不是我点的。	zhè bú shì wǒ diǎn de
I asked for …	我要的是…	wǒ yào de shì
There must be some mistake.	一定是搞错了。	yí-dìng shì gǎo cuò le
May I change this?	可以换这个吗？	kě-yǐ huàn zhè-ge ma
I asked for a small plate (for the child).	我要的是小盘的（给这 个孩子吃的）。	wǒ yào de shì xiǎo-pán de (gěi zhè-ge hái-zi chī de)
The meat is …	这肉…	zhè ròu
underdone	没熟	méi shóu
overdone	火太过了	huǒ tài guò le
I'm afraid this is too … for me.	我觉得这菜太…了。	wǒ jué-de zhè cài tài … le
bitter	苦	kǔ
oily	油腻	yóu-nì
salty	咸	xián
spicy (hot)	辣	là
sweet	甜	tián
I don't like this.	我不喜欢这个。	wǒ bù xǐ-huan zhè-ge
This dish is cold.	这个菜是凉的。	zhè-ge cài shì liáng de
I don't think this is fresh.	我觉得这不新鲜。	wǒ jué-de zhè bù xīn-xiān
There is something wrong with this dish.	这个菜味不对。	zhè ge cài wèi bú duì
What's taking so long?	做什么需要这么长的 时间？	zuò shén-me xū-yào zhè-me cháng de shí-jiān
Have you forgotten our drinks?	你忘了我们要的饮料 了吧？	nǐ wàng-le wǒ-men yào de yǐn-liào le ba
This isn't clean.	这不干净。	zhè bù gān-jìng
Would you ask the manager to come over?	请叫你们经理来。	qǐng jiào nǐ-men jīng-lǐ lái

The bill (check) 帐单

Even if you have enjoyed your meal very much, you should not attempt to press a tip on the waiter, as this custom is strongly discouraged in the People's Republic. If, at a special dinner or banquet, you would like to express your satisfaction with the meal, you can invite the chef over for a drink and offer him a toast.

I'd like to pay.	我想付钱。	wǒ xiǎng fù qián
We'd like to pay separately.	我们想各付各的。	wǒ-men xiǎng gè fù gè de
May I have the bill (check), please?	请给我帐单。	qǐng gěi wǒ zhàng-dān
I think there's a mistake in the bill.	这个帐单好象有错吧。	zhè-ge zhàng-dān hǎo-xiàng yǒu cuò ba
What is this amount for?	这项是付什么的钱？	zhè xiàng shì fù shén-me de qián
Is everything included?	都包括了吗？	dōu bāo-kuò le ma
Do you accept traveller's cheques?	你们这儿收旅行支票吗？	nǐ-men zhèr shōu lǚ-xíng zhī-piào ma
Can I pay with this credit card?	我能用这个信用卡付款吗？	wǒ néng yòng zhè-ge xìn-yòng-kǎ fù-kuǎn ma
That was a very good meal.	这顿饭吃得很好。	zhè dùn fàn chī-de hěn hǎo
We enjoyed it, thank you.	我们吃得很满意，谢谢。	wǒ-men chī-de hěn mǎn-yì. xiè-xie
Where should we pay?	我们该在哪儿付钱？	wǒ-men gāi zài nǎr fù qián

Snacks — picnic 小吃-野餐

Snacks can be found in every city and all over the city. The Chinese are inveterate snackers and the roadside stalls selling steamed savoury buns and other "fast food" have been in business for a very long time. If you're thirsty you can have a beer from a corner beer shop, and at the same time maybe try a small dish of sliced kidneys or a spring roll.

If you're in the South then it's worth having at least one meal in a dim sum (点心) restaurant. In the North you would go to a "small snack" (小吃) restaurant. This is where people meet, from mid-morning until mid-afternoon, to catch up on the latest news or even to discuss business. These restaurants are usually large, noisy and friendly. In dim sum restaurants waiters course around the room pushing trolleys loaded down with delicious bite-sized snacks, and you simply stop them and take your pick. In the North, more prosaically, you pick your snacks up at the counter. The food is normally quite light and non-greasy, and usually steamed rather than fried.

I'll have ..., please.	我要…	wǒ yào
one of those	一个那种的	yí-ge nà zhǒng de
some of those	几个那种的	jǐ-ge nà zhǒng de

炒面条
(chǎo miàn-tiáo)

Fried noodles.

汤面
(tāng miàn)

Noodles tossed in gravy or soup.

锅贴
(guō-tiē)

Parcels of thin pastry stuffed with a meat filling, or, in the south, with seafood. They are crispy at the bottom with a steamed filling.

元宵
(yuán-xiāo)

Tiny glutinous rice-flour balls with sweet fillings, usually served in soup.

烧卖
(shāo-mai)

Small open-topped dumplings that are stuffed with meat and steamed.

春卷儿
(chūn-juǎnr)

Spring rolls. A mixture of vegetables and meat, including water chestnuts, bean sprouts and spring onions, which is stir-fried and then wrapped in a thin pancake and deep-fried.

包子
(bāo-zi)

Steamed savoury buns. Meat and gravy are sealed in a yeast dough and then steamed.

江米饭
(jiāng-mǐ fàn)

Glutinous rice steamed with various dried fruit.

上饭馆儿

Here's a list of food and drink that might be useful if you want to organise a picnic.

Please give me a/an/some ...	请给我拿…	qǐng gěi wǒ ná
apples	几个苹果	jǐ-ge píng-guǒ
bananas	几个香蕉	jǐ-ge xiāng-jiāo
biscuits	一包饼干	yì-bāo bǐng-gān
bottle opener	一个开瓶器	yí-ge kāi-píng-qì
cake	一个蛋糕	yí-ge dàn-gāo
can opener	一个开罐器	yí-ge kāi-guàn-qì
chocolate bar	一块巧克力	yí-kuài qiǎo-kè-lì
coffee	一筒咖啡	yì-tǒng kā-fēi
cold cuts	一些熟肉	yì-xiē shóu-ròu
cookies (Am.)	一包饼干	yì-bāo bǐng-gān
cucumbers	几条黄瓜	jǐ tiáo huáng-guā
eggs	几个鸡蛋	jǐ-ge jī-dàn
ham	一些火腿	yì-xiē huǒ-tuǐ
ice cream	几个冰淇淋	jǐ-ge bīng-qí-lín
lemons	几个柠檬	jǐ-ge níng-méng
matches	几盒火柴	jǐ-hé huǒ-chái
milk	一瓶牛奶	yì-píng niú-nǎi
mustard	一些芥末	yì-xiē jiè-mo
oranges	几个柑子	jǐ-ge gān-zi
(paper) napkins	一打（纸）餐巾	yì-dá (zhǐ) cān-jīn
pepper	一些胡椒	yì-xiē hú-jiāo
potatoes	几个土豆	jǐ-ge tǔ-dòu
rolls (bread)	几个小圆面包	jǐ-ge xiǎo yuán miàn-bāo
salt	一些盐	yì-xiē yán
sandwiches	几个三明治	jǐ-ge sān-míng-zhì
soft drink	一瓶不带酒精的饮料	yì-píng bú dài jiǔ-jīng de yǐn-liào
soy sauce	一瓶酱油	yì-píng jiàng-yóu
sugar	一包糖	yì-bāo táng
tea	一包茶叶	yì-bāo chá-yè
tin opener	一个开罐器	yí-ge kāi-guàn-qì
tomatoes	几个西红柿	jǐ-ge xī-hóng-shì
wine	一瓶葡萄酒	yì-píng pú-tāo-jiǔ
yoghurt	一瓶酸奶	yì-píng suān-nǎi

bottle	瓶	píng
box	盒	hé
carton	箱	xiāng
jar	筒	tǒng
packet	包	bāo

Travelling around

Plane 飞机

Is there a flight to Beijing?	有去北京的航班吗？	yǒu qù běijīng de háng-bān ma
Is it a direct flight?	这是直达的航班吗？	zhè shì zhí-dá de háng-bān ma
When's the next flight to Shanghai?	下一班去上海的航班什么时间起飞？	xià yì-bān qù shànghǎi de háng-bān shén-me shí-jiān qǐ-fēi
Is there a connection to Guangzhou?	有去广州的联程航班吗？	yǒu qù guǎngzhōu de lián-chéng háng-bān ma
I'd like a ticket to Nanjing.	我想买一张去南京的机票。	wǒ xiǎng mǎi yì-zhāng qù nánjīng de jī-piào
single (one-way)	单程票	dān-chéng piào
return (roundtrip)	往返票	wǎng-fǎn piào
What time do we take off?	什么时间起飞？	shén-me shí-jiān qǐ-fēi
What time do I have to check in?	我什么时间到机场办登机手续？	wǒ shén-me shí-jiān dào jī-chǎng bàn dēng-jī shǒu-xù
Is there a bus to the airport?	有去机场的班车吗？	yǒu qù jī-chǎng de bān-chē ma
What's the flight number?	航班班次是多少？	háng-bān bān-cì shì duō-shao
What time do we arrive?	我们什么时间到？	wǒ-men shén-me shí-jiān dào
I'd like to ... my reservation on flight no. 123.	我想…我在一二三号航班的预定。	wǒ xiǎng ... wǒ zài 123 hào háng-bān de yù-dìng
cancel	取消	qǔ-xiāo
change	更换	gēng-huàn
confirm	确认	què-rèn
What's the rate for excess baggage?	超重的行李怎么计价？	chāo-zhòng de xíng-li zěn-me jì-jià

到达 dào-dá ARRIVAL	出发 chū-fā DEPARTURE	候机室 hòu-jī-shì WAITING ROOM

旅行

Trains 火车

The train system is well developed in China, however, independent train travel is not easy. Spur-of-the-moment journeys are almost impossible, as tickets can rarely be bought immediately before departure. All the seats will have been sold out, and the train will be full. Tickets are normally bought well in advance.

There are a number of possibilities when buying a ticket. You can choose between hard and soft seating, and, on longer journeys, between hard and soft sleeping. In practice, the choice is more limited as the Chinese prefer that foreign visitors travel "soft", together with the high-ranking Chinese. The main difference between the two categories lies, as the names suggest, in the degree of comfort. But price is also an important factor — soft sleeping can cost almost as much as an airline seat.

慢车 màn-chē SLOW TRAIN	快车 kuài-chē FAST TRAIN	特快车 tè-kuài-chē EXPRESS TRAIN

There are three types of train in terms of speed. The first are local trains, stopping at all the stations; these travel quite regularly. The second type — fast trains — stop only at larger towns and cities. Express trains are generally long-distance and connect major cities as well as providing the international service.

All trains are numbered and are referred to primarily by this number. However, both number and destination are mentioned in loudspeaker announcements.

Although independent travel is possible, it is extremely complicated and time-consuming to make the necessary arrangements. You would be advised to take advantage of the service provided by CITS.

To the railway station 去火车站

Where's the railway station?	火车站在哪儿？	huǒ-chē-zhàn zài nǎr
I'd like a taxi.	我想要一辆出租汽车。	wǒ xiǎng yào yí-liàng chū-zū qì-chē
Please take me to the railway station.	请送我去火车站。	qǐng sòng wǒ qù huǒ-chē-zhàn
What's the fare?	车费多少？	chē-fèi duō-shao
Can I have a receipt, please?	请开一张收据。	qǐng kāi yì-zhāng shōu-jù

入口	出口	至站台
rù-kǒu	chū-kǒu	zhì zhàn-tái
ENTRANCE	EXIT	TO THE PLATFORMS

Where's the ...? …在哪儿？

Where is/are the ...?	…在哪儿？	... zài nǎr
information office	问讯处	wèn-xùn-chù
left-luggage office (baggage check)	行李寄存处	xíng-li jì-cún-chù
lost property (lost-and-found) office	失物招领处	shī-wù zhāo-lǐng-chù
newsstand	售报亭	shòu-bào-tíng
platform 7	七号站台	qī hào zhàn-tái
restaurant	饭馆儿	fàn-guǎnr
ticket office	售票处	shòu-piào-chù
waiting room	候车室	hòu-chē-shì
Where are the toilets?	厕所在哪儿？	cè-suǒ zài nǎr

请勿吸烟
qǐng wù xī-yān
NO SMOKING

Smokers beware: on 1st June 1987 the whole of Beijing station officially became a non-smoking area.

旅行

Inquiries 问讯

When making inquiries about departure and arrival times of a particular train, refer to it by its number as well as its destination.

When is the … train to Tianjin?	去天津的…列车几点开车？	qù tiānjīn de … liè-chē jǐ diǎn kāi chē
last/next	最后一班/下一班	zuì-hòu yì-bān/xià yì-bān
What time does train no. 19 leave?	十九次列车什么时间开车？	19 cì liè-chē shén-me shí-jiān kāi chē
What's the fare to Shanghai?	去上海的票价是多少？	qù shànghǎi de piào-jià shì duō-shao
Is it an express train?	是特快列车吗？	shì tè-kuài liè-chē ma
Do I have to change trains?	我需要换车吗？	wǒ xū-yào huàn chē ma
How long will the train stop in Suzhou?	列车在苏州停多长时间？	liè-chē zài sūzhōu tíng duō-cháng shí-jiān
Is there enough time to change?	有足够的时间换车吗？	yǒu zú-gòu de shí-jiān huàn chē ma
Is the train running on time?	列车正点吗？	liè-chē zhèng-diǎn ma
What time does the train arrive in Nanjing?	列车什么时间到南京？	liè-chē shén-me shí-jiān dào nánjīng
Is there a … on the train?	车上有…吗？	chē-shang yǒu … ma
dining-car	餐车	cān-chē
sleeping-car	卧铺车厢	wò-pù chē-xiāng
Does the train stop in Jinan?	列车在济南停吗？	liè-chē zài jǐnán tíng ma
What platform does train no. 16 from Guangzhou arrive at?	从广州来的十六次列车在几号站台停？	cóng guǎngzhōu lái de 16 cì liè-chē zài jǐ hào zhàn-tái tíng
What platform does the train to Beijing leave from?	去北京的列车从哪个站台发车？	qù běi-jīng de liè-chē cóng nǎ-ge zhàn-tái fā chē
I'd like to buy a time-table.	我想买一本列车时刻表。	wǒ xiǎng mǎi yì-běn liè-chē shí-kè-biǎo

对不起，这次车的座位买完了。	I'm sorry, there are no seats left on that train.
…次列车客满。	Train no. … is full.
这是直达列车。	It's a through train.
你得在…换车。	You have to change at …
在…下车后换乘慢车。	Change at … and get a local train.
七号站台在…	Platform 7 is …
那边/左边/右边	over there/ on the left/ on the right
二次列车将于八号站台发车。	Train no. 2 will leave from platform 8.
列车将晚点…分钟。	There will be a delay of … minutes.

Tickets 车票

You can only buy single (one-way) tickets for the trains. If you should want to break your journey, go to the ticket office and enquire if there are any free seats on the train you would like to continue on.

I want a ticket to Nanjing.	我要一张去南京的车票。	wǒ yào yì-zhāng qù nánjīng de chē-piào
hard seating	硬座	yìng-zuò
soft seating	软座	ruǎn-zuò
hard sleeping	硬卧	yìng-wò
soft sleeping	软卧	ruǎn-wò
Is it cheaper for the child?	儿童票便宜吗？	ér-tóng-piào pián-yi ma
I want a …	我要一个…	wǒ yào yí-ge
seat (by the window)	（靠窗的）座位	(kào chuāng de) zuò-wèi
berth in the sleeping car	卧铺	wò-pù
upper berth	上铺	shàng-pù
middle berth	中铺	zhōng-pù
lower berth	下铺	xià-pù

All aboard 开车啦

Tickets are checked on entering and leaving the station, but there are also occasional checks on board.

Is this the platform for the train to Shanghai?	去上海是在这个站台上车吗？	qù shànghǎi shì zài zhèi-gè zhàn-tái shàng chē ma
Is this the train to Jinan?	这是去济南的列车吗？	zhè shì qù jǐnán de liè-chē ma
Excuse me. May I get past?	对不起，我可以过去吗？	duì-bu-qǐ. wǒ kě-yǐ guò qu ma
Is this seat taken?	这个座位有人吗？	zhèi-ge zuò-wèi yǒu rén ma
I think that's my seat.	这是我的座位吧。	zhè shì wǒ de zuò-wèi ba
Would you let me know before we get to Suzhou?	到苏州前请告诉我好吗？	dào sūzhōu qián qǐng gào-su wǒ hǎo ma
What station is this?	这是哪站？	zhè shì něi zhàn
How long does the train stop here?	列车在这儿停多长时间？	liè-chē zài zhèr tíng duō-cháng shí-jiān
When do we get to Suzhou?	列车什么时间到苏州？	liè-chē shén-me shí-jiān dào sūzhōu

硬席	软席
(yìng-xí)	(ruǎn-xí)
HARD SEATS	SOFT SEATS

Sleeping 卧铺

Are there any free berths in the sleeping car?	请问还有空着的卧铺吗？	qǐng wèn hái yǒu kōng-zhe de wò-pù ma
Where's the sleeping car?	卧铺车厢在哪儿？	wò-pù chē-xiāng zài nǎr
Where's my berth?	我的卧铺在哪儿？	wǒ de wò-pù zài nǎr
I'd like a lower berth.	我想要下铺。	wǒ xiǎng yào xià-pù
Would you make up our berths?	请把我们的卧铺整理一下。	qǐng bǎ wǒ-men de wò-pù zhěng-lǐ yí xià
Would you wake me at 7 o'clock?	请在七点叫醒我。	qǐng zài 7 diǎn jiào-xǐng wǒ

Eating 就餐

All long-distance trains have dining-cars in which you will be able to enjoy Chinese cuisine patterned after that which you would find in a good restaurant in Guangzhou or Beijing.

The dining-car is only open at meal times, but there is also often a snack bar trolley which supplies hot lunches, usually rice with fried meat and vegetables. Boiling water is brought around to make tea but the custom of providing tea leaves is dying out.

During station stops you will see platform carts selling local specialities: fruit, boiled eggs and very often a kind of hot steamed bread filled with meat and known as *bāo-zi*.

Where's the dining-car?	餐车在哪儿？	cān-chē zài nǎr
Can I have a lunch box?	请给我一盒盒饭。	qǐng gěi wǒ yì-hé hé-fàn
Please give me two of these and one of those.	请给我拿两个这种的和一个那种的。	qǐng gěi wǒ nā liǎng-ge zhè zhǒng de hé yí-ge nà zhǒng de

Baggage 行李

Chinese railway stations do not normally supply luggage trolleys, so if you have to carry your own luggage it would be wise to invest in a suitcase with wheels.

Where's the left-luggage office (baggage check)?	行李寄存处在哪儿？	xíng-li jì-cún-chù zài nǎr
I'd like to leave my luggage, please.	我想寄存我的行李。	wǒ xiǎng jì-cún wǒ de xíng-li
I'd like to register (check) my luggage?	我想托运我的行李。	wǒ xiǎng tuō-yùn wǒ de xíng-li

> **行李托运处**
> xíng-li tuō-yùn-chù
> REGISTERING (CHECKING) LUGGAGE

Coach (long-distance bus) 长途汽车

Coaches are not a practical alternative to trains as they are slow and not very comfortable. But you may need to travel by coach if you want to visit some of the less accessible sights.

When's the next coach to …?	下趟去…的长途汽车什么时间开车?	xià tàng qù … de cháng-tú qì-chē shén-me shí-jiān kāi chē
Does this coach stop in …?	这趟长途汽车在…停吗?	zhèi tàng cháng-tú qì-chē zài … tíng ma
How long does the journey (trip) take?	路上要用多长时间?	lù-shang yào yòng duō cháng shí-jiān

Bus — Tram (streetcar) 公共汽车-电车

Public transport is generally very crowded and it's not unusual to see passengers clinging onto the outside windows of buses. You buy your ticket from the conductor who will tell you when to get off if you give him or her a note of your destination written in Chinese characters. If a Chinese person offers you a seat, accept with a smile.

Which tram (street-car) goes to the National Art Gallery?	哪路电车去美术馆?	nǎ lù diàn-chē qù měi-shù-guǎn
Where can I get a bus to …?	我去…到哪儿去坐公共汽车?	wǒ qù … dào nǎr qù zuò gōng-gòng qì-chē
What bus do I take for …?	我去…乘哪路公汽车?	wǒ qù … chèng nǎ lù gōng-gòng qì-chē
Where's the …?	…在哪儿?	… zài nǎr
bus stop	公共汽车站	gōng-gòng qì-chē-zhàn
terminus	终点站	zhōng-diǎn-zhàn

公共汽车站
gōng-gòng qì-chē-zhàn
BUS STOP

When is the ... bus to the zoo?	去动物园的…公共汽车几点开？	qù dòng-wù-yuán de... gōng-gòng qì-chē jǐ-diǎn kāi
first/last	头班/ 末班	tóu-bān/ mò-bān
How often do the buses to the airport run?	去机场的公共汽车多长时间一趟？	qù jī-chǎng de gōng-gòng qì-chē duō cháng shí-jiān yí-tàng
How much is the fare to ...?	去…的票价多少？	qù ... de piào-jià duō-shao
Do I have to change buses?	我得换车吗？	wǒ děi huàn chē ma
How many bus stops are there to ...?	去…得坐几站？	qù ... děi zuò jǐ zhàn
How long does the journey (trip) take?	路上要用多长时间？	lù-shang yào yòng duō cháng shí-jiān
Will you tell me when to get off?	你能在该下车的时候告诉我吗？	nǐ néng zài gāi xià chē de shí-hou gào-su wǒ ma
I want to get off at the next stop.	我下站下车。	wǒ xià-zhàn xià chē

Underground (subway) 地铁

The Beijing underground — whose stations are recognized by the sign 地铁 *(dì-tiě)* — operates daily between 6 a.m. and 9 p.m., carrying more than 70 million passengers each year. Trains and stations are maintained in spotless condition.

Each station is visibly quite different from all the others by virtue of its colour scheme, the shape of the columns or other lesser details. Station names are written in Pinyin as well as Chinese, which also helps.

At present, the single-line system only covers 24km., but more lines are being built. An underground system is also under construction in Shanghai.

Where's the nearest underground station?	离这儿最近的地铁站在哪儿？	lí zhèr zuì jìn de dì-tiě-zhàn zài nǎr
Does this train go to ...?	这趟列车去…吗？	zhèi tàng liè-chē qù ... ma
Is the next station ...?	下站是…吗？	xià zhàn shì ... ma

旅行

Boat service 水路

If you have the chance, try to spend a few hours exploring the Shanghai waterfront, with its golden-sailed junks and big steamers, or go for a cruise down the Chang Jiang. Better still on a warm summer afternoon in Beijing you might like to go boating on one of the serene lakes that grace the capital's many parks.

If taking a longer cruise you will probably be more comfortable in second class, where there are two to four beds in each cabin, and often the use of a collective sitting room. Third and fourth classes are much more crowded, being based on dormitory-style accommodation.

Can I hire a rowing boat?	我可以租条游船吗？	wǒ kě-yǐ zū tiáo yóu-chuán ma
There are ... of us.	我们…个人。	wǒ-men ... ge rén
I'd like it for ...	我想租…	wǒ xiǎng zū
half an hour	半小时	bàn xiǎo-shí
1 hour	一小时	yì xiǎo-shí
What's the charge per hour?	每小时多少钱？	měi xiǎo-shí duō-shao qián
When does a boat for ... leave?	去…的船儿几点开？	qù ... de chuán jǐ diǎn kāi
Where's the embarkation point?	在哪儿上船？	zài nǎr shàng chuán
I'd like to take a tour of the harbour.	我想坐船游览一下儿港湾。	wǒ xiǎng zuò chuán yóu-lǎn yí xiàr gǎng-wān
boat	船	chuán
cabin	客舱	kè cāng
second class	二等	èr-děng
third class	三等	sān-děng
cruise	坐船游览	zuò chuán yóu-lǎn
deck	甲板	jiǎ-bǎn
life belt	救生衣	jiù-shēng-yī
life boat	救生艇	jiù-shēng-tǐng
port	码头	mǎ-tou
river cruise	河上坐船游览	hé shàng zuò chuán yóu-lǎn
ship	轮船	lún-chuán
I'd like to take a short cruise.	我想短途坐船游览。	wǒ xiǎng duǎn-tú zuò chuán yóu-lǎn

Pedicabs 三轮车

Pedicabs can still be encountered in certain large cities such as Shanghai, and are an ideal way of sightseeing. These man-powered three-wheelers take two passengers.

I'd like visit to the town centre.	我想去市区观光。	wǒ xiǎng qù shì-qū guān-guāng
How much do you charge?	要付多少钱？	yào fù duō-shao qián

Car 包车

You will not be able to hire a self-drive car, but you can hire a car and driver for the day or longer.

I'd like to hire a car with a guide and driver.	我想租一辆有导游和司机的汽车。	wǒ xiǎng zū yí-liàng yǒu dǎo-yóu hé sī-jī de qì-chē
I'd like it for ...	我想用…	wǒ xiǎng yòng
a day/ ... days	一天/…天	yì-tiān/ ... tiān
a week/ ... weeks	一个星期/…个星期	yí-ge xīng-qī/ ... ge xīng-qī
What's the charge per day?	一天多少钱？	yì-tiān duō-shao qián

Accidents — Police 事故-警察

Here are a few phrases that may be useful should you be involved in or witness an accident.

Please call a doctor, quickly.	请快叫一位大夫来。	qǐng kuài jiào yí-wèi dài-fu lái
Please call the police.	请叫警察来。	qǐng jiào jǐng-chá lái
There's been an accident.	出事了。	chū shì le
There are people injured.	有人受伤了。	yǒu rén shòu shāng le
I'd like an interpreter.	我想请一位口译。	wǒ xiǎng qǐng yí-wèi kǒu-yì
Here's my name and address.	这是我的姓名和地址。	zhè shì wǒ de xìng-míng hé dì-zhǐ

Bicycle hire 租自行车

Even on a tightly-scheduled tour, you may be able to fit in a bike ride around town. Machines can be hired at Friendship Stores and large bicycle repair shops.

I'd like to hire a bicycle ...	我想租一辆自行车…	wǒ xiǎng zū yí-liàng zì-xíng-chē
for ... hours	骑…小时	qí ... xiǎo-shí
for 1 day	骑一天	qí yì tiān
for a ride around the town	在市区骑	zài shì-qū qí
What is the hire charge?	租金多少？	zū-jīn duō-shao
How much is the deposit?	押金多少？	yā-jīn duō-shao
When must I return the bicycle?	我该在什么时候还自行车？	wǒ gāi zài shén-me shí-hou huán zì-xíng-chē

行，我能租给你一辆自行车。 Yes, I can rent you a bicycle.

不行，我不能把自行车租给你。 No, I can't rent you a bicycle.

请交…块钱押金。 Please leave a deposit of ... yuan.

这辆自行车你能用… You can keep the bicycle ...

…小时 for ... hours

到…点钟为止 until ... o'clock

到明天 until tomorrow

Other means of transport 其它交通工具

helicopter	直升飞机	zhí-shēng fēi-jī
moped	小摩托车	xiǎo mó-tuō-chē
motorbike	摩托车	mó-tuō-chē

Or perhaps you prefer:

to hike	徒步旅行	tú-bù lǚ-xíng
to hitchhike	搭车	dā chē
to walk	走路	zǒu lù

Asking the way – Street directions 问路-指路

Excuse me.	请问	qǐng wèn
What is the name of this street?	这条街叫什么名字？	zhèi tiáo jiē jiào shén-me míng-zi
Could you show me on this map where I am?	你能在这张地图上指出我在哪儿吗？	nǐ néng zài zhèi zhāng dì-tú shang zhǐ-chū wǒ zài nǎr ma
Where can I find this address?	我怎么才能找到这个地方？	wǒ zěn-me cái néng zhǎo dào zhèi-ge dì-fang
Can you tell me the way to ...?	你能告诉我去…的路吗？	nǐ néng gào-su wǒ qù ... de lù ma
How do I get to ...?	去…怎么走？	qù ... zěn-me zǒu
How long does it take on foot?	走路去要用多少时间？	zǒu lù qù yào yòng duō-shao shí-jiān
Where can I find this place?	我怎么能找到这个地方？	wǒ zěn-me néng zhǎo dào zhèi-ge dì-fang
Where's this?	这在哪儿？	zhèi zài nǎr
How far is it to ... from here?	…离这儿有多远？	... lí zhèr yǒu duō yuǎn
Which bus should I take?	我该坐几路汽车？	wǒ gāi zuò jǐ-lù qì-chē

你走错路了。	You're going the wrong way.
一直走。	Go straight ahead.
往那边走，在马路…	It's down there on the ...
左边/右边	left/right
对面/在…后面	opposite/behind ...
在…旁边儿/过了…之后	next to/after ...
北/南/东/西	north/south/east/west
走到第一个/第二个十字路口。	Go to the first/second crossroads (intersection).
在红绿灯处向左拐。	Turn left at the traffic lights.
在下一个路口往右拐。	Turn right at the next corner.

旅行

SIGHTSEEING

Sightseeing

Is there a Lüxingshe (CITS) office here?	旅行社在哪儿？	lǚ-xíng-shè zài nǎr
What are the main points of interest?	这儿都有些什么名胜古迹？	zhèr dōu yǒu xiē shén-me míng-shèng gǔ-jī
We're here for ...	我们在这里停留…	wǒ-men zài zhè-li tíng-liú
a few hours	几小时	jǐ xiǎo-shí
a day	一天	yì-tiān
a week	一星期	yì xīng-qī
Can you recommend a sightseeing tour?	请推荐一个集体游览路线。	qǐng tuī-jiàn yí-ge jí-tǐ yóu-lǎn lù-xiàn
Where do we leave from?	从哪儿出发？	cóng nǎr chū-fā
Will the bus pick us up at the hotel?	汽车来旅馆接我们吗？	qì-chē lái lǚ-guǎn jiē wǒ-men ma
How much does the tour cost?	游览一趟要花多少钱？	yóu-lǎn yí-tàng yào huā duō-shao qián
What time do we leave?	我们什么时间出发？	wǒ-men shén-me shí-jiān chū-fā
Is lunch included?	包括午饭吗？	bāo-kuò wǔ-fàn ma
What time do we get back?	我们什么时间回来？	wǒ-mén shén-me shí-jiān huí-lai
Do we have free time in ...?	我们在…有自由活动的时间吗？	wǒ-men zài ... yǒu zì-yóu huó-dòng de shí-jiān ma
I'd like to hire an English-speaking private guide for ...	我想请一位私人英语导游，工作…	wǒ xiǎng qǐng yí-wèi sī-rén yīng-yǔ dǎo-yóu gōng-zuò
half a day	半天	bàn-tiān
a day	一天	yì-tiān

and if you'd like a close-up of someone on your travels it's polite to ask:

May I take a photo of you, please?	我可以给你照像吗？	wǒ kě-yǐ gěi nǐ zhào-xiàng ma

游览

Admission 入场

Is ... open on Sundays?	…星期天开门吗？	… xīng-qī-tiān kāi mén ma
When does it open?	几点开门？	jǐ diǎn kāi mén
When does it close?	几点关门？	jǐ diǎn guān mén
How much is the entrance fee?	门票多少钱？	mén-piào duō-shao qián

免费入场
miǎn-fèi rù chǎng
ADMISSION FREE

禁止摄影
jìn-zhǐ shè-yǐng
NO CAMERAS ALLOWED

Is there any reduction for ...?	…买票减价吗？	… mǎi piào jiǎn-jià ma
children	儿童	ér-tóng
the disabled	残废人	cán-fèi-rén
groups	团体	tuán-tǐ
pensioners	退休的	tuì-xiū de
students	学生	xué-sheng
Do you have a guide-book (in English)?	你这儿有（英文）旅游指南吗？	nǐ zhèr yǒu (yīng-wén) lǚ-yóu zhǐ-nán ma
Can I buy a catalogue?	可以买一份简介吗？	kě-yǐ mǎi yí-fèn jiǎn-jiè ma
Is it all right to take pictures?	可以照相吗？	kě-yǐ zhào-xiàng ma
Is there an English-speaking guide?	有会说英语的导游吗？	yǒu huì shuō yīng-yǔ de dǎo-yóu ma

Where is ...? …在哪儿？

Where is/ Where are the ...?	…在哪儿？	… zài nǎr
aquarium	水族馆	shuǐ-zú-guǎn
art gallery	画店	huà-diàn
botanical gardens	植物园	zhí-wù-yuán
bridge	桥	qiáo
building	建筑	jiàn-zhù

cathedral	大教堂	dà-jiào-táng
cave	岩洞	yán-dòng
cemetery	公墓	gōng-mù
church	教堂	jiào-táng
city centre	市中心	shì zhōng-xīn
commune	公社	gōng-shè
concert hall	音乐厅	yīn-yuè-tīng
courtyard	庭院	tíng-yuàn
department store	百货商店	bǎi-huò shāng-diàn
docks	码头	mǎ-tou
downtown area	市中心	shì zhōng-xīn
exhibition	展览会	zhǎn-lǎn-huì
factory	工厂	gōng-chǎng
fortress	要塞	yào-sài
fountain	泉	quán
gardens	园林	yuán-lín
grotto	小岩洞	xiǎo yán-dòng
harbour	港湾	gǎng-wān
island	岛	dǎo
lake	湖	hú
market	农贸市场	nóng-mào shì-chǎng
memorial (museum)	纪念馆	jì-niàn-guǎn
memorial (stone)	纪念碑	jì-niàn-bēi
monument	纪念碑	jì-niàn-bēi
mosque	清真寺	qīng-zhēn-sì
museum	博物馆	bó-wù-guǎn
observatory	天文台	tiān-wén-tái
old town	老城	lǎo chéng
opera house (Chinese)	戏院	xì-yuàn
pagoda	宝塔	bǎo-tǎ
palace	宫殿	gōng-diàn
park	公园	gōng-yuán
pavilion	亭子	tíng-zi
planetarium	天文馆	tiān-wén guǎn
river	河	hé
... ruins	…旧址	... jiù-zhǐ
shopping area	商业区	shāng-yè-qū
square	广场	guǎng-chǎng
stadium	体育场	tǐ-yù-chǎng
statue	雕像	diāo-xiàng
temple (Buddhist)	佛寺	fó-sì
(Taoist)	道观	dào-guàn
theatre	剧场	jù-chǎng
tomb	陵墓	líng-mù
tower	塔	tǎ
university	大学	dà-xué
zoo	动物园	dòng-wù-yuán

What are your special interests? 你对什么特别感兴趣？

I'd like to see a/ the ...	我想看…	wǒ xiǎng kàn
Buddhist temple	佛寺	fó-sì
carved lacquerware factory	雕漆厂	diāo-qī chǎng
cloisonné factory	景泰蓝厂	jǐng-tài-lán chǎng
hot springs	温泉	wēn-quán
jade factory	玉器厂	yù-qì chǎng
Mao Zedong Memorial Hall	毛主席纪念堂	máo zhǔ-xí jì-niàn-táng
National Art Gallery	中国美术馆	zhōng-guó měi-shù-guǎn
Nationalities' Cultural Palace	民族文化宫	mín-zú wén-huà-gōng
rock carvings	石雕	shí-diāo
silk factory	丝绸厂	sī-chóu chǎng
Summer Palace	颐和园	yí-hé-yuán
Taoist temple	道观	dào-guàn
Temple of Heaven	天坛	tiān-tán

We're interested in ...	我们对…感兴趣。	wǒ-men duì ... gǎn xìng-qu
acupuncture	针灸	zhēn-jiǔ
antiques	古董	gǔ-dǒng
archaeology	考古学	kǎo-gǔ-xué
architecture	建筑学	jiàn-zhù-xué
art	艺术	yì-shù
botany	植物学	zhí-wù-xué
calligraphy	书法	shū-fǎ
ceramics	陶瓷	táo-cí
furniture	家具	jiā-jù
geology	地质学	dì-zhì-xué
handicrafts	手工艺品	shǒu-gōng-yì-pǐn
history	历史	lì-shǐ
ivory carvings	牙雕	yá-diāo
jade carvings	玉器	yù-qì
medicine	医学	yī-xué
musical instruments	乐器	yuè-qì
natural history	自然博物	zì-rán bó-wù
painting	画儿	huàr
porcelain	细瓷器	xì-cí-qì
sculpture	雕塑	diāo-sù
silk painting	绢画	juàn-huà
zoology	动物学	dòng-wù-xué

Where's the ... department?	…部在哪儿？	... bù zài nǎr

游览

Who — What — When? 哪位-什么-什么时代？

What's that building?	那个建筑是什么？	nà-ge jiàn-zhù shì shén-me
When was it built?	是什么时候建的？	shì shén-me shí-hou jiàn de
Who was the …?	是哪位…的作品？	shì nǎ-wèi … de zuò-pǐn
architect	建筑师	jiàn-zhù-shī
artist	艺术家	yì-shù-jiā
painter	画家	huà-jiā
sculptor	雕塑家	diāo-sù-jiā
When did he live?	他是什么时代的人？	tā shì shén-me shí-dài de rén
Who painted this?	这是谁画的？	zhè shì shéi huà de
It's …	这真…	zhè zhēn
beautiful	美丽	měi-lì
interesting	有趣	yǒu qù
magnificent	雄伟	xióng-wěi
strange	奇怪	qí-guài

Religious services 作礼拜

If you want to attend a religious service, give your guide advance warning so that your request can be accommodated in the general schedule.

Is there a … near here?	附近有…吗？	fù-jìn yǒu … ma
Catholic church	天主教教堂	tiān-zhǔ-jiào jiào-táng
mosque	清真寺	qīng-zhēn-sì
Protestant church	新教教堂	xīn-jiào jiào-táng
synagogue	犹太教堂	yóu-tài jiào-táng
Is it open to visitors?	对旅游者开放吗？	duì lǚ-yóu-zhě kāi-fàng ma
What time is mass/ the service?	几点作弥撒/礼拜？	jǐ diǎn zuò mí-sa/lǐ-bài
Where can I find a priest/minister who speaks English?	哪儿有说英语的神父/牧师？	nǎr yǒu shuō yīng-yǔ de shén-fù/mù-shī

The table of dynasties and major events, opposite, provides a useful frame of reference for Chinese history.

Chinese dynasties and major events

夏   *Xià* (approx. 21st–16th centuries B.C.): Legendary first Chinese dynasty.

商   *Shāng* (16th–11th centuries B.C.): Cultivation of silkworm first documented.

周   *Zhōu* (11th–5th centuries B.C.): *Zhōu* establish a state near Xi'an, later relocating their capital at Luoyang.

战国   *Zhàn Guó* (Warring States, 403–221 B.C.): Development of iron-working.

秦   *Qín* (221–206 B.C.): Building of the Great Wall as protection against the Huns.

汉   *Hàn* (206 B.C.–A.D. 220): Great advance in agriculture, commerce, learning and historical writing.

三国   *Sān Guó* (Three Kingdoms, 220–265): Taoism and Buddhism spread throughout China.

晋   *Jìn* (265–420): Following partition of empire under previous dynasty, China now enjoys a brief period of unification.

南北朝   *Nán Běi Cháo* (Southern and Northern dynasties, 386–581): North splinters into numerous small states, while South makes spectacular progress.

隋   *Suí* (581–618): Imperial Canal started, for transport of cereals from Yangtze.

唐   *Táng (618–907): China is paramount power in eastern Asia; highest flowering of Chinese culture and science. Gunpowder invented.*

五代十国   *Wǔ Dài — Shí Guó* (Five Dynasties and Ten Kingdoms, 907–960): Expansion of trade in China.

宋   *Sòng* (960–1279): Printing promotes communications. Paper currency in circulation.

元   *Yuán* (1279–1368): Moslem and European explorers and traders link China with the West.

明   *Míng* (1368–1644): Empire reaches new heights. Power is further centralized. Bureaucracy, the economy and agriculture are reorganized.

清   *Qīng* (1644–1911): Population explosion. Opium War (1839–1842). Hong Kong ceded to British. War with Japan, 1894. Advent of the republic in 1912.

SIGHTSEEING

In the countryside 在农村

Is there a scenic route to …?	去…有风景好的路吗？	qù … yǒu fēng-jǐng hǎo de lù ma
How far is it to …?	到…有多远？	dào … yǒu duō yuǎn
Can we get there on foot?	能走路去吗？	néng zǒu-lù qù ma
How high is that mountain?	那座山有多高？	nà-zuò shān yǒu duó gāo
What's the name of that …?	那是什么…？	nà shì shén-me
animal/bird	动物/鸟儿	dòng-wù/niǎor
flower/tree	花儿/树	huār/shù

Landmarks 风景

bridge	桥	qiáo
canal	运河	yùn-hé
cliff	山崖	shān-yá
farm (state run)	（国营）农场	(guó-yíng) nóng-chǎng
field	农田	nóng-tián
footpath	小路	xiǎo lù
forest	森林	sēn-lín
garden	花园	huā-yuán
Great Wall	长城	cháng-chéng
hill	小山	xiǎo shān
house	房屋	fáng-wū
island	岛	dǎo
lake	湖	hú
meadow	草场	cǎo-chǎng
mountain (pass)	山（口）	shān (kǒu)
paddy field	稻田	dào-tián
path	小路	xiǎo lù
peak	山峰	shān-fēng
plantation	种植园	zhòng-zhí-yuán
pond	池塘	chí-táng
river	河	hé
road	路	lù
sea	海	hǎi
spring	泉	quán
swamp	沼泽	zhǎo-zé
valley	山谷	shān-gǔ
village	村庄	cūn-zhuāng
vineyard	葡萄园	pú-táo-yuán
waterfall	瀑布	pù-bù
wood	树林	shù-lín

ASKING THE WAY, see page 77

游览

Relaxing

Whether you are visiting China on your own or as part of a group your travel schedule will be worked out in advance down to the last detail. Your days will be well filled: a visit to a people's commune, a trip to the Great Wall, a shopping expedition to a Friendship Store, etc. Back at the hotel, you will certainly be happy to take things easy for a while.

However, for the benefit of those who don't want to waste a minute of their precious time, hotels sometimes put on typical Chinese shows of interest to tourists. Table-tennis and billiards buffs will often find facilities for these sports in their hotel. Savvy travellers will have brought a chess or scrabble set or pack of cards along with which to while away idle evening hours.

In all probability, your visit to China will include an evening or two of organized entertainment. Popular items are concerts, acrobat shows, Chinese ballet and opera, the circus, and, of course, the banquets which will be unforgettable highlights of your trip.

Theatre — Opera, etc.

If your places have been booked in advance, all you have to do is to turn up at the appointed meeting place on time. However, if you are travelling alone or for some other reason find yourself left to your own devices, the phrases given on the following pages will enable you to communicate your wishes – preferably to your hotel receptionist who will then make the appropriate reservations for you.

娱乐

A number of favourites from the traditional Chinese theatre have resurfaced over recent years, and modern plays are often staged depicting heroic episodes from the Long March or the setting up of a people's commune; but the star attraction of the Beijing (Peking) stage is the renowned Peking Opera. You will be enchanted by the sumptuous costumes, the daring leaps, the virtuoso performances. The action takes place on a sparsely decorated stage where it is the actor's gestures which indicate whether he is opening a door, riding a horse or travelling aboard a vessel on a river.

These works are rich in intrigue and surprise developments, and in the simplest and often most touching plots the focal point may be a brief argument, a quarrel, a unique situation such as a chance meeting, a misunderstanding or a reconciliation. What's more, the libretto is extremely adaptable: it gets rewritten, developed, abbreviated — to the delight and pleasure of connoisseurs.

The roles can be categorized according to sex, age and type of character. One of the leading male parts is generally that of *lǎo shēng*, a venerable gentleman with a long beard and a fine baritone voice. *Xiǎo shēng* is a young lover or a student. His make-up is like that of a girl and he often speaks in a high-pitched voice. *Wǔ shēng* is a soldier who appears in a great number of operas of the classical repertoire. He is led to perform acrobatic feats that will leave you breathless. One of the main female roles you'll notice is that of *qīng yī* ("blue dress"), a lady with a falsetto voice who represents either a mistress or the faithful and virtuous wife. Her movements are graceful and she sings with her eyes modestly lowered. *Huā dàn* ("flower") is agile and alert. The actress playing this part wears some of the most elegant costumes; her gestures are seductive and coquettish. A wide range of other characters represent valiant warriers, dishonest government ministers, ruthless bandits, incorruptible judges and loyal servants of the state, not to mention deities and other supernatural beings.

You will certainly not understand all of the actors' gestures, let alone the songs and the words, but the rhythm, the colours, the mime and the music will capture your imagination as little else can.

Theatre 戏剧

What's playing at the Capital Theatre?	首都剧场现在正上演什么？	shǒu-dū jù-chǎng xiàn-zài zhèng shàng-yǎn shén-me
What sort of play is it?	这是哪种戏剧？	zhè shì nǎ zhǒng xì-jù
Who's it by?	剧作者是谁？	jù-zuò-zhě shì shéi
Who's playing the lead?	主角是谁？	zhǔ-jué shì shéi
Are there any tickets for tonight?	还有今晚的票吗？	hái yǒu jīn wǎn de piào ma
How much are the tickets?	这些票多少钱？	zhè xiē piào duō-shao qián
What time does it begin?	什么时间开演？	shén-me shí-jiān kāi yǎn
Can I have a ticket for the matinée?	我想买一张早场的票。	wǒ xiǎng mǎi yì-zhāng zǎo-chǎng de piào
I want a seat in the stalls (orchestra).	我要一张楼下的票。	wǒ yào yì-zhāng lóu-xià de piào
Not too far back.	不要太后边。	bú yào tài hòu-bian
Somewhere in the middle.	要中间的。	yào zhōng-jiān de
May I have a programme, please?	请给我一份节目单。	qǐng gěi wǒ yí-fèn jié-mù-dān
Where's the cloakroom?	衣帽间在哪儿？	yī-mào-jiān zài nǎr

对不起，票卖完了。
只剩几张楼上的票了。

我可以看看你的票吗？

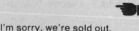

I'm sorry, we're sold out.
There are only a few seats left in the circle (mezzanine).

May I see your ticket?

Opera — Ballet — Concert 歌剧－芭蕾舞－音乐会

Can you recommend a/an …?	你能推荐一场…吗？	nǐ néng tuī-jiàn yì-chǎng … ma
ballet	芭蕾舞	bā-léi-wǔ
concert	音乐会	yīn-yuè-huì
opera	歌剧	gē-jù
Where's the opera house/concert hall?	歌剧院/音乐厅在哪儿？	gē-jù-yuàn/yīn-yuè-tīng zài nǎr
Is the Beijing Opera putting on a performance?	北京京剧团现在演出吗？	běijīng jīng-jù-tuán xiàn-zài yǎn-chū ma
Who's the singer/dancing the lead?	独唱/跳主角的是谁？	dú-chàng/tiào zhǔ-jué de shì shéi
Which orchestra is playing?	是由哪个乐队演奏的？	shì yóu nǎ-ge yuè-duì yǎn-zòu de
Who's the conductor/soloist?	指挥/独奏演员是谁？	zhǐ-huī/dú-zòu yǎn-yuán shì shéi

Cinema 电影院

What's on at the cinema tonight?	这个电影院今晚有什么电影？	zhè-ge diàn-yǐng-yuàn jīn-wǎn yǒu shén-me diàn-yǐng
Can you recommend a …?	你能推荐一个…吗？	nǐ néng tuī-jiàn yí-ge … ma
good film	好电影	hǎo diàn-yǐng
comedy	喜剧片	xǐ-jù piàn
Who's in it?	有些什么演员？	yǒu xiē shén-me yǎn-yuán
Who's the director?	导演是谁？	dǎo-yǎn shì shéi
What time does It begin?	几点开演？	jǐ diǎn kāi yǎn

Nightclubs — Discos 夜总会－迪斯科舞会

Where is there a nightclub/disco?	哪儿有夜总会/迪斯科舞会？	nǎr yǒu yè-zǒng-huì/dí-sī-kē wǔ-huì
Where can we go dancing?	我们可以去什么地方跳舞？	wǒ-men kě-yǐ qù shén-me dì-fang tiào-wǔ
Is evening dress required?	要穿晚礼服吗？	yào chuān wǎn-lǐ-fú ma

Sports 体育运动

Early-risers taking their morning stroll along the city streets are likely to encounter numerous groups of Chinese earnestly engaged in practising tai chi chuan (太极拳 *tài-jí-quán*). To the casual observer it may look as though the participants are merely shadow-boxing or performing slow dance movements, but the adept will tell you that tai chi chuan is, in effect, a physical-philosophical discipline that tones up all the body's muscles and composes the mind and spirit.

Swimming is another popular pastime, and many swimming pools have been housed in converted excavation sites. For most public swimming pools you will need a health certificate from a Chinese clinic, but your tour guide can organise this quite easily.

Is it possible to play tennis?	这儿能打网球吗？	zhèr néng dǎ wǎng-qiú ma
Where are the tennis courts?	网球场在哪儿？	wǎng-qiú-chǎng zài nǎr
Can I hire (rent) ...?	我能租用…吗？	wǒ néng zū-yòng ... ma
equipment	体育器材	tǐ-yù qì-cái
rackets	球拍	qiú-pāi

badminton	羽毛球	yǔ-máo-qiú
basketball	蓝球	lán-qiú
boxing	拳击	quán-jī
cycling	骑自行车	qí zì-xíng-chē
football (soccer)	足球	zú-qiú
gymnastics	体操	tǐ-cāo
skating	滑冰	huá-bīng
swimming	游泳	yóu-yǒng
table-tennis	乒乓球	bīng-bāng-qiú
tennis	网球	wǎng-qiú
volleyball	排球	pái-qiú

What's the charge per hour/per day?	一小时/一天的租金多少？	yì xiǎo-shí/yì-tiān de zū-jīn duō-shao

I'd like to see a …	我想看一场…	wǒ xiǎng kàn yì-chǎng
table-tennis match	乒乓球比赛	bīng-bāng-qiú bǐ-sài
gymnastics display	体操表演	tǐ-cāo biǎo-yǎn
What's the admission charge?	门票多少钱？	mén-piào duō-shao qián
Is a national team playing?	有国家队上场吗？	yǒu guó-jiā-duì shàng-chǎng ma
Can you get me a ticket?	你能帮我搞张票吗？	nǐ néng bāng wǒ gǎo zhāng piào ma
Is there a skating-rink near here?	这附近有滑冰场吗？	zhè fù-jìn yǒu huá-bīng-chǎng ma
Can I hire skates?	我能租到冰鞋吗？	wǒ néng zū-dào bīng-xié ma
Is there any good fishing around here?	附近有可以钓鱼的地方吗？	fù-jìn yǒu kě-yǐ diào-yú de dì-fang ma
Do I need a permit to fish?	钓鱼需要争得许可吗？	diào-yú xū-yào zhēng-dé xǔ-kě ma

---

禁止钓鱼
jìn-zhǐ diào-yú
NO FISHING ALLLOWED

Can one swim in the lake/river?	可以在这个湖/河里游泳吗？	kě-yǐ zài zhè-ge hú/hé li yóu-yǒng ma
Is there a swimming pool here?	这儿有游泳池吗？	zhèr yǒu yóu-yǒng-chí ma
Is it open-air or indoor?	是室外的还是室内的？	shì shì-wài de hái-shì shì-nèi de
Is it heated?	是温水的吗？	shì wēn-shuǐ de ma
What's the temperature of the water?	水温多少度？	shuǐ-wēn duō-shao dù
Is there a sandy beach?	有沙滩吗？	yǒu shā-tān ma

禁止入内
jìn-zhǐ rù nèi
NO ENTRANCE

On the beach 在海滩上

As Chinese women are rather modest, bikinis are rarely seen at swimming pools or on the beach, and they aren't encouraged. It's a good idea to pack a discreet one-piece suit.

Is it safe to swim here?	这儿游泳安全吗？	zhèr yóu-yǒng ān-quán ma
Is there a lifeguard?	有救生员吗？	yǒu jiù-shēng-yuán ma
Are there any dangerous currents?	有危险的潮流吗？	yǒu wēi-xiǎn de cháo-liú ma
When does the tide come in/go out?	什么时间涨/落潮？	shén-me shí-jiān zhǎng/luò cháo
Is it safe for children?	儿童在这儿游泳安全吗？	ér-tóng zài zhèr yóu-yǒng ān-quán ma
There are some big waves.	有大浪。	yǒu dà-làng
The sea is very calm.	海上风平浪静。	hǎi-shang fēng-píng làng-jìng
Is it deep here?	这儿水深吗？	zhèr shuǐ shēn ma
Can I hire a/an/ some …?	我能租用…吗？	wǒ néng zū-yòng … ma
air mattress	一条汽褥子	yì-tiáo qì-rù-zi
bathing suit	一件游泳衣	yí-jiàn yóu-yǒng-yī
deck chair	一把躺椅	yì-bǎ tǎng-yǐ
motorboat	汽艇	qì-tǐng
pedalo	脚踏游艇	jiǎo-tà yóu-tǐng
rowing boat	游船	yóu-chuán
sailing boat	帆船	fān-chuán
skin-diving equipment	潜水装备	qián-shuǐ zhuāng-bèi
sunshade (umbrella)	遮阳伞	zhē-yáng-sǎn
water skis	滑水板	huá-shuǐ-bǎn
What's the charge per hour?	一小时租金多少？	yì xiǎo-shí zū-jīn duō-shao

禁止游泳
jìn-zhǐ yóu-yǒng
NO BATHING

MAKING FRIENDS

Making friends

Introductions 互相介绍

Let me introduce you to each other.	让我来介绍一下。	ràng wǒ lái jiè-shào yí xià
John, this is …	约翰，这是…	yuē-hàn zhè shì
My name is …	我叫…	wǒ jiào
How do you do?	你好，很高兴能认识你。	nǐ hǎo. hěn gāo-xìng néng rèn-shi nǐ
What's your name?	你叫什么名字？	nǐ jiào shén-me míng-zi
How are you?	你好吗？	nǐ hǎo ma
Fine, thanks. And you?	很好，谢谢。你呢？	hěn hǎo xiè-xie. nǐ ne

Follow up 进一步交谈

How long have you been here?	你来这儿有多久了？	nǐ lái zhèr yǒu duō-jiǔ le
We've been here a week.	我们来了一个星期了。	wǒ-men lái le yí-ge xīng-qī le
Is this your first visit?	这是你们第一次来吗？	zhè shì nǐ-men dì-yī-cì lái ma
No, we came here last year.	不，我们去年来过。	bù wǒ-men qù-nián lái guò
Are you enjoying your stay?	你们在这儿过得愉快吗？	nǐ-men zài zhèr guò-de yú kuài ma
Yes, I like it very much.	过得很愉快。	guò de hěn yú-kuài
I like the landscape a lot.	我非常喜欢这儿的风景。	wǒ fēi-cháng xǐ-huan zhèr de fēng-jǐng
Do you travel a lot?	你经常旅行吗？	nǐ jīng-cháng lǚ-xíng ma
Where do you come from?	你是从哪来的？	nǐ shì cóng nǎr lái de
I'm from …	我从…来的。	wǒ cóng … lái de
What nationality are you?	你是哪国人？	nǐ shì nǎ guó rén

COUNTRY, see page 148

交朋友

I'm ...	我是…	wǒ shì
American	美国人	měi-guó rén
British	英国人	yīng-guó rén
Canadian	加拿大人	jiā-ná-dà rén
Irish	爱尔兰人	ài-ěr-lán rén
Where are you staying?	你住在哪儿？	nǐ zhù zài nǎr
Are you on your own?	你是一个人来的吗？	nǐ shì yí-ge rén lái de ma
I'm with my ...	我和我…一同来的。	wǒ hé wǒ ... yì-tóng lái de
wife	妻子	qī-zi
husband	丈夫	zhàng-fu
family	家属	jiā-shǔ
children	孩子	hái-zi
parents	父母	fù-mǔ
boyfriend/girlfriend	男朋友/女朋友	nán-péng-you/ nǚ-péng-you

father/mother	父亲/母亲	fù-qin/mǔ-qin
son/daughter	儿子/女儿	ér-zi/nǚ-er
older brother/ younger brother	哥哥/弟弟	gē-ge/dì-di
older sister/younger sister	姐姐/妹妹	jiě-jie/mèi-mei

Are you married?	你已经结婚了吗？	nǐ yǐ-jīng jié-hūn le ma
Are you single?	你还没有结婚吗？	nǐ hái méi-yǒu jié-hūn ma
Do you have children?	你有孩子吗？	nǐ yǒu hái-zi ma
What do you think of the country?	你觉得这个国家怎么样？	nǐ jué-de zhè-ge guó-jiā zěn-me yàng
What do you do? (work)	你是做什么工作的？	nǐ shì zuò shén-me gōng-zuò de
I'm a student.	我是学生。	wǒ shì xué-sheng
What are you studying?	你在学什么？	nǐ zài xué shén-me
I'm here on a business trip.	我来这儿出差。	wǒ lái zhèr chū-chāi
Do you play cards?	你会玩儿牌吗？	nǐ huì wánr pái ma

The weather 天气

The weather in China tends not to be as changeable as in Europe and parts of America, so there is less opportunity to discuss it. Nevertheless, a few of these phrases could be used to break the ice.

What a lovely day!	天气真好！	tiān-qì zhēn hǎo
What awful weather!	天气真坏！	tiān-qì zhēn hùai
Is it usually as warm as this?	这儿的天气总是这么热吗？	zhèr de tiān-qì zǒng-shì zhè-me rè ma
Do you think it's going to … tomorrow?	你觉得明天会…吗？	nǐ jué-de míng-tiān huì … ma
be a nice day	是晴天	shì qíng-tiān
rain	下雨	xià yǔ
snow	下雪	xià xuě
What is the weather forecast?	天气预报怎么说的？	tiān-qì yù-bào zěn-me shuō de

cloud	云	yún
fog	雾	wù
frost	霜	shuāng
ice	冰	bīng
lightning	闪电	shǎn-diàn
monsoon	季风	jì-fēng
moon	月亮	yuè-liang
rain	雨	yǔ
sky	天空	tiān-kōng
snow	雪	xuě
star	星星	xīng-xing
sun	太阳	tài-yáng
thunder	雷	léi
thunderstorm	暴风雨	bào-fēng-yǔ
typhoon	台风	tái-fēng
wind	风	fēng

Invitations 邀请

Would you like to have dinner with us on …?	咱们…一起吃晚饭好吗？	zán-men … yì-qǐ chī wǎn-fàn hǎo ma
May I invite you to lunch?	我可以请你吃午饭吗？	wǒ kě-yǐ qǐng nǐ chī wǔ-fàn ma

DAYS OF THE WEEK, see page 153

交朋友

Can you come over for a drink this evening?	今晚你能来喝一杯吗？	jīn-wǎn nǐ néng lái hē yì-bēi ma
There's a party. Are you coming?	今晚有个晚会，你来吗？	jīn-wǎn yǒu ge wǎn-huì. nǐ lái ma
That's very kind of you.	你真客气。	nǐ zhēn kè-qi
Great. I'd love to come.	太好了，我很愿意。	tài hǎo le. wǒ hěn yuàn-yì
What time shall we come?	我们该几点到？	wǒ-men gāi jǐ-diǎn dào
May I bring a friend?	我能带个朋友吗？	wǒ néng dài ge péng-you ma
May I bring my girlfriend/boyfriend?	我能带我的女朋友/男朋友吗？	wǒ néng dài wǒ-de nǚ-péng-you/nán-péng-you ma
I'm afraid we have to leave now.	对不起，我们得走了。	duì-bu-qǐ. wǒ-men děi zǒu le
Next time you must come to visit us.	下次你一定来我们这儿玩儿。	xià-cì nǐ yí-dìng lái wǒ-men zhèr wánr
Thanks for the evening. It was great.	今晚过得很高兴，十分感谢。	jīn-wǎn guò de hěn gāo-xìng. shí-fēn gǎn-xiè

Dating 约会

Do you mind if I smoke?	我可以吸烟吗？	wǒ kě-yǐ xī yān ma
Would you like a cigarette?	你吸烟吗？	nǐ xī yān ma
Do you have a light, please?	你有火儿吗？	nǐ yǒu huǒr ma
Why are you laughing?	你笑什么？	nǐ xiào shén-me
Is my Chinese that bad?	我汉语说得那么糟糕吗？	wǒ hàn-yǔ shuō de nà-me zāo-gāo ma
Do you mind if I sit here?	我能坐这儿吗？	wǒ néng zuò zhèr ma
Can I get you a drink?	你要喝什么？	nǐ yào hē shén-me

Are you waiting for someone?	你在等人吗？	nǐ zài děng rén ma
Are you free this evening?	你今晚有空吗？	nǐ jīn-wǎn yǒu kòng ma
Would you like to go out with me tonight?	今晚你愿意和我一起去玩儿吗？	jīn-wǎn nǐ yuàn-yì hé wǒ yì-qǐ qù wánr ma
Would you like to go dancing?	你想去跳舞吗？	nǐ xiǎng qù tiào-wǔ ma
Would you like to dance?	你想跳舞吗？	nǐ xiǎng tiào-wǔ ma
Shall we go to the cinema (movies)?	咱们去看电影好吗？	zán-men qù kàn diàn-yǐng hǎo ma
Where shall we meet?	咱们在什么地方见面？	zán-men zài shén-me dì-fang jiàn-miàn
Let's meet in the hotel bar.	咱们在旅馆酒吧见面吧。	zán-men zài lǚ-guǎn jiǔ-bā jiàn-miàn ba
I'll pick you up at …	我…点来接你。	wǒ … diǎn lái jiē nǐ
I'll call for you at 8.	我八点来找你。	wǒ bā-diǎn lái zhǎo nǐ
May I take you home?	我可以送你回家吗？	wǒ kě-yǐ sòng nǐ huí jiā ma
Can I see you again tomorrow?	咱们明天能再见面吗？	zán-men míng-tiān néng zài jiàn-miàn ma
What's your telephone number?	你的电话号码是多少？	nǐ-de diàn-huà hào-mǎ shì duō-shao

and you might answer:

I'd love to, thank you.	我很愿意，谢谢。	wǒ hěn yuàn-yì xiè-xie
No. I'm not interested, thank you.	我不感兴趣，谢谢。	wǒ bù gǎn xìng-qu xiè-xie
Thank you, but I'm busy.	谢谢，但我很忙。	xiè-xie dàn wǒ hěn máng
Leave me alone, please.	请别管我。	qǐng bié guǎn wǒ
Thank you, it's been a wonderful evening.	谢谢，这个晚上过得真痛快。	xiè-xie zhè-ge wǎn-shang guò de zhēn tòng-kuai
I've enjoyed myself.	我玩得很痛快。	wǒ wánr de hěn tòng-kuai

Shopping guide

This shopping guide is designed to help you find what you want with ease, accuracy and speed. It features:

1. A list of all major shops, stores and services (p. 98).
2. Some general expressions required when shopping to allow you to be specific and selective (p.100).
3. Full details of the shops and services most likely to concern you. Here you'll find advice, alphabetical lists of items, and conversion charts listed under the headings below.

		page
Antiques	antiques, artist's supplies, jewellery	104
Bookshop — Stationer's	books, stationery	105
Chemist's (drugstore)	medecine, first-aid, toiletry	107
Clothing	clothes and accessories	111
Electrical appliances	radios, cassette-recorders etc …	119
Grocery	some general expressions and measures	120
Household	some everyday items	120
Jeweller's — Watchmaker's	jewellery, watches, watch repairs	121
Optician	glasses, lenses, binoculars	123
Photography	cameras, films, developing, accessories	124
Smoker's supplies	everything for the smoker	126
Souvenirs	gifts to take back home	126
Miscellaneous	records, cassettes, toys	128

LAUNDRY, see page 30/HAIRDRESSER'S, see page 31

采购指南

Shops, stores and services 商店，百货商店及服务行业

Most of your shopping will be done in Friendship Stores which offer certain Western goods as well as a wide range of Chinese goods made for export. They are generally open every day between 9 a.m. and 7 or 8 p.m. You should also try a Chinese department store, these are normally open from 9 a.m. to 6 or 7 p.m.

Some shops may be organised a little differently from Western shops. You will find jewellery sold in antique shops, and watches at the optician's. And if you're looking for a baker's you will probably have no luck at all — bread simply isn't as common in China.

As a general rule prices are fixed so don't try bargaining for anything.

Since the distribution system is unpredictable, old China hands say you shouldn't take a chance: if you find something you like, buy it, for it may be on sale nowhere else in China.

营业 yíng-yè OPEN	休息 xiū-xi CLOSED

Where's the nearest ...?	离这儿最近的…在哪儿？	lí zhèr zuì jìn de ... zài nǎr
antique shop	古董店	gǔ-dǒng-diàn
baker's	面包店	miàn-bāo-diàn
bank	银行	yín-háng
barber's	理发店	lǐ-fà-diàn
beauty salon	美容院	měi-róng-yuàn
bookshop	书店	shū-diàn
butcher's	肉店	ròu-diàn
cake shop	糕点店	gāo-diǎn-diàn
camera shop	照相器材商店	zhào-xiàng qì-cái shāng-diàn
chemist's	药店	yào-diàn
dairy	奶制品店	nǎi-zhì-pǐn-diàn

delicatessen	地方风味食品店	dì-fāng fēng-wèi shí-pǐn-diàn
dental clinic	牙科门诊部	yá-kē mén-zhěn-bù
department store	百货商店	bǎi-huò shāng-diàn
dressmaker's	裁缝店	cái-feng-diàn
drugstore	药店	yào-diàn
electrician	电器修理部	diàn-qì xiū-lǐ-bù
fishmonger's	鱼店	yú-diàn
florist's	花店	huā-diàn
Friendship Store	友谊商店	yǒu-yì shāng-diàn
furrier's	皮货店	pí-huò-diàn
greengrocer's	蔬菜店	shū-cài-diàn
grocery	副食店	fù-shí-diàn
hairdresser's (ladies/men)	理发店（女/男）	lǐ-fà-diàn (nǚ/nán)
hardware store	五金商店	wǔ-jīn shāng-diàn
hospital	医院	yī-yuàn
ironmonger's	五金商店	wǔ-jīn shāng-diàn
jeweller's	珠宝首饰店	zhū-bǎo shǒu-shì diàn
laundry	洗衣店	xǐ-yī-diàn
library	图书馆	tú-shū-guǎn
market	农贸市场	nóng-mào shì-chǎng
optician's	眼镜店	yǎn-jìng-diàn
pastry shop	糕点店	gāo-diǎn-diàn
photographer's	照像馆	zhào-xiàng-guǎn
police station	公安局	gōng-ān-jú
post office	邮电局	yóu-diàn-jú
shoemaker's (repair)	补鞋店	bǔ-xié-diàn
shoe shop	鞋店	xié-diàn
shopping centre	商场	shāng-chǎng
souvenir shop	旅游纪念品商店	lǚ-yóu jì-niàn-pǐn shāng-diàn
sporting goods shop	体育用品商店	tǐ-yù yòng-pǐn shāng-diàn
stationer's	文具店	wén-jù-diàn
supermarket	自选商场	zì-xuǎn shāng-chǎng
tailor's	裁缝店	cái-feng-diàn
toy shop	玩具店	wán-jù-diàn
travel agency	旅行社	lǚ-xíng-shè
vegetable store	蔬菜店	shū-cài-diàn
veterinarian	兽医	shòu-yī
watchmaker's	钟表店	zhōng-biǎo diàn

入口	出口	太平门
rù-kǒu	chū-kǒu	tài-píng-mén
ENTRANCE	EXIT	EMERGENCY EXIT

General expressions 一般语汇

Where? 哪儿？

Where's there a good …?	哪儿有好的…？	nǎr yǒu hǎo de
Where's the nearest …?	离这儿最近的…在哪儿？	lí zhèr zuì jìn de … zài nǎr
Where can I find a …?	哪儿有…？	nǎr yǒu
Where do they sell …?	哪儿卖…？	nǎr mài
Where's the main shopping area?	主要商业区在哪儿？	zhǔ-yào shāng-yè-qū zài nǎr
Is it far from here?	离这儿远吗？	lí zhèr yuǎn ma
How do I get there?	我怎么去那儿？	wǒ zěn-me qù nàr

Service 服务

Can you help me?	你能帮助我吗？	nǐ néng bāng-zhù wǒ ma
I'm just looking.	我先看看。	wǒ xiān kàn-kan
Do you sell …?	你这儿卖…吗？	nǐ zhèr mài … ma
I'd like …	我想要…	wǒ xiǎng-yào
Can you show me some …?	请拿些…给我看看。	qǐng ná xiē … gěi wǒ kàn-kan
Do you have any …?	你这儿有…？	nǐ zhèr yǒu
Where's the … department?	…部在哪儿？	… bù zài nǎr
Where's the lift (elevator)?	电梯在哪儿？	diàn-tī zài nǎr

That one 那个

Can you show me …?	请你把…拿来看看。	qǐng nǐ bǎ … ná lai kàn-kan
this one/that one	这个/那个	zhè-ge/nà-ge
the one in the window	橱窗里的那个	chú-chuāng li de nà-ge

Defining the article 说明所要物

I'd like a …	我想要…	wǒ xiǎng-yào
I want a … one.	我要…的。	wǒ yào … de
big	大	dà
cheap	便宜	pián-yi
dark	深色	shēn sè
good	好	hǎo
heavy	重	zhòng
light (weight)	轻	qīng
light (colour)	浅色	qiǎn sè
oval	椭圆	tuǒ-yuán
rectangular	长方	cháng-fāng
round	圆	yuán
small	小	xiǎo
square	方	fāng
sturdy	结实	jiē-shi
wide	宽	kuān
I don't want anything too expensive.	太贵的我不要。	tài guì de wǒ bú yào

Preference 喜好

I'd prefer something of better quality	我喜欢质量好些的。	wǒ xǐ-huan zhì-liàng hǎo xiē de
Can you show me some others?	请再拿几个给我看看。	qǐng zài ná jǐ go gěi wǒ kàn-kan
Do you have anything …?	你这儿有…的吗？	nǐ zhèr yǒu … de ma
cheaper/better	便宜些/好些	pián-yi xiē/hǎo xiē
larger/smaller	大些/小些	dà xiē/xiǎo xiē

How much? 多少？

How much is this?	这个多少钱？	zhè-ge duō-shao qián
How much are they?	这些有多少？	zhè xiē yǒu duō-shao
I don't understand. Please write it down.	我不懂。请写下来。	wǒ bù dǒng. qǐng xiě xia lai
I don't want to spend more than … yuan.	我不想买…块钱以上的东西。	wǒ bù xiǎng mǎi … kuài qián yǐ-shàng de dōng-xi

COLOURS, see page 112

Decision 决定

It's not quite what I want.	这个不太理想。	zhè-ge bú tài lǐ-xiǎng
No, I don't like it.	我不喜欢这个。	wǒ bù xǐ-huan zhè-ge
I'll take it.	我决定买这个。	wǒ jué-dìng mǎi zhè-ge

Ordering 订购

| Can you order it for me? | 我能订购吗？ | wǒ néng dìng-gòu ma |
| How long will it take? | 要多长时间？ | yào duō cháng shí-jiān |

Delivery 寄送

I'll take it with me.	我带走。	wǒ dài zǒu
Please deliver it to the … Hotel.	请把这个送到…旅馆。	qǐng bǎ zhè-ge sòng dào … lǚ-guǎn
Please send it to this address.	请寄到地址上的地方。	qǐng jì dào dì-zhǐ shang de dì-fang
Will I have any difficulty with the customs?	在海关会有麻烦吗？	zài hǎi-guān huì yǒu má-fan ma

Paying 付款

How much is it?	多少钱？	duō-shao qián
Can I pay by traveller's cheque?	能用旅行支票付款吗？	néng yòng lǚ-xíng zhī-piào fù kuǎn ma
Do you accept credit cards?	能用信用卡付款吗？	néng yòng xìn-yòng-kǎ fù kuǎn ma
I think there's a mistake in the bill.	这个帐单好象有错吧。	zhè-ge zhàng-dān hǎo xiàng yǒu cuò ba
Can I have a receipt?	请开张收据。	qǐng kāi zhāng shōu-jù

103

SHOPPING GUIDE

Anything else? 还要别的吗？

No, thanks, that's all.	不要了，谢谢，就这些。	bú yào le. xiè-xie jiù zhè-xiē
Yes, I'd like ...	对，我要…	duì. wǒ yào
Can you wrap it up, please?	请包一下。	qǐng bāo yí xià
May I have a bag, please?	能给我一个袋子吗？	néng gěi wǒ yí-ge dài-zi ma
Thank you. Goodbye.	谢谢。再见。	xiè-xie. zài-jiàn

Dissatisfied? 不满意？

Can you exchange this, please?	可以换一个吗？	kě-yǐ huàn yí-ge ma
I want to return this.	我想退掉这个。	wǒ xiǎng tuì diào zhè-ge
I'd like a refund.	我要求退款。	wǒ yāo-qiú tuì kuǎn
Here's the receipt.	这是收据。	zhè shì shōu-jù

我能为你做点什么？	Can I help you?
你要什么？	What would you like?
你要什么…的？	What ... would you like?
颜色/样子	colour/shape
质量/数量	quality/quantity
对不起，我们这儿没有。	I'm sorry, we don't have any.
我们这儿卖完了	We're out of stock.
要我们寄去吗？	Shall we send it?
还要别的吗？	Anything else?
请付…元钱。	That's ... yuan, please.
我们不收…	We don't accept ...
信用卡	credit cards
旅行支票	traveller's cheques
收款处在那儿。	The cash desk is over there.

采购指南

Antiques 古董

Antique shops specialize in old pottery, jewellery, carvings and calligraphy, as well as high quality reproductions. Chinese customs regulations prohibit the export of any cultural relics except those marked with special wax seals. And only fairly recent objects are given the seal. (As in all other shops, do not forget your receipt if you buy anything). The no-haggling rule applies in the case of antiques, too — prices are fixed.

Do you have any …?	你们这儿有…吗？	nǐ-men zhèr yǒu … ma
ancient coins	古币	gǔ-bì
bronzeware	青铜制品	qīng-tóng zhì-pǐn
calligraphy	书法	shū-fǎ
carpets	地毯	dì-tǎn
ceramics	陶瓷	táo-cí
camel	骆驼	luò-tuo
dog	狗	gǒu
horse	马	mǎ
pig	猪	zhū
chinaware	瓷器	cí-qì
cloisonné-ware	景泰蓝	jǐng-tài-lán
folding screens	折叠屏风	zhé-dié píng-fēng
ivory	象牙制品	xiàng-yá zhì-pǐn
jade	玉石制品	yù-shí zhì-pǐn
jewels	珠宝首饰	zhū-bǎo shǒu-shi
lacquerware	漆器	qī-qì
pearls	珍珠	zhēn-zhū
porcelain	细瓷器	xì cí-qì
scrolls	卷轴	juàn-zhóu
snuff bottles	鼻烟壶	bí-yān-hú
What period does this date from?	这是哪个时期的？	zhè shì nǎ-ge shì-qī de
How old is it?	这东西有多长的历史？	zhè dōng-xi yǒu duō cháng de lì-shǐ
Who made it?	这是谁的作品？	zhè shì shéi de zuò-pǐn
There's a fault here.	这里有一个残痕。	zhè-li yǒu yí-ge cán-hén
I'd like to see some other items.	我想看看别的品种。	wǒ xiǎng kàn-kan bié de pǐn-zhǒng
I like this one.	我喜欢这件。	wǒ xǐ-huan zhè jiàn
How much is it?	这要多少钱？	zhè yào duō-shao qián

Bookshop — Stationer's 书店-文具店

Those fortunate travellers with a reading knowledge of Chinese will, of course, have no problem finding a book to interest them in a bookshop. Works published in translation are on sale in foreign-language bookshops found in the main cities. Foreign newspapers and magazines are only sold in Friendship Stores and in major hotels.

Where's the nearest ...?	离这儿最近的…在哪儿？	lí zhèr zuì jìn de ... zài nǎr
(foreign language) bookshop	（外文）书店	(wài-wén) shū-diàn
stationer's	文具店	wén-jù-diàn
newsstand	售报亭	shòu-bào-tíng
Where can I buy an English-language newspaper?	哪儿能买到英文报纸？	nǎr néng mǎi dào yīng-wén bào-zhǐ
Do you sell stationery?	你这儿卖文具吗？	nǐ zhèr mài wén-jù ma
Where's the guidebook section?	哪儿卖旅游指南？	nǎr mài lǚ-yóu zhǐ-nán
Where do you keep the English books?	英文书在哪儿？	yīng-wén shū zài nǎr
Is there an English translation of ...?	有…的英译本吗？	yǒu ... de yīng-yì-běn ma
Do you have second-hand books?	这儿卖旧书吗？	zhèr mài jiù-shū ma
I want to buy a/an/some ...	我想买…	wǒ xiǎng mǎi ...
abacus	一把算盘	yì-bǎ suàn-pan
address book	一本通讯薄	yì-běn tōng-xùn-bù
adhesive tape	一卷胶条	yì-juǎn jiāo-tiáo
ball-point pen	一支圆珠笔	yì-zhī yuán-zhū-bǐ
book	一本书	yì-běn shū
calendar	一本日历	yì-běn rì-lì
carbon paper*	一盒复写纸	yì-hé fù-xiě-zhǐ
colouring pencils	一盒彩色铅笔	yì-hé cǎi-sè qiān-bǐ

* Where in English we can use the general word "some", the Chinese language is more specific. For example, the English "some carbon paper" is translated by "a box of carbon paper" to indicate quantity. Some other qualifiers used are "a pad of ..." and "a bottle of ...".

采购指南

crayons	一盒腊笔	yì-hé là-bǐ
dictionary	一本…字典	yì-běn … zì-diǎn
Chinese-English	汉英	hàn-yīng
English-Chinese	英汉	yīng-hàn
pocket	袖珍	xiù-zhēn
drawing paper	一本图画纸	yì-běn tú-huà-zhǐ
drawing pins	一盒图钉	yì-hé tú-dīng
envelopes	一打信封	yì-dá xìn-fēng
eraser	一块橡皮	yí-kuài xiàng-pí
exercise book	一本练习本	yì-běn liàn-xí-běn
felt-tip pen	一支软芯笔	yì-zhī ruǎn-xīn-bǐ
fountain pen	一支钢笔	yì-zhī gāng-bǐ
glue	一瓶胶水儿	yì-píng jjāo-shuǐr
guidebook	一本旅游指南	yì-běn lǚ-yóu zhǐ-nán
ink	一瓶…墨水儿	yì-píng … mò-shuǐr
black/red/blue	黑/红/蓝	hēi/hóng/lán
labels	一盒签条	yì-hé qiān-tiáo
magazine	一本杂志	yì-běn zá-zhì
map	一张地图	yì-zhāng dì-tú
map of the city	市区地图	shì-qū dì-tú
map of China	中国地图	zhōng-guó dì-tú
mechanical pencil	一支自动铅笔	yì-zhī zì-dòng qiān-bǐ
notebook	一本笔记本	yì-běn bǐ-jì-běn
note paper	一本信纸	yì-běn xìn-zhǐ
paintbox	一个油画箱	yí-ge yóu-huà-xiāng
paper	一张纸	yì-zhāng zhǐ
paperback	一本简装本	yì-běn jiǎn-zhuāng-běn
paperclips	一盒曲别针	yì-hé qū-bié-zhēn
pen	一支钢笔	yì-zhī gāng-bǐ
pencil	一支铅笔	yì-zhī qiān-bǐ
pencil sharpener	一个转笔刀	yí-ge zhuàn-bǐ-dāo
playing cards	一副扑克	yí-fù pū-kè
pocket calculator	一个袖珍计算器	yí-ge xiù-zhēn jì-suàn-qì
postcards	几张明信片	jǐ-zhāng míng-xìn-piàn
propelling pencil	一支自动铅笔	yì-zhī zì-dòng qiān-bǐ
refill (for a pen)	一个钢笔芯	yí-ge gāng-bǐ-xīn
rubber	一块橡皮	yí-kuài xiàng-pí
rubber bands	几根橡皮筋儿	jǐ-gēn xiàng-pí-jīnr
ruler	一把尺子	yì-bǎ chǐ-zi
staples	一盒钉书钉	yì-hé dìng-shū-dīng
string	一根绳子	yì-gēn shéng-zi
thumbtacks	一盒图钉	yì-hé tú-dīng
travel guide	一本旅游指南	yì-běn lǚ-yóu zhǐ-nán
typewriter ribbon	一卷打字机色带	yì-juǎn dǎ-zì-jī sè-dài
typing paper	一打打字纸	yì-dá dǎ-zì-zhǐ
wrapping paper	一张包装纸	yì-zhāng bāo-zhuāng-zhǐ
writing pad	一本拍纸薄	yì-běn pāi-zhǐ-bù

Chemist's (drugstore) 药店

There are two types of pharmacy in China: those dealing with Western medicine and those specializing in traditional Chinese medicine. Some shops have counters for both services. Though the range of pharmaceutical goods to be found in China should generally be sufficient for your trip, it would be wise to take along a supply of any drugs that you use regularly. Products that you may not find readily available include tampons, sanitary towels, cold and indigestion remedies, insect repellent and adhesive plasters.

If trying a traditional pharmacy then you should describe your pain or problem to the person in charge who will sell you a herb-based remedy.

Toiletries cannot be bought at the chemist's; for these you should go to a department store.

This section has been divided into two parts:

1. Pharmaceutical — medicine, first-aid etc.
2. Toiletry — toilet articles, cosmetics

General 一般询问

Where's the nearest (all-night) chemist's?	离这儿最近的（夜营）药店在哪儿？	lí zhèr zuì jìn de (yè-yíng) yào-diàn zài nǎr
What time does the chemist's open/close?	药店几点开门/关门？	yào-diàn jǐ diǎn kāi mén/guān mén

1 — Pharmaceutical 药品

I want something for (a) ...	我要一些治…的药。	wǒ yào yì-xiē zhì ... de yào
cold/cough	感冒/咳嗽	gǎn-mào/ké-sou
hay fever	枯草热	kū-cǎo-rè
insect bites	虫咬伤	chóng-yǎo-shāng
sunburn	晒伤	shài-shāng
travel sickness	晕车	yūn-chē
upset stomach	反胃	fǎn wèi

DOCTOR, see page 138

采购指南

I'd like Western medicine.	我想要西药。	wǒ xiǎng-yào xī-yào
Can I get it without a prescription?	没有处方能买这药吗？	méi-yǒu chǔ-fāng néng mǎi zhè yào ma
Can you make up this prescription for me?	请按这个处方配药。	qǐng àn zhè-ge chǔ-fāng pèi yào
Shall I wait?	我得等吗？	wǒ děi děng ma
Can I have a/an/some ...?	请给我拿一些…	qǐng gěi wǒ ná yì-xiē

analgesic	止疼药	zhǐ-téng-yào
aspirin	阿司匹林	ā-sī-pǐ-lín
bandage	绷带	bēng-dài
elastic bandage	弹性绷带	tán-xìng bēng-dài
Band-Aids	带药垫橡皮膏	dài yào-diàn xiàng-pí-gāo
chlorine tablets	氯片	lǜ-piàn
contraceptives	避孕药	bì-yùn-yào
corn plasters	鸡眼膏	jī-yǎn-gāo
cotton wool (absorbent cotton)	脱脂棉	tuō-zhī-mián
cough syrup	止咳糖浆	zhǐ ké táng-jiāng
disinfectant	消毒剂	xiāo-dú-jì
ear drops	滴耳药水	dī ěr yào-shuǐ
Elastoplast	带药垫橡皮膏	dài yào-diàn xiàng-pí-gāo
eye drops	眼药水	yǎn-yào-shuǐ
gauze	纱布	shā-bù
insect repellent	除虫剂	chú-chóng-jì
insect spray	除虫喷雾剂	chú-chóng pēn-wù-jì
iodine	碘酒	diǎn-jiǔ
laxative	缓泻剂	huǎn-xiè jì
mouthwash	漱口药水	shù kǒu yào-shuǐ
nose drops	滴鼻药	dī-bí-yào
quinine tablets	奎宁片	kuí-níng piàn
sanitary towels (napkins)	妇女卫生巾	fù-nǚ wèi-shēng-jīn
suppositories	栓剂	shuān-jì
... tablets	…片	... piàn
thermometer	体温表	tǐ-wēn-biǎo
throat lozenges	喉咙含片	hóu-lóng hán-piàn

| 只可外用
zhǐ kě wài yòng
FOR EXTERNAL USE ONLY | 有毒
yǒu dú
POISON |

2 — Toiletry 盥洗卫生用品及化妆品

Friendship Stores now carry a much wider range of Western goods, and the best selection will be found in the main cities. However, there are certain things that are still quite difficult to find, and it is worth taking a supply of them along with you. These things include shampoo, Western cosmetics and suntanning preparations.

I'd like a/an/some …	我想要…	wǒ xiǎng-yào
after-shave lotion*	一瓶修面后香水	yì-píng xiū miàn hòu xiāng-shuǐ
bath essence	一瓶洗澡液	yì-píng xǐ-zǎo-yè
bath salts	一袋洗澡粉	yí-dài xǐ-zǎo-fěn
blusher	一盒胭脂	yì-hé yān-zhī
cream	一瓶雪花膏	yì-píng xuě-huā-gāo
cleansing cream	一瓶下妆面霜	yì-píng xià-zhuāng miàn-shuāng
foundation cream	一瓶底层面霜	yì-píng dǐ-céng miàn-shuāng
moisturizing cream	一瓶润肤霜	yì-píng rùn-fū-shuāng
cuticle remover	一瓶除皮屑剂	yì-píng chú pí-xiè jì
deodorant	一瓶除体臭液	yì-píng chú tǐ-xiù yè
emery board	一打锉指甲砂纸	yì-dá cuò zhǐ-jia shā-zhǐ
eye liner	一支眼线笔	yì-zhī yǎn-xiàn-bǐ
eyebrow pencil	一支画眉笔	yì-zhī huà-méi-bǐ
eye shadow	一管眼影膏	yì-guǎn yǎn-yǐng gāo
face powder	一盒脸粉	yì-hé liǎn-fěn
hand cream	一瓶润手霜	yì-píng rùn-shǒu-shuāng
lipsalve	一盒防唇裂油膏	yì-hé fáng chún liè yóu-gāo
lipstick	一管口红	yì-guǎn kǒu-hóng
make-up remover pads	一袋下妆棉球	yí-dài xià-zhuāng mián-qiú
mascara	一瓶染睫毛油	yì-píng rǎn jié-máo yóu
mirror	一面镜子	yí-miàn jìng-zi
nail brush	一把指甲油刷子	yì-bǎ zhǐ-jia-yóu shuā-zi
nail clippers	一把指甲刀	yì-bǎ zhī-jia-dāo
nail file	一把指甲锉	yì-bǎ zhī-jia-cuò

---

* Where in English we use the word "some", the Chinese is more specific when necessary, using the translation "a bottle of …".

nail polish	一瓶指甲油	yì-píng zhī-jia-yóu
nail polish remover	一瓶退指甲油水	yì-píng tuì zhī-jia-yóu shuǐ
nail scissors	一把指甲剪刀	yì-bǎ zhī-jia jiǎn-dāo
perfume	一瓶香水	yì-píng xiāng-shuǐ
powder puff	一个粉扑	yí-ge fěn-pū
razor	一把剃须刀	yì-bǎ tì-xū-dāo
razor blades	一盒剃须刀片	yì-hé tì-xū-dāo-piàn
safety pins	一盒别针	yì-hé bié-zhēn
shaving brush	一把剃须肥皂刷	yì-bǎ tì-xū féi-zào-shuā
shaving soap	一瓶剃须皂液	yì-píng tì-xū zào-yè
soap	一块肥皂	yí-kuài féi-zào
sponge	一块海绵	yí-kuài hǎi-mián
sun-tan cream	一盒晒黑膏	yì-hé shài-hēi-gāo
sun-tan oil	一瓶晒黑油	yì-píng shài-hēi-yóu
talcum powder	一盒爽身粉	yì-hé shuǎng-shēn-fěn
tissues	一包纸手绢儿	yì-bāo zhǐ shǒu-juànr
toilet paper	一卷卫生纸	yì-juǎn wèi-shēng-zhǐ
toilet water	一瓶爽身香水	yì-píng shuǎng-shēn xiāng-shuǐ
toothbrush	一把牙刷	yì-bǎ yá-shuā
(tube of) toothpaste	(一筒) 牙膏	(yì-tǒng) yá-gāo
towel	一条毛巾	yì-tiáo máo-jīn
tweezers	一把镊子	yì-bǎ niè-zi

For your hair 洗发用品

bobby pins	几个卡子	jǐ-ge qiǎ-zi
colour shampoo	一瓶染发洗发膏	yì-píng rǎn-fà xǐ-fà-gāo
comb	一把梳子	yì-bǎ shū-zi
curlers	几个卷发夹子	jǐ-ge juǎn-fà jiǎ-zi
dry shampoo	一袋干性洗发剂	yí-dài gān-xìng xǐ-fà-jì
dye	一瓶染发剂	yì-píng rǎn-fà-jì
hairbrush	一把发刷	yì-bǎ fà-shuā
hairgrips	几个卡子	jǐ-ge qiǎ-zi
hair lotion	一瓶护发液	yì-píng hù-fà-yè
hair spray	一瓶喷雾发浆	yì-píng pēn-wù fà-jiāng
setting lotion	一瓶冷烫水	yì-píng lěng-tàng-shuǐ
shampoo	一瓶…洗发剂	yì-píng … xǐ-fà-jì
for dry hair	抗干发	kàng gān fà
greasy (oily) hair	抗多油发	kàng duō yóu fà
wig	一副假发	yí-fù jiǎ-fà

For the baby 婴儿用品

baby food	婴儿食品	yīng-ér shí-pǐn
dummy (pacifier)	橡皮奶嘴儿	xiàng-pí nǎi-zuǐr
feeding bottle	奶瓶	nǎi-píng
nappies (diapers)	纸尿布	zhǐ niào-bù

Clothing 衣服

If you want to buy something specific, prepare yourself in advance. Look at the list of clothing on page 116. Get some idea of the colour, material and size you want. They are all listed in the next few pages.

Provided you have brought a pattern along with you, you can have a shirt, blouse or simple silk dress made up in about 48 hours. Men's suits made to measure take a little longer. The tailoring is generally high quality and extremely reasonable in price. See phrases on page 114.

General 一般询问

I'd like …	我想要…	wǒ xiǎng-yào
I want something for a …	我要买给…穿的衣服	wǒ yào mǎi gěi … chuān de yī-fu
boy/girl	男孩儿/女孩儿	nán-háir/nǚ-háir
man/woman	男人/女人	nán-rén/nǚ-rén
I like the one in the window.	我喜欢橱窗里的那个。	wǒ xǐ-huan chú-chuāng li de nà-ge
Could you show me another one?	可以再给我看一个别的吗？	kě-yǐ zài gěi wǒ kàn yí-ge bié de ma
I want something like this.	我要一件像这个样子的。	wǒ yào yí-jiàn xiàng zhè-ge yàng-zi de

1 centimetre (cm.)	= 0.39 in.	1 inch = 2.54 cm.
1 metre (m.)	= 39.37 in.	1 foot = 30.5 cm.
10 metres	= 32.81 ft.	1 yard = 0.91 m.

Although the metric system has been adopted in China, part of the population continues to use the following units for length measurement:

1 市尺 (shì-chǐ)	= 0.33 m.	= 1.094 ft.
3 市尺 (shì-chǐ)	= 1 m.	= 3.281 ft.

Colour 颜色

I want something in …	我想要…的。	wǒ xiǎng-yào … de
I want a … shade.	我想要颜色…的。	wǒ xiǎng-yào yán-sè … de
darker	深些	shēn xiē
lighter	浅些	qiǎn xiē
I want something to match this.	我想要和这个相配的。	wǒ xiǎng-yào hé zhè-ge xiāng pèi de
I don't like the colour.	我不喜欢这种颜色。	wǒ bù xǐ-huan zhè-zhǒng yán-sè
Is it colour-fast?	这料子退色吗？	zhè liào-zi tuì sè ma

beige	浅咖啡色	qiǎn kā-fēi-sè
black	黑色	hēi-sè
blue	蓝色	lán-sè
brown	褐色	hè-sè
fawn	浅黄褐色	qiǎn huáng-hè-sè
golden	金黄色	jīn-huáng-sè
green	绿色	lǜ-sè
grey	灰色	huī-sè
mauve	紫红色	zǐ-hóng-sè
orange	桔红色	jú-hóng-sè
pink	粉红色	fěn-hóng-sè
purple	紫色	zǐ-sè
red	红色	hóng-sè
scarlet	鲜红色	xiān-hóng-sè
silver	银灰色	yín-huī-sè
turquoise	青绿色	qīng-lǜ-sè
white	白色	bái-sè
yellow	黄色	huáng-sè
light	浅色	qiǎn-sè
dark	深色	shēn-sè

一色
(yí-sè)

直条纹
(zhí-tiáo-wén)

小圆点
(xiǎo yuán-diǎn)

方格
(fāng-gé)

图案
(tú-àn)

Material 布料

Do you have anything in …?	你这儿有…的吗？	nǐ zhèr yǒu … de ma
Is it …?	这是…的吗？	zhè shì … de ma
colour fast	不退色	bú tuì sè
crease resistant	抗皱	kàng zhòu
pure cotton/silk	纯棉/真丝	chún mián/zhēn sī
synthetic	人造纤维	rén-zào xiān-wéi
hand-made	手工制	shǒu-gōng zhì
imported	进口	jìn-kǒu
made here	本地生产	běn-dì shēng-chǎn
Will it shrink?	这料子缩水吗？	zhè liào-zi suō-shuǐ ma
I'd like something …	我想要…的料子。	wǒ xiǎng-yào … de liào-zi
thicker/thinner	厚些/薄些	hòu xiē/báo xiē
Do you have any better quality?	你这儿有质量好些的吗？	nǐ zhèr yǒu zhí-liàng hǎo xiē de ma
What is it made of?	这是什么料子？	zhè shì shén-me liào-zi
How much is it per metre?	一公尺多少钱？	yì gōng-chǐ duō-shao qián

brocade	织锦缎	zhī-jǐn-duàn
corduroy	灯芯绒	dēng-xīn-róng
cotton	棉布	mián-bù
crepe	绉绸	zhòu-chóu
denim	劳动布	láo-dòng-bù
felt	毡	zhān
flannel	法兰绒	fǎ-lán-róng
gabardine	华达呢	huá-dá-ní
lace	钩织布料	gōu-zhī bù-liào
leather	皮子	pí-zi
linen	亚麻布	yà-má-bù
poplin	府绸	fǔ-chóu
satin	缎子	duàn-zi
silk	丝绸	sī-chóu
raw silk	生丝	shēng-sī
suede	翻毛皮	fān-máo-pí
towelling	毛巾布	máo-jīn-bù
velvet	天鹅绒	tiān-é-róng
wool	纯毛	chún-máo

Tailor's — Dressmaker's 裁缝店

I'd like a ... made to measure.	我想订做…	wǒ xiǎng dìng zuò
blouse	女衬衫	nǚ chèn-shān
dress	连衣裙	lián-yī-qún
jacket	上衣	shàng-yī
shirt	衬衫	chèn-shān
skirt	裙子	qún-zi
Do you have any material samples?	你有料子的样品吗？	nǐ yǒu liào-zi de yàng-pǐn ma
How much material do I need for a ...?	我做一件…要用多少布料？	wǒ zuò yí-jiàn ... yào yòng duō-shao bù-liào
Can you copy this?	你能照这个样子做吗？	nǐ néng zhào zhè-ge yàng-zi zuò ma
I have some material.	我有一些布料。	wǒ yǒu yì-xiē bù-liào
I have a pattern.	我有样子。	wǒ yǒu yàng-zi
Please make up ... (quantity) to the same pattern.	请照这个样子做…件。	qǐng zhào zhè-ge yàng-zi zuò ... jiàn
How long will the job take?	多长时间能做好？	duō cháng shí-jiān néng zuò hǎo
How many fittings will be necessary?	要试几次样子？	yào shì jǐ cì yàng-zi
When must I come back?	我什么时间再来？	wǒ shén-me shí-jiān zài lái

button	钮扣	niǔ-kòu
collar	衣领	yī-lǐng
cuff	袖口	xiù-kǒu
elastic	松紧带	sōng-jǐn-dài
hem	衣边	yī-biān
lapel	翻领	fān-lǐng
lining	衬里	chèn-lǐ
ribbon	彩带	cǎi-dài
seam	接缝	jiē-fèng
sleeve	袖子	xiù-zi
waist	腰	yāo
longer	长些	cháng xiē
shorter	短些	duǎn sie

FOR A GOOD FIT, see page 115

Sizes 尺寸

Clothing sizes in China are still being standardized, and do not correspond to those in the West. In Friendship Stores, where clothes are made for export, you'll find three sizes — small, medium and large. As a general rule, though, clothes are designed for smaller people than in the West and are also cut more generously.

If you want to buy clothes in a department store you will find that the sizes are based on a combination of two measurements — one of which is usually height. For example, a jacket may be sized 165-88. This means it should fit someone who is 1 metre 65cm. tall, and has an 88cm. chest. Trousers will be sized according to height and waist.

When buying shoes the best bet is to try a few pairs on, if you can find any large enough (39/UK 6/US 7 ½ is considered large).

I don't know the Chinese sizes.	我不知道中国尺寸。	wǒ bù zhī-dao zhōng-guó chǐ-cùn
Could you measure me?	请你给我量量好吗？	qǐng nǐ gěi wǒ liáng-liang hǎo ma

小 xiǎo SMALL	中 zhōng MEDIUM	大 dà LARGE

A good fit? 合适吗？

Can I try it on?	我可以试穿一下儿吗？	wǒ kě-yǐ shì-chuān yí xiàr ma
Where's the changing room?	试衣室在哪儿？	shì-yī-shì zài nǎr
Is there a mirror?	这儿有镜子吗？	zhèr yǒu jìng-zi ma
It fits very well.	这很合适。	zhè hěn hé-shì
It doesn't fit.	这不合适。	zhè bù hé-shì

NUMBERS, see page 149

采购指南

It's too …	这太…	zhè tài
tight/loose	紧/肥	jǐn/féi
short/long	短/长	duǎn/fèi
How long will it take to alter?	改一下需要多长时间？	gǎi yí-xià xū-yào duō cháng shí-jiān

Clothes and accessories 服装及有关用品

I'd like a/an/some …	我想要…	wǒ xiǎng-yào
anorak	一件登山服	yí-jiàn dēng-shān-fú
bathrobe	一件浴衣	yí-jiàn yù-yī
bathing cap	一顶游泳帽	yì-dǐng yóu-yǒng-mào
bathing suit	一件游泳衣	yí-jiàn yóu-yǒng-yī
blouse	一件女衬衫	yí-jiàn nǚ chèn-shān
bra	一副乳罩	yí-fù rǔ-zhào
braces (Br.)	一副背带	yí-fù bēi-dài
briefs	一条内裤	yì-tiáo nèi-kù
cap	一顶帽子	yì-dǐng mào-zi
cardigan	一件开身毛衣	yí-jiàn kāi shēn máo-yī
cheongsam	一件旗袍	yí-jiàn qí-páo
coat	一件大衣	yí-jiàn dà-yī
dress	一件连衣裙	yí-jiàn lián-yī-qún
dressing gown	一件浴衣	yí-jiàn yù-yī
evening dress (woman's)	一件女晚礼服	yí-jiàn nǚ wǎn-lǐ-fú
girdle	一条健美内裤	yì-tiáo jiàn-měi nèi-kù
gloves	一副手套	yí-fù shǒu-tào
handbag	一个手提包	yí-ge shǒu-tí-bāo
handkerchief	一条手绢儿	yì-tiáo shǒu-juànr
hat	一顶礼帽	yì-dǐng lǐ-mào
jacket	一件上衣	yí-jiàn shàng-yī
silk-padded jacket	一件丝棉袄	yí-jiàn sī mián-ǎo
cotton-padded jacket	一件棉袄	yí-jiàn mián-ǎo
jeans	一条牛仔裤	yì-tiáo niú-zǎi-kù
kimono	一件和服	yí-jiàn hé-fú
leotard	一件体操服	yí-jiàn tǐ-cāo-fú
nightdress	一件长睡衣	yí-jiàn cháng shuì-yī
overalls	一条工装裤	yì-tiáo gōng-zhuāng-kù
pair of …	一双…	yi-shuāng
panties	一条内裤	yì-tiáo nèi-kù
pants (Am.)	一条长裤	yì-tiáo cháng kù
panty hose	一条裤袜	yì-tiáo kù-wà
parka	一件登山服	yí-jiàn dēng-shān-fú
pullover	一件…毛衣	yí-jiàn … máo-yī
polo-neck (turtle-neck)	高领	gāo lǐng

round neck	圆领	yuán lǐng
V-neck	鸡心领	jī-xīn lǐng
with long/short sleeves	长袖/短袖	cháng xiù/duǎn xiù
sleeveless pullover	一件毛背心	yí-jiàn máo bèi-xīn
pyjamas	一套睡衣	yí-tào shuì-yī
raincoat	一件雨衣	yí-jiàn yǔ-yī
scarf	一条围巾	yì-tiáo wéi-jīn
shirt	一件衬衫	yí-jiàn chèn-shān
shorts	一条短裤	yì-tiáo duǎn-kù
skirt	一条裙子	yì-tiáo qún-zi
slip	一条衬裙	yì-tiáo chèn-qún
socks (a pair of)	一双袜子	yì-shuāng wà-zi
sports jacket	一件运动衫	yí-jiàn yùn-dòng-shān
stockings (a pair of)	一双长袜	yì-shuāng cháng wà
suit (men)	一套男西服	yí-tào nán xī-fú
suit (women)	一套女西服	yí-tào nǚ xī-fú
suspenders (Am.)	一副背带	yí-fù bēi-dài
sweater	一件毛衣	yí-jiàn máo-yī
sweatshirt	一件长袖运动衫	yí-jiàn cháng xiù yùn-dòng-shān
swimming trunks	一条游泳裤	yì-tiáo yóu-yǒng-kù
swimsuit	一件游泳衣	yí-jiàn yóu-yǒng-yī
T-shirt	一件针织衬衫	yí-jiàn zhēn-zhī chèn-shān
tie	一条领带	yì-tiáo lǐng-dài
tights	一条裤袜	yì-tiáo kù-wà
tracksuit	一套运动衫	yí-tào yùn-dòng-shān
trousers	一条长裤	yì-tiáo cháng kù
umbrella	一把雨伞	yì-bǎ yǔ-sǎn
underpants	一条男内裤	yì-tiáo nán nèi-kù
undershirt	一件背心	yí-jiàn bèi-xīn
vest (Am.)	一件西服坎肩	yí-jiàn xī-fú kǎn-jiān
vest (Br.)	一件背心	yí-jiàn bèi-xīn
waistcoat	一件西服坎肩	yí-jiàn xī-fú kǎn-jiān

belt	腰带	yāo-dài
buckle	带扣	dài-kòu
button	钮扣	niǔ-kòu
pocket	衣袋	yī-dài
press stud (snap fastener)	按扣	àn-kòu
zip (zipper)	拉锁	lā-suǒ

Shoes 鞋

I'd like a pair of ...	我想买一双…	wǒ xiǎng mǎi yì-shuāng
boots	靴子	xuē-zi
plimsolls (sneakers)	球鞋	qiú-xié
sandals	凉鞋	liáng-xié
shoes	…鞋	… xié
flat	平底	píng-dǐ
with a heel	有跟的	yǒu gēn de
slippers	拖鞋	tuō-xié
These are too ...	这些都太…	zhè xiē dōu tài
narrow/wide	紧/肥	jǐn/féi
big/small	大/小	dà/xiǎo
Do you have a larger/smaller size?	你有大些/小些的吗？	nǐ yǒu dà-xiē/xiǎo-xiē de ma
Do you have the same in black?	你们这儿有这种式样的黑颜色的吗？	nǐ-men zhèr yǒu zhèi zhǒng shì-yàng de hēi yán-sè de ma
cloth	布料	bù-liào
leather	皮子	pí-zi
rubber	橡胶	xiàng-jiāo
suede	翻毛皮	fān-máo-pí
Is it genuine leather?	这是真皮子的吗？	zhè shì zhēn pí-zi de ma
I'd like some shoe polish.	我想买一筒鞋油。	wǒ xiǎng mǎi yì-tǒng xié-yóu
I'd like some shoelaces.	我要买鞋带。	wǒ yào mǎi xié-dài

Shoes worn out? Here's the key to getting them fixed again:

Can you repair these shoes?	你能修这些鞋子吗？	nǐ néng xiū zhè-xiē xié-zi ma
Can you stitch this?	你能缝补这个吗？	nǐ néng féng-bǔ zhè-ge ma
I want new soles and heels.	我要换新鞋底和鞋跟。	wǒ yào huàn xīn xié-dǐ hé xié-gēn
When will they be ready?	什么时候能修好？	shén-me shí-hou néng xiū hǎo

COLOURS, see page 112

Electrical appliances 电器

Electrical current is 220 volts, 50 cycles. It is advisable to take your own appliances with you as well as a plug adaptor — plug sizes vary throughout China. The electric current supply is not always stable, so be prepared for occasional power fluctuations.

Do you have a battery for this?	你这儿有适用于这个…的电池吗？	nǐ zhèr yǒu shì-yòng yú zhè-ge … de diàn-chí ma
Do you have a plug for this?	你这儿有适用于这个…的插头吗？	nǐ zhèr yǒu shì-yòng yú zhè-ge … de chā-tóu ma
This is broken. Can you repair it?	这个坏了。你这儿能修吗？	zhè-ge huài le. nǐ zhèr néng xiū ma
Can you show me how it works?	能教我怎么用吗？	néng jiāo wǒ zěn-me yòng ma
I'd like to hire a video cassette/video recorder.	我想租一盘录像带/一台录像机	wǒ xiǎng zū yì-pán lù-xiàng-dài/yì-tái lù-xiàng-jī
I'd like a/an/some …	我想要…	wǒ xiǎng-yào
adaptor	一个多路插座	yí-ge duō-lù chā-zuò
amplifier	一台扩音机	yì-tái kuò-yīn-jī
battery	几节电池	jǐ-jié diàn-chí
bulb	一个灯泡	yí-ge dēng-pào
clock	一座钟	yí-zuò zhōng
extension lead (cord)	一根接长电线	yì-gēn jiē-cháng diàn-xiàn
hair dryer	一个电吹发器	yí-ge diàn chuī-fà-qì
headphones	一副耳机	yí-fù ěr-jī
iron	一个熨斗	yí-ge yùn-dǒu
lamp	一盏灯	yì-zhǎn dēng
plug	一个插头	yí-ge chā-tóu
portable …	袖珍…	xiù-zhēn
radio	一台收音机	yì-tái shōu-yīn-jī
record player	一台留声机	yì-tái liú-shēng-jī
shaver	一个电动剃须刀	yí-ge diàn-dòng tì-xū-dāo
speakers	一个扬声器	yí-ge yáng-shēng-qì
(cassette) tape recorder	一台（盒式）磁带录音机	yì-tái (hé-shì) cí-dài lù-yīn-jī
(colour) television	一台（彩色）电视机	yì-tái (cǎi-sè) diàn-shì-jī
transformer	一个变压器	yí-ge biàn-yā-qì
video recorder	一台录像机	yì-tái lù-xiàng-jī

Grocery 副食店

Here are a few phrases to help you out when buying food for a picnic or journey.

I'd like a loaf of bread, please.	我想要一个面包。	wǒ xiǎng-yào yí-ge miàn-bāo
I'll have one of those, please.	我要一块那种的。	wǒ yào yí-kuài nèi-zhǒng de
May I help myself?	我能自己拿吗？	wǒ néng zì-jǐ ná ma
I'd like …	我想要…	wǒ xiǎng-yào
a kilo of eggs	一公斤鸡蛋	yì gōng-jīn jī-dàn
half a kilo of tomatoes	半公斤西红柿	bàn gōng-jīn xī-hóng-shì
100 grams of butter	一百克黄油	100 kè huáng-yóu
a bottle of milk	一瓶牛奶	yì-píng niú-nǎi
half a dozen apples	六个苹果	6 ge píng-guǒ
4 slices of ham	四片火腿	4 piàn huǒ-tuǐ
a packet of tea	一包茶叶	yì-bāo chá-yè
a jar of jam	一瓶果酱	yì-píng guǒ-jiàng
a tin (can) of peaches	一筒桃子罐头	yì-tǒng táo-zi guàn-tou
a box of chocolates	一盒巧克力	yì-hé qiǎo-kè-lì

Household 日用品

These everyday items could come in handy on your trip.

I'd like a…	我想要…	wǒ xiǎng-yào
bottle opener	一个开瓶器	yí-ge kāi-píng-qì
can opener	一个开罐器	yí-ge kāi-guàn-qì
chopsticks	几双筷子	jǐ shuāng kuài-zi
corkscrew	一把拔塞钻	yì-bǎ bá-sāi-zuān
crockery	一件陶瓷餐具	yí-jiàn táo-cí cān-jù
cutlery	一套刀叉餐具	yí-tào dāo-chā cān-jù
first-aid kit	一个急救箱	yí-ge jí-jiù-xiāng
flashlight	一只手电筒	yì-zhī shǒu-diàn-tǒng
lamp	一盏灯	yì-zhǎn dēng
mosquito net	一幅蚊帐	yì-fú wén-zhàng
paper napkins	一打纸餐巾	yì-dá zhǐ-cān-jīn
penknife	一把小刀	yì-bǎ xiǎo-dāo
rucksack	一个帆布背包	yí-ge fān-bù bēi-bāo
scissors	一把剪刀	yì-bǎ jiǎn-dāo
screwdriver	一把改锥	yì-bǎ gǎi-zhuī
tin opener	一个开罐器	yí-ge kāi-guàn-qì
torch	一只手电筒	yì-zhī shǒu-diàn-tǒng
vacuum flask	一个暖水瓶	yí-ge nuǎn-shuǐ-píng
water flask	一个水壶	yí-ge shuǐ-hú

FOOD, see also page 63

Jeweller's — Watchmaker's 首饰店-钟表店

Jewellery is sold in antique shops. Look out for jade objects — the Chinese excel in the art of jade carving. If buying ivory check that it is the real thing and not a substitute — they are virtually indistinguishable.

Could I see that, please?	我可以看看那个吗？	wǒ kě-yǐ kàn-kan nèi-ge ma
Do you have anything in gold?	你这儿有金制品吗？	nǐ zhèr yǒu jīn-zhì-pǐn ma
How many carats is this?	这是几开金的？	zhè shì jǐ kāi jīn de
Is this real silver?	这是银的吗？	zhè shì yín de ma
Can you repair this watch?	你这儿能修这块表吗？	nǐ zhèr néng xiū zhè-kuài biǎo ma
I'd like a/an/some ...	我想要…	wǒ xiǎng-yào
alarm clock	一个闹钟	yí-ge nào-zhōng
bangle	一副手镯	yí-fù shǒu-zhuó
battery	几节电池	jǐ-jié diàn-chí
bracelet	一副手镯	yí-fù shǒu-zhuó
chain bracelet	链手镯	liàn-shǒu-zhuó
charm bracelet	带饰物链手镯	dài shì-wù liàn-shǒu-zhuó
brooch	一枚胸针	yì-méi xiōng-zhēn
chop (uncarved Chinese seal)	一块印章石料	yí-kuài yìn-zhāng shí-liào
chop (carved)	一枚印章	yì-méi yìn-zhāng
cigarette case	一个烟盒	yí-ge yān-hé
cigarette lighter	一个打火机	yí-ge dǎ-huǒ-jī
clip	一个夹子	yí-ge jiā-zi
clock	一座钟	yí-zuò zhōng
cuff links	一枚袖口链扣	yì-méi xiù-kǒu liàn-kòu
cutlery	一套刀叉餐具	yí-tào dāo-chā cān-jù
earrings	一副耳环	yí-fù ěr-huán
gem	一枚宝石	yì-méi bǎo-shí
jewel box	一个首饰箱	yí-ge shǒu-shì-xiāng
mechanical pencil	一支自动铅笔	yì-zhī zì-dòng qiān-bǐ
music box	一个八音盒	yí-ge bā-yīn-hé
necklace	一副项链	yí-fù xiàng-liàn
pendant	一些悬饰物	yì-xiē xuán-shì-wù
pin	一个别针	yí-ge bié-zhēn
pocket watch	一块怀表	yí-kuài huái-biǎo
powder compact	一个小粉盒	yí-ge xiǎo fěn-hé
propelling pencil	一枝自动铅笔	yì-zhī zì-dòng qiān-bǐ

ring	一枚戒指	yì-méi jiè-zhi
engagement ring	定婚戒指	dìng-hūn jiè-zhi
wedding ring	结婚戒指	jié-hūn jiè-zhi
silverware	一件银器	yí-jiàn yín-qì
tie clip	一枚领带夹子	yì-méi lǐng-dài jiā-zi
tie pin	一枚领带别针	yì-méi lǐng-dài bié-zhēn
watch	一块（…）表	yí-kuài (…) biǎo
automatic	自动	zì-dòng
digital	电子显示	diàn-zǐ xiǎn-shì
quartz	石英	shí-yīng
with a secondhand	带秒针的	dài miǎo-zhēn de
watchstrap	一条表带	yì-tiáo biǎo-dài
wristwatch	一块手表	yí-kuài shǒu-biǎo

amber	琥珀	hǔ-pò
amethyst	紫水晶	zǐ-shuǐ-jīng
chromium	铬	luò
copper	铜	tóng
coral	珊瑚	shān-hú
crystal	水晶	shuǐ-jīng
cut glass	雕玻璃	diāo bō-li
diamond	金钢石	jīn-gāng-shí
ebony	乌木	wū-mù
emerald	绿刚玉	lǜ-gāng-yù
enamel	搪瓷	táng-cí
gold	金	jīn
gold-plated	镀金的	dù-jīn de
ivory	象牙	xiàng-yá
jade	玉	yù
onyx	缟玛瑙	gǎo mǎ-nǎo
pearl	珍珠	zhēn-zhū
pewter	锡镴器皿	xī-là qì-mǐn
platinum	白金	bái-jīn
ruby	红宝石	hóng-bǎo-shí
sapphire	蓝宝石	lán-bǎo-shí
silver	银	yín
silver-plated	镀银的	dù-yín de
stainless steel	不锈钢	bú-xiù-gāng
topaz	黄玉	huáng-yù
turquoise	绿松石	lǜ-sōng-shí

Optician's 眼镜店

I've broken my glasses.	我的眼镜坏了。	wǒ de yǎn-jìng huài le
Can you repair them for me?	你这儿能修吗？	nǐ zhèr néng xiū ma
I need them in a hurry.	我想尽快能用上。	wǒ xiǎng jìn kuài néng yòng shang
When will they be ready?	什么时候能修好？	shén-me shí-hou néng xiū hǎo
Can you change the lenses?	你这儿能换镜片吗？	nǐ zhèr néng huàn jìng-piàn ma
I want tinted lenses.	我想要着色镜片。	wǒ xiǎng-yào zhuó-sè jìng-piàn
The frame is broken.	这个镜架坏了。	zhè-ge jìng-jià huài le
I'd like a spectacle case.	我要一个眼镜盒。	wǒ yào yí-ge yǎn-jìng-hé
I'd like to have my eyesight checked.	我想验光。	wǒ xiǎng yàn guāng
I'm short-sighted/long-sighted.	我是近视/远视。	wǒ shì jìn-shi/yuǎn-shi
I want some contact lenses.	我想要角膜接触镜。	wǒ xiǎng-yào jiǎo-mó jiē-chù-jìng
I've lost one of my contact lenses.	我的角膜接触镜丢了一片。	wǒ de jiǎo-mó jiē-chù-jìng diū le yí-piàn
Could you give me another one?	你能给我配一片吗？	nǐ néng gěi wǒ pèi yí-piàn ma
I have hard/soft lenses.	我的角膜接触镜是硬/软的。	wǒ de jiǎo-mó jiē-chù-jìng shì yìng/ruǎn de
Do you have any contact-lens fluid?	你这儿有角膜接触镜清洗液吗？	nǐ zhèr yǒu jiǎo-mó jiē-chù-jìng qīng-xǐ-yè ma
I'd like to buy a pair of sunglasses.	我想买一副墨镜。	wǒ xiǎng mǎi yí-fù mò-jìng
May I look in a mirror?	这儿有镜子吗？	zhèr yǒu jìng-zi ma
I'd like to buy a pair of binoculars.	我想买一架双筒望远镜。	wǒ xiǎng mǎi yí-jià shuāng-tǒng wàng-yuǎn-jìng

124

Photography 摄影

Some international brands of film are now available in China and can be found in Friendship Stores. But it is better to take a good supply of the film that you are used to. It is forbidden to take pictures of soldiers, bridges and tunnels, and if you want to take a close-up photo of a Chinese person, ask permission first.

May I take a photo of you, please?	我可以给你照像吗？	wǒ kě-yǐ gěi nǐ zhào-xiàng ma

In the shop 在商店

I want a(n) ... camera.	我想买一个…照像机。	wǒ xiǎng mǎi yí-ge ... zhào-xiàng-jī
automatic	自动的	zì-dòng de
inexpensive	便宜的	pián-yi de
simple	简单的	jiǎn-dān de
Show me some ..., please.	请让我看看…	qǐng ràng wǒ kàn-kan
cine (movie) cameras	摄影机	shè-yǐng-jī
video cameras	摄像机	shè-xiàng-jī
I'd like to have some passport photos taken.	我想照几张护照像片。	wǒ xiǎng zhào jǐ zhāng hù-zhào xiàng-piàn

Film 胶卷

I'd like a film for this camera.	我想要一卷适于这种照像机的胶卷。	wǒ xiǎng-yào yì-juǎn shì-yú zhè-zhǒng zhào-xiàng-jī de jiāo-juǎn
black and white	黑白的	hēi-bái de
colour	彩色的	cǎi-sè de
colour negative	彩色底片	cǎi-sè dǐ-piàn
colour slide	彩色幻灯片	cǎi-sè huàn-dēng-piàn
video cassette	录像带	lù-xiàng-dài
24/36 exposures	二十四/三十六张的	èr-shí-sì/sān-shí-liù zhāng de
this size	这个型号的	zhè-ge xíng-hào de
artificial light type	灯光片	dēng-guāng piàn
daylight type	日光片	rì-guāng piàn
fast (high-speed)	快速的	kuài-sù de
fine grain	细颗粒的	xì kē-lì de

Developing 冲洗

How much do you charge for processing?	冲洗这卷胶卷多少钱？	chōng-xǐ zhè-juǎn jiāo-juǎn duō-shao qián
I'd like ... prints of each negative.	每张底片洗…张。	měi-zhāng dǐ-piàn xǐ ... zhāng
with a mat finish	要绒面纸的	yào wén-miàn-zhǐ de
with a glossy finish	要光面纸的	yào guāng-miàn-zhǐ de
Will you enlarge this, please?	请把这张放大一下。	qǐng bǎ zhè-zhāng fàng-dà yí-xià
When will the photos be ready?	什么时候能取？	shén-me shí-hou néng qǔ

Accessories and repairs 零配件和修理

I'd like a/an/some ...	我想要…	wǒ xiǎng-yào
battery	几节电池	jǐ-jié diàn-chí
cable release	一个连线快门	yí-ge lián-xiàn kuài-mén
camera case	一个像机盒	yí-ge xiàng-jī-hé
(electronic) flash	一个（电子）闪光灯	yí-ge (diàn-zǐ) shǎn-guāng-dēng
filter	一片滤色镜	yí-piàn lǜ-sè-jìng
for black and white	用于黑白底片的	yòng yú hēi-bái dǐ-piàn de
for colour	用于彩色底片的	yòng yú cǎi-sè dǐ-piàn de
lens	镜头	jìng-tóu
telephoto lens	望远镜头	wàng-yuǎn jìng-tóu
wide angle lens	广角镜头	guǎng-jiǎo jìng-tóu
lens cap	镜头盖	jìng-tóu-gài
Can you repair this camera?	你这儿能修理这个像机吗？	nǐ zhèr néng xiū zhè-ge xiàng-jī ma
The film is jammed.	胶卷被卡住了。	jiāo-juǎn bèi qiǎ zhù le
There's something wrong with the ...	…有毛病。	... yǒu máo-bìng
exposure counter	胶片计数器	jiāo-piàn jì-shù-qì
film winder	缠绕胶卷柄	chán-rào jiāo-juǎn bǐng
flash attachment	闪光灯接口	shǎn-guāng-dēng jiē-kǒu
lens	镜头	jìng-tóu
light meter	测光表	cè-guāng-biǎo
rangefinder	测距器	cè-jù-qì
shutter	快门	kuài-mén

NUMBERS, see page 149

Smoker's supplies 香烟、烟草及烟具

There are no tobacconist's or kiosks specializing in cigarettes, instead you should go to a department store or a beer
and wine shop or ask at your hotel service desk. You will
find a wide variety of Chinese cigarettes as well as foreign
cigarettes made under licence. Pipe fans are advised to bring
along an adequate supply of their favourite blend, or buy it
Chinese style — by the leaf.

A packet of cigarettes, please.	请拿一包香烟。	qǐng ná yì-bāo xiāng-yān
Do you have any American/English cigarettes?	你这儿有美国/英国香烟吗？	nǐ zhèr yǒu měi-guó/yīng-guó xiāng-yān ma
I'd like a carton.	我要一条。	wǒ yào yì-tiáo
Give me a/some …, please.	请给我拿…	qǐng gěi wǒ ná
chewing tobacco	一包口嚼烟草	yì-bāo kǒu-jiáo yān-cǎo
cigarettes	一包…香烟	yì-bāo … xiāng-yān
filter-tipped	带过滤嘴的	dài guò-lǜ-zuǐ de
without filter	不带过滤嘴的	bú dài guò-lǜ-zuǐ de
mild/strong	柔和的/有劲的	róu-hé de/yǒu jìn de
king-size	加长的	jiā-cháng de
cigars	一盒雪茄	yì-hé xuě-jiā
lighter	一个打火机	yí-ge dǎ-huǒ-jī
lighter fluid	打火机液体燃料	dǎ-huǒ-jī yè-tǐ rán-liào
lighter gas	打火机气体燃料	dǎ-huǒ-jī qì-tǐ rán-liào
matches	一盒火柴	yì-hé huǒ-chái
pipe	一个烟斗	yí-ge yān-dǒu
pipe cleaners	清洗烟斗的器具	qīng-xǐ yān-dǒu de qì-jù
pipe tobacco	一包烟斗烟草	yì-bāo yān-dǒu yān-cǎo
pipe tool	抽烟斗的用具	chōu yān-dǒu de yòng-jù
snuff	鼻烟	bí-yān
wick	灯芯	dēng-xīn

Souvenirs 纪念品

Few countries can offer such a varied selection of souvenirs
as China. Here is a list of some of the most popular ones:

abacus	算盘	suàn-pan
acupuncture poster	针灸经络穴位图	zhēn-jiǔ jīng-luò xué-wèi tú

bamboo products	竹制品	zhú zhì-pǐn
basketware	藤编器具	téng-biān qì-jù
bronzeware	青铜制品	qīng-tóng zhì-pǐn
carpet	地毯	dì-tǎn
cashmere	开司米	kāi-sī-mǐ
chinaware	瓷器	cí-qì
chop (carved seal)	印章	yìn-zhāng
chopsticks	筷子	kuài-zi
cloisonné-ware	景泰兰	jǐng-tài-lán
craft products	工艺品	gōng-yì-pǐn
fan	扇子	shàn-zi
folding screen	折叠屏风	zhé-dié píng-fēng
fur	毛皮	máo-pí
furniture	家具	jiā-jù
ginseng	人参	rén-shēn
hand embroidery	手工刺绣	shǒu-gōng cì-xiù
herbal remedies	草药	cǎo-yào
ink (Chinese)	墨	mò
ivory	象牙制品	xiàng-yá zhì-pǐn
jade	玉石制品	yù-shí zhì-pǐn
kimono	和服	hé-fú
kite	风筝	fēng-zheng
lacquerware	漆器	qī-qì
carved lacquerware	雕漆	diāo-qī
lamp shade	灯罩	dēng-zhào
lantern	安全风灯	ān-quán fēng-dēng
linen	亚麻布	yà-má-bù
mahjong	麻将	má-jiàng
musical instrument	乐器	yuè-qì
Chinese fiddle	胡琴儿	hú-qinr
cymbals	钹	bó
drum	鼓	gǔ
flute	笛子	dí-zi
gong	锣	luó
guitar	吉他	jí-tā
mouth organ	口琴	kǒu-qín
seven-stringed lute	古琴	gǔ-qín
porcelain	细瓷器	xì cí-qì
pottery	陶器	táo-qì
prints	版画儿	bǎn-huàr
rubbings	拓片	tà-piàn
rug	小地毯	xiǎo dì-tǎn
scrolls	卷轴	juàn-zhóu
silk	丝绸	sī-chóu
spices	作料	zuò-liào
tea	茶叶	chá-yè
teacup (with lid)	茶杯（带盖的）	chá-bēi (dài gài de)
teapot	茶壶	chá-hú
toys	玩具	wán-jù

Miscellaneous 其他物品

Records — Cassettes 唱片－盒式磁带

Records can be bought in record shops, musical instrument shops, and in the record department of bookshops.

Do you have any records by …?	你这儿有…的唱片吗？	nǐ zhèr yǒu … de chàng-piàn ma
Can I listen to this record?	我可以试听这张唱片吗？	wǒ kě-yǐ shì-tīng zhè-zhāng chàng-piàn ma
I'd like a cassette.	我想要一盒盒式磁带。	wǒ xiǎng-yào yì-hé hé-shì cí-dài
chamber music	室内乐	shì-nèi-yuè
classical Chinese music	中国古典音乐	zhōng-guó gǔ-diǎn yīn-yuè
classical music	古典音乐	gǔ-diǎn yīn-yuè
folk music	民间音乐	mín-jiān yīn-yuè
instrumental music	器乐演奏音乐	qì-yuè yǎn-zòu yīn-yuè
jazz	爵士乐	jué-shì-yuè
light music	轻音乐	qīng yīn-yuè
orchestral music	管弦乐	guǎn-xián-yuè

Toys 玩具

Toys in China tend to be simpler than in the West. You can buy a hoop and stick for a bowling game, or a kind of shuttlecock (毽子 jiàn-zi) made of three feathers stuck to a flat disc. The Chinese like to bounce this off the sides of their feet — rather like footballers controlling the ball.

I'd like a toy/game …	我想要…的玩具/智力游戏。	wǒ xiǎng-yào … de wán-jù/zhì-lì yóu-xì
for a boy	给男孩儿玩儿的	gěi nán-háir wánr de
for a 5-year-old girl	给一个五岁女孩儿玩儿的	gěi yí-ge wǔ-suì nǚ-háir wánr de
ball	球	qiú
bucket and spade (pail and shovel)	小桶和小铲子	xiǎo tǒng hé xiǎo chǎn-zi
building blocks (bricks)	积木	jī-mù
chess set	国际象棋	guó-jì xiàng-qí
Chinese chequers	中国象棋	zhōng-guó xiàng-qí
doll	娃娃	wá-wa
hoop	铁环	tiě-huán

Your money: banks — currency

While foreign currency and traveller's cheques may be brought into the country in unlimited amounts, provided they are declared upon arrival, no local currency whatsoever (unless in foreign exchange certificates) may be either imported or exported. Money and traveller's cheques can only be exchanged at authorized currency exchange counters at main ports and airports, leading hotels, banks and Friendship Stores. Exchange rates are the same everywhere.

Hours 营业时间

Exchange counters in Friendship Stores have the same opening hours as the shop itself, i.e.: 9 a.m. to 7 p.m. (8 p.m. in summer), seven days a week.

Banks in hotels open from 7.30 or 8 a.m. to around 7 p.m., with a break for lunch. (Generally, the larger the hotel, the later the foreign exchange facility stays open.) Money may also be changed on Sunday mornings.

Currency 货币

China's two-tier currency system is almost bound to confuse you. The standard currency, called *renminbi* or people's money (RMB) is based on the *yuán* （元） divided into 10 *jiǎo* （角） or *máo* （毛） and 100 *fen* （分）.

However, foreign exchange bureaus also dispense a second currency called Foreign Exchange Certificates (FEC) in denominations of 1 and 5 jiao (= 10 and 50 fen) and 1, 5, 10, 50 and 100 yuan.

Friendship Stores and other establishments catering primarily to foreigners accept only FEC, not RMB. In some small towns, merchants may not accept FEC, simply because they have never heard of them. FEC may be taken out of China, but RMB may not.

Currency exchange 兑换外汇

Foreign currency and traveller's cheques may be exchanged for FEC in hotels and Friendship Stores. You'll have to show your passport. Keep the receipt as proof of the amount changed. You'll also need it if you want to convert excess Chinese money to a foreign currency when leaving the country.

Credit cards — Traveller's cheques 信用卡-旅行支票

Credit cards are accepted more and more in tourist areas. (Note: a 4% commission is charged to users of credit cards.) In some major cities personal cheques are accepted on presentation of certain credit cards, though it may entail a trip to the bank. Traveller's cheques are recognized at the money-exchange counters of hotels and shops almost everywhere in China.

General 一般询问

Is there a currency exchange office in the hotel?	旅馆里有外汇兑换处吗？	lǚ-guǎn li yǒu wài-huì duì-huàn-chù ma
Where's the nearest bank?	离这儿最近的银行在哪儿？	lí zhèr zuì jìn de yín-háng zài nǎr
At what time does it open/close?	什么时候开门/关门？	shén-me shí-hou kāi mén/guān mén

At the bank 在银行

I want to change some	我想用…兑换。	wǒ xiǎng yòng … duì-huàn
U.S. dollars	美元	měi-yuán
Hongkong dollars	港币	gǎng-bì
Japanese yen	日元	rì-yuán
pounds sterling	英镑	yīng-bàng
I want to cash a traveller's cheque.	我想兑现一张旅行支票。	wǒ xiǎng duì-xiàn yì-zhāng lǚ-xíng-zhī-piào

NUMBERS, see page 149

銀行

Here's my currency declaration form.	这是我的外汇申报单。	zhè shì wǒ de wài-huì shēn-bào-dān
What's the exchange rate?	兑换率是多少？	duì-huàn-lǜ shì duō-shao
How much commission do you charge?	要付多少手续费？	yào fù duō-shao shǒu-xù-fèi
Can you cash a personal cheque?	这儿能兑现私人支票吗？	zhèr néng duì-xiàn sī-rén zhī-piào ma
How long will it take to clear?	兑现要等多少时间？	duì-xiàn yào děng duō-shao shí-jiān
Can you telex my bank in …?	你能给我在…的银行发个电传吗？	nǐ néng gěi wǒ zài … de yín-háng fā ge diàn-chuán ma
I have a/an …	我有…	wǒ yǒu
credit card	一张信用卡	yì-zhāng xìn-yòng-kǎ
introduction from …	一封…的介绍信	yì-fēng … de jiè-shào-xìn
letter of credit	一封银行存款证明信	yì-fēng yín-háng cún-kuǎn zhèng-míng-xìn
I'm expecting some money from …	我在等从…汇来的一笔钱。	wǒ zài děng cóng … huì lái de yì-bǐ qián
Has it arrived yet?	已经到了吗？	yǐ-jīng dào le ma
Could you please check that again?	能再查对一次吗？	néng zài chá-duì yí-cì ma
Please give me …	请给我…	qǐng gěi wǒ
large/small notes (bills)	面值大的/小的钞票	miàn-zhí dà de/ xiǎo de chāo-piào
small change	零钱	líng-qián
coins	硬币	yìng-bì

Deposits — Withdrawals 存-取

I'd like to …	我想…	wǒ xiǎng
open an account	开个帐户	kāi ge zhàng-hù
withdraw … (yuan/ U.S. dollars)	取…（元/美元）	qǔ (yuán/ měi-yuán)
I want to pay this into my account.	我想把这笔钱存入我的帐户。	wǒ xiǎng bǎ zhè bǐ qián cún-rù wǒ-de zhàng-hù
Where should I sign?	我该在哪儿签名？	wǒ gāi zài nǎr qiān-míng

NUMBERS, see page 149

Business and banking terms 贸易及银行术语

amount	数额	shù-é
balance	结余	jié-yú
bond	公债券	gōng-zhài-quàn
(to) borrow	借	jiè
(to) buy	买	mǎi
capital	资本	zī-běn
cheque (check)	支票	zhī-piào
contract	合同	hé-tong
discount	折扣	zhé-kòu
expenses	开支	kāi-zhī
export	出口	chū-kǒu
import	进口	jìn-kǒu
interest	利息	lì-xī
investment	投资	tóu-zī
invoice	发票	fā-piào
(to) lend	借给	jiè-gěi
loan	贷款	dài-kuǎn
loss	亏损	kuī-sǔn
mortgage	抵押	dǐ-yā
payment	付款	fù-kuǎn
percentage	百分比	bǎi-fēn-bǐ
price	价钱	jià-qián
profit	利润	lì-rùn
purchase	买进的货品	mǎi jìn de huò-pǐn
sale	卖出的货品	mài chū de huò-pǐn
(to) sell	卖	mài
share	股份	gǔ-fèn
transfer (of funds)	转账	zhuǎn-zhàng
value	价值	jià-zhí

Doing business 做生意

My name is ...	我叫…	wǒ jiào
Here's my card.	这是我的名片。	zhè shì wǒ de míng-piàn
I represent ...	我是…的代表。	wǒ shì ... de dài-biǎo
I have an appointment with ...	我和…约了个会谈。	wǒ hé ... yuē le gè huì-tán
What's your name, please?	您贵姓？	nín guì xìng
Please write it down for me.	请你写下这个。	qǐng nǐ xiě xià zhè-ge

Can you provide me with a/an ...?	能为我找一位…吗？	néng wèi wǒ zhǎo yí-wèi ... ma
interpreter	口译	kǒu-yì
secretary	秘书	mì-shū
translator	翻译	fān-yì
I need an interpreter who specializes in ...	我需要一位专于…的口译。	wǒ xū-yào yí-wèi zhuān-yú ... de kǒu-yì
agriculture	农业	nóng-yè
chemistry	化学	huà-xué
electronics	电子	diàn-zǐ
engineering	工程	gōng-chéng
foodstuffs	食品	shí-pǐn
handicrafts	手工艺	shǒu-gōng-yì
machinery	机械	jī-xiè
mining	矿业	kuàng-yè
native produce	土特产	tǔ-tè-chǎn
textiles	纺织	fǎng-zhī
I'd like to see a sample of your latest collection.	我想看你们最新产品的样品。	wǒ xiǎng kàn nǐ-men zuì xīn chǎn-pǐn de yàng-pǐn
Do you have a photo of ...?	你有…的照片吗？	nǐ yǒu ... de zhào-piàn ma
Do you have any statistics?	你们有有关的统计吗？	nǐ-men yǒu yǒu-guān de tǒng-jì ma
Can you give me an estimate of the cost?	能给个成本预算吗？	néng gěi ge chéng-běn yù-suàn ma

goods	货品	huò-pǐn
joint venture	合营	hé-yíng
licence	许可证	xǔ-kě-zhèng
product	产品	chǎn-pǐn
(to) send (goods)	发货	fā-huò
(to) send back (goods)	退货	tuì-huò
shipment	一批货	yì-pī-huò
tax	税	shuì

| Where can I make photocopies? | 哪儿能复印？ | nǎr néng fù-yìn |
| What's the rate of inflation? | 通货膨胀率是多少？ | tōng-huò péng-zhàng-lǜ shì duō-shao |

At the post office

Hotels have branch post offices or postal service desks, open 7 days a week, selling stamps, writing paper, and postcards. But you can also go to a post office, recognized by the sign 邮电局 *(yóu-diàn-jú)*. If you are sending a parcel, don't seal it until it has been checked at the post office.

The Chinese post office has no facilities for poste-restante (general delivery) mail. As confirmed hotel reservations are rare, this poses a problem. If you expect to receive mail while in China, ask correspondents to address letters c/o CITS in the various cities on your itinerary; if you're on a package tour, they should also write on the envelope your tour number, as well as the tour operator's name.

Where's the nearest post office?	离这儿最近的邮局在哪儿？	lí zhèr zuì-jìn de yóu-jú zài nǎr
What time does the post office …	邮局几点…？	yóu-jú jǐ diǎn
open/close	开门/关门	kāi mén/guān mén
I want some stamps, please.	我要几张邮票。	wǒ yào jǐ zhāng yóu-piào
A stamp for this letter, please.	请给一张寄这封信的邮票。	qǐng gěi yì-zhāng jì zhè fēng xìn de yóu-piào
What's the postage for a postcard, please?	一张明信片的邮费是多少？	yì-zhāng míng-xìn-piàn de yóu-fèi shì duō-shao
Where's the letter box (mailbox)?	邮筒在哪儿？	yóu-tǒng zài nǎr

邮票 yóu-piào STAMPS	包裹 bāo-guǒ PARCELS

I'd like to send this parcel.	我要寄这个包裹。	wǒ yào jì zhèi-ge bāo-guǒ
I want to send this (by) ...	我想寄…	wǒ xiǎng jì
airmail	航空	háng-kōng
express (special delivery)	快递	kuài-dì
registered mail	挂号	guà-hào
surface mail	平信	píng-xìn
At which counter can I cash an international money order?	哪个柜台可以兑现国际汇票？	nǎ-ge guì-tái kě-yǐ duì-xiàn guó-jì huì-piào

汇款
huì-kuǎn
MONEY ORDERS

Telegrams — Telex 电报－电传

If your hotel does not have a service that deals with telegrams and telexes, you'll have to go to a post office. Only main post offices in the largest cities will have these facilities.

Can I send a telex from here?	我能在这儿发电传吗？	wǒ néng zài zhèr fā diàn-chuán ma
I want to send a ...	我想拍发…	wǒ xiǎng pāi-fā
letter telegram (night letter)	一封夜信电	yì-fēng yè-xìn-diàn
phototelegram	一封传真电报	yì-fēng chuán-zhēn diàn-bào
telegram	一封电报	yì-fēng diàn-bào
telex	一封电传	yì-fēng diàn-chuán
May I have a form, please?	可以给我一张电报纸吗？	kě-yǐ gěi wǒ yì-zhāng diàn-bào-zhǐ ma
What's the basic charge?	基价是多少？	jī-jià shì duō-shao
How much is it per word?	一个字多少钱？	yí-ge zì duō-shao qián
Can I have the charges transferred?	能请对方付费吗？	néng qǐng duì-fāng fù-fèi ma

Telephoning 打电话

Through your hotel switchboard you will be able to phone inland subscribers and numbers abroad. Local calls are usually free of charge. To phone home, you should book your call well in advance. You can also book calls at the post office. There are few telephone booths, but you will see signs for public telephones. These are found in private houses, but are designated for public use.

Where's the nearest public telephone?	离这儿最近的公用电话在哪儿？	lí zhèr zuì-jìn de gōng-yòng-diàn-huà zài-nǎr
May I use your phone?	可以用你这儿的电话吗？	kě-yǐ yòng nǐ zhèr de diàn-huà ma
Could you look up this company for me in the telephone directory?	能帮我在电话簿上找到这个公司的名字吗？	néng bāng wǒ zài diàn-huà-bù shang zhǎo-dào zhèi-ge gōng-sī de míng-zi ma
Can you help me get this number?	请接这个号码。	qǐng-jiē zhèi-ge hào-mǎ
I'd like to make a long-distance call.	我想打长途电话。	wǒ xiǎng dǎ cháng-tú-diàn-huà
I want to telephone to …	我想给…打电话。	wǒ xiǎng gěi … dǎ diàn-huà

Operator 总机

Operator?	喂，总机？	wéi zǒng-jī
Could you get me this number …?	请接…	qǐng jiē
What number must I dial …?	…我该拨什么号码？	… wǒ gāi bō shén-me hào-mǎ
to get an outside line	接外线	jiē wài-xiàn
to call room no. …	接…号房间	jiē … hào fáng-jiān

公用电话
gōng-yòng-diàn-huà
PUBLIC TELEPHONE

NUMBERS, see page 149

| Can I dial direct? | 能直拨吗？ | néng zhí bō ma |
| I want to reverse the charges (call collect). | 我想让对方付费。 | wǒ xiǎng ràng duì-fāng fù fèi |

Speaking 通话

Hello! This is …	喂，我是…	wéi wǒ shì
I want to speak to …	我想和…说话。	wǒ xiǎng hé … shuō huà
I want extension …	请转…	qǐng zhuǎn
Is that …?	是…吗？	shì … ma
Speak louder, please.	请大点儿声。	qǐng dà diǎnr shēng
Speak more slowly, please.	请说慢点儿。	qǐng shuō màn diǎnr
Would you please try again later?	请过会儿再试试。	qǐng guò huǐr zài shì-shi
You put me through to the wrong number.	你接错号码了。	nǐ jiē cuò hào-mǎ le
Operator, we've been cut off.	总机，线断了。	zǒng-jī xiàn duàn le

Not there 不在

When will he/she be back?	他/她什么时候能回来？	tā/tā shén-me shí-hou néng huí-lai
Please tell him/her I called. My name is …	请你告诉他/她，我来过电话。我叫…	qǐng nǐ gào-su tā/tā wǒ lái-guo diàn-huà. wǒ jiào
Please ask him/her to call me.	麻烦你让他/她给我回电话。	má-fan nǐ ràng tā/tā gěi wǒ huí diàn-huà
Would you take a message, please?	你能转告他吗？	nǐ néng zhuǎn-gào tā ma

Charges 费用

| What was the cost of that call? | 电话费是多少？ | diàn-huà-fèi shì duō-shao |
| I want to pay for the call. | 我要付电话费。 | wǒ yào fù diàn-huà-fèi |

Doctor

大夫

Should you require medical care in China, your guide, hotel desk clerk or the local CITS office will call a doctor, or arrange for you to be taken to a hospital. Considering the language problem, it's a relief to have an interpreter on hand when discussing symptoms and treatment: there is no reason to expect that your doctor, however well-qualified in medicine, understands a single word of English.

Treatment may involve a combination of modern and traditional medicine — perhaps some tablets to swallow and some herbs to take in an infusion. You may also come across the traditional Chinese art of acupuncture.

Warning: In the extreme event of an emergency blood transfusion, those with Rhesus-negative blood should be warned that the Chinese are virtually all Rhesus-positive.

General 一般询问

Can you get me a doctor?	请找一位大夫。	qǐng zhǎo yí-wèi dài-fu
Is there a doctor here?	这儿有大夫吗？	zhèr yǒu dài-fu ma
I need a doctor, quickly.	我得马上见大夫。	wǒ děi mǎ-shàng jiàn dài-fu
Where can I find a doctor who speaks English?	这儿有会说英语的大夫吗？	zhèr yǒu huì shuō yīng-yǔ de dài-fu ma
Where's the surgery (doctor's office)?	外科门诊在哪儿？	wài-kē mén-zhěn zài nǎr
What are the surgery (office) hours?	外科门诊几点开门？	wài-kē mén-zhěn jǐ-diǎn kāi mén
Could the doctor come to see me here?	大夫能来这儿吗？	dài-fu néng lái zhèr ma
What time can the doctor come?	大夫什么时间到？	dài-fu shén-me shí-jiān dào

CHEMIST'S, see page 107

Can you recommend a/an …?	请推荐一位…	qǐng tuī-jiàn yí-wèi
general practitioner	门诊大夫	mén-zhěn dài-fu
children's doctor	儿科大夫	ér-kē dài-fu
eye specialist	眼科大夫	yǎn-kē dài-fu
gynaecologist	妇科大夫	fù-kē dài-fu
I'd like to get in touch with a doctor who uses acupuncture.	我想见会扎针灸的大夫	wǒ xiǎng jiàn huì zhā zhēn-jiǔ de dài-fu
I've been referred to Dr. … This is his address.	有人介绍我见…大夫，这是他的地址。	yǒu rén jiè-shào wǒ jiàn … dài-fu. zhè shì tā de dì-zhǐ
Can you contact him for me?	能和他联系一下吗？	néng hé tā lián-xì yí-xià ma
Can I have an appointment as soon as possible?	能约个尽早的看病时间吗？	néng yuē ge jìn-zǎo de kàn-bìng shí-jiān ma

Parts of the body 身体各部名称

abdomen	腹部	fù-bù
ankle	脚腕	jiǎo-wàn
appendix	阑尾	lán-wěi
arm	胳膊	gē-bo
artery	动脉	dòng-mài
back	背	bèi
bladder	膀胱	páng-guāng
blood	血	xuè
bone	骨	gǔ
bowel	大肠	dà-cháng
brain	脑	nǎo
breast	乳房	rǔ-fáng
chest	胸部	xiōng-bù
coccyx	尾骨	wěi-gǔ
collar-bone	锁骨	suǒ-gǔ
ear	耳朵	ěr-duo
elbow	肘	zhǒu
eye	眼	yǎn
face	脸	liǎn
finger	手指	shǒu-zhǐ
foot	脚	jiǎo
forehead	前额	qián-é
gall-bladder	胆囊	dǎn-náng
genitals	生殖器	shēng-zhí-qì
gland	分泌腺	fēn-mì-xiàn
hand	手	shǒu

head	头	tóu
heart	心脏	xīn-zàng
heel	脚后跟	jiǎo-hòu-gēn
hip	屁股	pì-gu
intestines	肠	cháng
jaw	下巴	xià-ba
joint	关节	guān-jié
kidney	肾	shèn
knee	膝盖	xī-gài
knee-cap	膝盖骨	xī-gài-gǔ
leg	腿	tuǐ
ligament	韧带	rèn-dài
lip	嘴唇	zuǐ-chún
liver	肝	gān
lung	肺	fèi
mouth	嘴	zuǐ
muscle	肌肉	jī-ròu
nail	指甲	zhī-jia
nape	后颈	hòu-jìng
neck	脖子	bó-zi
nerve	神经	shén-jīng
nervous system	神经系统	shén-jīng-xì-tǒng
nose	鼻子	bí-zi
rib	肋骨	lèi-gǔ
scalp	头皮	tóu-pí
shoulder	肩膀	jiān-bǎng
shoulder blade	肩胛骨	jiān-jiá-gǔ
skin	皮肤	pí-fū
spine	脊椎	jǐ-zhuī
spleen	脾	pí
stomach	胃	wèi
tendon	肌腱	jī-jiàn
thigh	大腿	dà-tuǐ
throat	嗓子	sǎng-zi
thumb	拇指	mǔ-zhǐ
toe	脚趾	jiǎo-zhǐ
tongue	舌头	shé-tou
tonsils	扁桃腺	biǎn-táo-xiàn
vein	静脉	jìng-mài
wrist	手腕	shǒu-wàn

| 左
zuǒ
LEFT | 右
yòu
RIGHT |

大夫

Accident — Injury 事故-受伤

There's been an accident.	出事了。	chū shì le
My child has had a fall.	我的孩子摔倒了。	wǒ de hái-zi shuāi-dǎo le
He/She has hurt his/her head.	他/她的头碰伤了。	tā/tā de tóu pèng shāng le
He's/She's unconscious.	他/她昏过去了。	tā/tā hūn-guo-qu le
He's/She's bleeding.	他/她在流血。	tā/tā zài liú xuě
He's/She's injured.	他/她受伤了。	tā/tā shòu shāng le
It's serious.	伤得很重。	shāng de hěn zhòng
His/Her arm is broken.	他/她的胳膊断了。	tā/tā de gē-bo duàn le
His/Her ankle is swollen.	他/她的脚腕子肿了。	tā/tā de jiǎo-wàn-zi zhǒng le
I've been stung.	我被蜇伤了。	wǒ bèi zhē shāng le
I've been bitten by something.	我被什么虫子咬了。	wǒ bèi shén-me chóng-zi yǎo le
I've got something in my eye.	我眼睛进东西了。	wǒ yǎn-jīng jìn dōng-xi le
I've got a …	我有…	wǒ yǒu
blister	一个水疱	yí-ge shuǐ-pào
boil	一个疖子	yí-ge jiē-zi
bruise	一块青紫	yí-kuài qīng-zǐ
lump	一个肿块	yí-ge zhǒng-kuài
rash	一片疹子	yí-piàn zhěn-zi
swelling	一块红肿	yí-kuài hóng-zhǒng
wound	一个伤口	yí-ge shāng-kǒu
I've … myself.	我被…	wǒ bèi
scalded	烫伤了	tàng shāng le
burned	烧伤了	shāo shāng le
cut	割破了	gē pò le
grazed	擦破了	cā pò le
Could you have a look at it?	请诊治一下。	qǐng zhěn-zhì yí-xià
I can't move my …	我…动不了啦。	wǒ … dòng-bu-liǎo la
It hurts.	这儿疼。	zhèr téng

大夫

哪儿疼？	Where does it hurt?
哪种疼？	What kind of pain is it?
纯疼	dull
刺疼	sharp
一跳一跳的疼	throbbing
持续的疼	constant
一阵阵的疼	on and off
这儿…	It's …
断了	broken
脱臼了	dislocated
扭伤了	sprained
撕裂了	torn
需要去照张 X 光片子。	I want you to have an X-ray.
需要用石膏固定。	You'll have to have a plaster.
感染了。	It's infected.
你注射过预防破伤风的疫苗吗？	Have you been vaccinated against tetanus?
我会给你开止痛药的。	I'll give you a painkiller.

Illness 生病

I'm not feeling well.	我不舒服。	wǒ bù shū-fu
I'm ill.	我病了。	wǒ bìng le
I feel …	我觉得…	wǒ jué-de
dizzy	头晕	tóu-yūn
nauseous	恶心	ě-xīn
shivery	发冷	fā-lěng
I've got a fever.	我在发烧。	wǒ zài fā-shāo
My temperature is 38 degrees.	我的体温是摄氏38°。	wǒ de tǐ-wēn shì shè-shì 38 dù
I've been vomiting.	我一直在呕吐。	wǒ yì-zhí zài ǒu-tù
I'm constipated/ I've got diarrhoea.	我便秘/ 我腹泻。	wǒ biàn-bì/ wǒ fù-xiè
My … hurt(s).	我的…疼。	wǒ de … téng
I've got (a/an) …	我…	wǒ

asthma	哮喘	xiào-chuǎn
backache	腰疼	yāo-téng
cough	咳嗽	ké-sou
cramps	肚子绞痛	dù-zi jiǎo-tòng
earache	耳朵疼	ěr-duo téng
headache	头疼	tóu téng
indigestion	消化不良	xiāo-huà bù liáng
nosebleed	流鼻血	liú bí-xuě
palpitations	心悸	xīn-jì
sore throat	嗓子疼	sǎng-zi téng
stiff neck	脖子发硬	bó-zi fā yìng
stomach ache	胃疼	wèi téng
sunstroke	中暑了	zhòng-shǔ le
I've got (an) …	我有…	wǒ yǒu
arthritis	关节炎	guān-jié-yán
hay fever	枯草热	kū-cǎo-rè
haemorrhoids	痔疮	zhì-chuāng
rheumatism	风湿	fēng-shī
ulcer	胃溃疡	wèi-kuì-yáng
I have difficulties breathing.	我呼吸困难。	wǒ hū-xī kùn-nan
I have a pain in my chest.	我胸部疼。	wǒ xiōng-bù téng
I had a heart attack … years ago.	我…年以前曾有过一次心肌梗塞。	wǒ … nián yǐ-qián céng yǒu guo yí-cì xīn-jī gěng-sè
My blood pressure is too high/too low.	我的血压过高/过低。	wǒ de xuě-yā guò gāo/guò dī
I'm allergic to …	我对…过敏。	wǒ duì … guò-mǐn
I've got diabetes.	我有糖尿病。	wǒ yǒu táng-niào-bìng

Women's section 妇产科

I have period pains.	我有痛经。	wǒ yǒu tòng-jīng
I have a vaginal infection.	我阴道发炎了。	wǒ yīn-dào fā-yán le
I'm on the pill.	我一直服避孕药。	wǒ yì-zhí fú bì-yùn-yào
I haven't had my period for 3 months.	我停经有三个月了。	wǒ tíng-jīng yǒu sān-ge yuè le
I'm (3 months) pregnant.	我怀孕（有三个月）了。	wǒ huái-yùn (yǒu sān-ge yuè) le
I have morning sickness.	我早晨恶心呕吐。	wǒ zǎo-chen ě-xīn ǒu-tù

大夫

你这么不舒服有多长时间了？	How long have you been feeling like this?
这是你第一次有这种症状吗？	Is this the first time you've had this?
我给你测一下体温。	I'll take your temperature.
我给你量一下血压。	I'll take your blood pressure.
请卷起衣袖。	Roll up your sleeve, please.
请脱掉衣服。	Please undress.
请躺在这儿。	Please lie down over here.
张开嘴。	Open your mouth.
深呼吸。	Breathe deeply.
咳嗽一下。	Cough, please.
哪儿疼？	Where does it hurt?
你得了…	You've got (a/an) …
…发炎	inflammation of …
肺炎	pneumonia
黄疸	jaundice
阑尾炎	appendicitis
流感	flu
麻疹	measles
膀胱炎	cystitis
食物中毒	food poisoning
胃炎	gastritis
性病	venereal disease
这病（不）传染。	It's (not) contagious.
需要打针。	I'll give you an injection.
你得去取血化验。	I want a specimen of your blood.
你得去留大便/尿化验。	I want a specimen of your stools/urine.
你必须卧床休息…天。	You must stay in bed for … days
我得把你转到…科去。	I want you to see a … specialist.
你需要到医院做一个全面查体。	I want you to go to hospital for a general checkup.

Prescription — Treatment 处方-治疗

This is my usual medicine.	这是我常用的药。	zhè shì wǒ cháng-yòng de yào
Can you give me a prescription for this?	能给我开这种药吗？	néng gěi wǒ kāi zhè zhǒng yào ma
Can you prescribe a/an/some …?	请给我开一些…？	qǐng gěi wǒ kāi yì-xiē
antidepressant	抗抑郁药	kàng yì-yù yào
sleeping pills	安眠药	ān-mián yào
tranquillizer	镇静药	zhèn-jìng yào
I'm allergic to …	我对…过敏。	wǒ duì … guò-mǐn
antibiotics	抗菌素	kàng-jūn-sù
aspirin	阿司匹林	ā-sī-pǐ-lín
penicillin	青霉素	qīng-méi-sù
I don't want anything too strong.	我不要太厉害的药。	wǒ bú yào tài lì-hai de yào
How many times a day should I take it?	一天吃几次？	yì-tiān chī jǐ-cì
Must I swallow them whole?	我必须吞服吗？	wǒ bì-xū tūn-fú ma

你目前在进行哪些治疗？	What treatment are you having?
你正在服用什么药？	What medicine are you taking?
是注射还是口服？	By injection or orally?
这种药每服…汤匙。	Take … teaspoons of this medicine.
每服一片…	Take one pill …
每隔…小时一服	every … hours
每日…次	… times a day
饭前/饭后	before/after each meal
晨服/睡前服	in the morning/at night
痛时服	if there is any pain
连续服…天	for … days

CHEMIST'S, see page 107

大夫

DOCTOR

Fee 医药费

How much do I owe you?	我该付多少钱？	wǒ gāi fù duō-shao qián
May I have a receipt?	请开张收据。	qǐng kāi zhāng shōu-jù
Can I have a medical certificate?	请开张医生证明。	qǐng kāi zhāng yī-shēng zhèng-míng
Would you fill in this health insurance form, please?	请填写这张健康保险单。	qǐng tián-xiě zhè zhāng jiàn-kāng bǎo-xiǎn-dān

Hospital 医院

Please notify my family.	请通知我的家属。	qǐng tōng-zhī wǒ de jiā-shǔ
What are the visiting hours?	什么时间能探视？	shén-me shí-jiān néng tàn-shì
When can I get up?	我什么时候可以下床活动？	wǒ shén-me shí-hou kě-yǐ xià chuáng huó-dòng
When will the doctor come?	大夫什么时候来？	dài-fu shén-me shí-hou lái
I'm in pain.	我很疼。	wǒ hěn téng
I can't eat.	我吃不下。	wǒ chī-bu-xià
I can't sleep.	我睡不着。	wǒ shuì-bu-zháo
Where is the bell?	铃在哪儿？	líng zài nǎr

nurse	护士	hù-shì
patient	病人	bìng-rén
anaesthetic	麻药	má-yào
blood transfusion	输血	shū-xuě
injection	注射	zhù-shè
operation	手术	shǒu-shù
bed	床	chuáng
bedpan	便盆儿	biàn-pénr
thermometer	体温表	tǐ-wēn-biǎo

大夫

Dentist 牙科大夫

Can you recommend a good dentist?	你能推荐一位好牙科大夫吗？	nǐ néng tuī-jiàn yí-wèi hǎo yá-kē dài-fu ma
Can I make an (urgent) appointment?	我能约个（急诊）看牙的时间吗？	wǒ néng yuē ge (jí-zhěn) kàn yá de shí-jiān ma
Couldn't you make it earlier than that?	能早点儿吗？	néng zǎo diǎnr ma
I have a broken tooth.	我的牙碰断了。	wǒ de yá pèng duàn le
I have a toothache.	我牙疼。	wǒ yá téng
I have an abscess.	我的牙化脓了。	wǒ de yá huà-nóng le
This tooth hurts.	这颗牙很疼。	zhè kē yá hěn téng
at the top	在上边	zài shàng-bian
at the bottom	在下边	zài xià-bian
in the front	在前边	zài qián-bian
at the back	在后边	zài hòu-bian
Can you fix it temporarily?	你能暂时把它治疗一下吗？	nǐ néng zàn-shí bǎ tā zhì-liáo yí xià ma
I don't want it extracted.	请不要拔这颗牙。	qǐng bú yào bá zhè kē yá
Could you give me an anaesthetic?	请给我打麻药。	qǐng gěi wǒ dǎ má-yào
I've lost a filling.	我牙里的镶补物丢了。	wǒ yá-li de xiāng-bǔ-wù diū le
The gum is very sore.	牙龈很疼。	yá-yín hěn téng
The gum is bleeding.	牙龈流血。	yá-yín liú xuě
I've broken this denture.	我把这副假牙弄坏了。	wǒ bǎ zhè fù jiǎ-yá nòng huài le
Can you repair this denture?	你能修这副假牙吗？	nǐ néng xiū zhè fù jiǎ-yá ma
When will it be ready?	什么时候能修好？	shén-me shí-hou néng xiū hǎo

Reference section

Where do you come from? 你是从哪儿来的？

Africa	非洲	fēi-zhōu
Asia	亚洲	yà-zhōu
Australia	澳大利亚	āo-dà-lì-yà
Europe	欧洲	ōu-zhōu
North America	北美洲	běi-měi-zhōu
South America	南美洲	nán-měi-zhōu
Afghanistan	阿富汗	ā-fù-hàn
Bangladesh	孟加拉	mèng-jiā-lā
Belgium	比利时	bǐ-lì-shí
Bhutan	不丹	bù-dān
Burma	缅甸	miǎn-diàn
Canada	加拿大	jiā-ná-dà
China	中国	zhōng-guó
England	英格兰	yīng-gé-lán
France	法国	fǎ-guó
Germany	德国	dé-guó
Great Britain	英国	yīng-guó
Hong Kong	香港	xiāng-gǎng
India	印度	yìn-dù
Indonesia	印度尼西亚	yìn-dù-ní-xī-yà
Ireland	爱尔兰	ài-ěr-lán
Israel	以色列	yǐ-sè-liè
Italy	意大利	yì-dà-lì
Japan	日本	rì-běn
Korea	朝鲜	cháo-xiǎn
Laos	老挝	lǎo-wō
Mongolia	蒙古	měng-gǔ
Nepal	尼泊尔	ní-bó-ěr
Netherlands	荷兰	hé-lán
New Zealand	新西兰	xīn-xī-lán
Pakistan	巴基斯坦	bā-jī-sī-tǎn
Philippines	菲律宾	fēi-lǜ-bīn
Scotland	苏格兰	sū-gé-lán
Singapore	新加坡	xīn-jiā-pō
South Africa	南非	nán-fēi
Spain	西班牙	xī-bān-yá
Taiwan	台湾	tái-wān
Thailand	泰国	tài-guó
United States	美国	měi-guó
Vietnam	越南	yuè-nán
Wales	威尔士	wēi-ěr-shì

Numbers 数字

In Chinese, counting is based on the decimal system. From eleven to nineteen, numbers are formed by addition. E.g.: 11 is 10 plus 1, 19 is 10 plus 9; 20 to 90 are formed by multiplication. E.g.: 30 is expressed as "3 times 10". The numerals between the tens are expressed in multiples of ten plus the remainder. E.g. 33 is "3 times ten plus 3".

Alongside their traditional system of numerals, the Chinese are also familiar with Western figure notation, which facilitates communication where money, the telephone and room location, etc., are concerned.

0	零	líng
1	一	yī
2	二	èr
3	三	sān
4	四	sì
5	五	wǔ
6	六	liù
7	七	qī
8	八	bā
9	九	jiǔ
10	十	shí
11	十一	shí-yī
12	十二	shí-èr
13	十三	shí-sān
14	十四	shí-sì
15	十五	shí-wǔ
16	十六	shí-liù
17	十七	shí-qī
18	十八	shí-bā
19	十九	shí-jiǔ
20	二十	èr-shí
21	二十一	èr-shí yī
22	二十二	èr-shí èr
23	二十三	èr-shí sān
24	二十四	èr-shí sì
25	二十五	èr-shí wǔ
26	二十六	èr-shí liù
27	二十七	èr-shí qī
28	二十八	èr-shí bā
29	二十九	èr-shí jiǔ
30	三十	sān-shí
31	三十一	sān-shí yī
32	三十二	sān-shí èr

33	三十三	sān-shí sān
40	四十	sì-shí
41	四十一	sì-shí yī
42	四十二	sì-shí èr
43	四十三	sì-shí sān
50	五十	wǔ-shí
51	五十一	wǔ-shí yī
52	五十二	wǔ-shí èr
53	五十三	wǔ-shí sān
60	六十	liù-shí
61	六十一	liù-shí yī
62	六十二	liù-shí èr
63	六十三	liù-shí sān
70	七十	qī-shí
71	七十一	qī-shí yī
72	七十二	qī-shí èr
73	七十三	qī-shí sān
80	八十	bā-shí
81	八十一	bā-shí yī
82	八十二	bā-shí èr
83	八十三	bā-shí sān
90	九十	jiǔ-shí
91	九十一	jiǔ-shí yī
92	九十二	jiǔ-shí èr
93	九十三	jiǔ-shí sān
100	一百	yì-bǎi
101	一百零一	yì-bǎi líng-yī
102	一百零二	yì-bǎi líng-èr
110	一百一十	yì-bǎi yī-shí
120	一百二十	yì-bǎi èr-shí
130	一百三十	yì-bǎi sān-shí
140	一百四十	yì-bǎi sì-shí
150	一百五十	yì-bǎi wǔ-shí
160	一百六十	yì-bǎi liù-shí
170	一百七十	yì-bǎi qī-shí
180	一百八十	yì-bǎi bā-shí
190	一百九十	yì-bǎi jiǔ-shí
200	二百	èr-bǎi
300	三百	sān-bǎi
400	四百	sì-bǎi
500	五百	wǔ-bǎi
600	六百	liù-bǎi
700	七百	qī-bǎi
800	八百	bā-bǎi
900	九百	jiǔ-bǎi
1,000	一千	yì-qiān
1,100	一千一百	yì-qiān yì-bǎi
1,200	一千二百	yì-qiān èr-bǎi
2,000	二千	èr-qiān

5,000	五千	wǔ-qiān
10,000	一万	yí-wàn
50,000	五万	wǔ-wàn
100,000	十万	shí-wàn
1,000,000	一百万	yì-bǎi-wàn
1,000,000,000	十亿	shí-yì
first	第一	dì-yī
second	第二	dì-èr
third	第三	dì-sān
fourth	第四	dì-sì
fifth	第五	dì-wǔ
sixth	第六	dì-liù
seventh	第七	dì-qī
eighth	第八	dì-bā
ninth	第九	dì-jiǔ
tenth	第十	dì-shí
once	一次	yí-cì
twice	两次	liǎng-cì
three times	三次	sān-cì
a half/half a …	一半/半…	yí-bàn/bàn
half of …/half (adj.)	…的一半/半	… de yí-bàn/bàn
a quarter	四分之一	sì-fēn-zhī-yī
a third	三分之一	sān-fēn-zhī-yī
a pair of	一双	yì-shuāng
a dozen	一打	yì-dá
one per cent	百分之一	bǎi-fēn-zhī-yī
3.4%	百分之三点四	bǎi-fēn zhī sān-diǎn-sì
1981	一九八一	yī jiǔ bā yī
1992	一九九二	yī jiǔ jiǔ èr
2003	二零零三	èr líng líng sān

Year and age 年份和岁数

year	年	nián
leap year	闰年	rùn-nián
decade	十年	shí nián
century	世纪	shì-jì
this year	今年	jīn-nián
last year	去年	qù-nián
next year	明年	míng-nián
every year	每年	měi nián
… years ago	两年前	liǎng nián qián
in one year	一年后	yì nián hòu

in the eighties	在八十年代	zài bā-shí nián-dài
the 16th century	十六世纪	shí-liù shì-jì
in the 20th century	在二十世纪	zài èr-shí shì-jì
How old are you?	你今年多大岁数？	nǐ jīn-nián duō dà suì-shu
I'm 30 years old.	我今年三十岁。	wǒ jīn-nián sān-shí suì
He/She was born in 1960.	他/她是一九六零年出生的。	tā/tā shì yī liù jiǔ líng nián chū-shēng de
What is his/her age?	他/她今年多大岁数？	tā/tā jīn-nián duō dà suì-shu

Seasons 季节

spring/summer	春/夏	chūn/xià
autumn/winter	秋/冬	qiū/dōng
in spring	在春天	zài chūn-tiān
during the summer	在夏天的时候	zài xià-tiān de shí-hou
in autumn	在秋天	zài qiū-tiān
during the winter	在冬天的时候	zài dōng-tiān de shí-hou
high season	旺季	wàng-jì
low season	淡季	dàn-jì

Months 月份

China adopted the Gregorian calendar at the beginning of this century. However, the traditional lunar calendar still holds sway in matters of local customs and festivals. The lunar calendar divides the year into 24 parts, each of which has agricultural significance.

January	一月	yī-yuè
February	二月	èr-yuè
March	三月	sān-yuè
April	四月	sì-yuè
May	五月	wǔ-yuè
June	六月	liù-yuè
July	七月	qī-yuè
August	八月	bā-yuè
September	九月	jiǔ-yuè
October	十月	shí-yuè
November	十一月	shí-yī yuè
December	十二月	shí-èr yuè

since June	六月以来	liù-yuè yǐ-lái
during August	在八月份里	zài bā-yuè-fèn li
last month	上个月	shàng-ge yuè
next month	下个月	xià-ge yuè

Days and date 日期

What day is it today?	今天星期几？	jīn-tiān xīng-qī jǐ
Sunday	星期天/星期日	xīng-qī-tiān/xīng-qī-rì
Monday	星期一	xīng-qī-yī
Tuesday	星期二	xīng-qī-èr
Wednesday	星期三	xīng-qī-sān
Thursday	星期四	xīng-qī-sì
Friday	星期五	xīng-qī-wǔ
Saturday	星期六	xīng-qī-liù
It's …	今天…	jīn-tiān
March 1	三月一号	sān-yuè yī-hào
December 7	十二月七号	shí-èr-yuè qī-hào
in the morning	在上午	zài shàng-wǔ
during the day	在白天	zài bái-tiān
in the afternoon	在下午	zài xià-wǔ
in the evening	在晚上	zài wǎn-shang
at night	在夜里	zài yè-li
the day before yesterday	前天	qián-tiān
yesterday	昨天	zuó-tiān
today	今天	jīn-tiān
tomorrow	明天	míng-tiān
the day after tomorrow	后天	hòu-tiān
the day before	前一天	qián yì-tiān
the next day	第二天	dì-èr tiān
two days ago	两天前	liǎng-tiān qián
in three days' time	三天后	sān tiān hòu
last week	上个星期	shàng-ge xīng-qī
next week	下个星期	xià-ge xīng-qī
for a fortnight (two weeks)	两个星期	liǎng-ge xīng-qī
birthday	生日	shēng-rì
day off	休息日	xiū-xi-rì
(public) holiday	假日	jià-rì
holidays/vacation	假期	jià-qī
week	星期	xīng-qī
weekend	周末	zhōu-mò
working day	工作日	gōng-zuò-rì

Public holidays and festivals 节假日

Lunar calendar holidays 农历节假日

Some Chinese holidays are fixed according to the lunar calendar, not our Gregorian calendar, so precise dates cannot be given. Here are the main festivals:

春节 (chūn-jié)	Spring Festival (Chinese New Year)/Lunar New Year (late January/early February). This is the biggest Chinese festival of them all. Lasting three days, it's predominantly a family celebration.
清明节 (qīng-míng-jié)	The festival of *Qing-ming*, in April, is a time for honouring ancestors. The sweeping of graves is a traditional family obligation.
端午节 (duān-wǔ-jié)	The Dragon Boat Festival at the end of May is celebrated in memory of the ancient poet and statesman *Qu Yuan* who drowned in Hunan Province. Sweet rice cakes containing dates or nuts are served.
中秋节 (zhōng-qiū-jié)	Autumn ''Moon'' Festival. Takes place in September or October, when everyone turns out to look at the full moon, hope for a good harvest, and eat moon-shaped cakes.

Greetings and wishes 问候和祝愿

Merry Christmas!	圣诞快乐！	shèng-dàn kuài-lè
Happy New Year!	新年快乐！	xīn-nián kuài-lè
Happy birthday!	生日快乐！	shēng-rì kuài-lè
Best wishes!	祝一切顺利！	zhù yí-qiè shùn-lì
Congratulations!	祝贺！	zhù-hè
Good luck!	祝你好运！	zhù nǐ hǎo-yùn
Have a good trip!	旅行愉快！	lǚ-xíng yú-kuài
Have a good holiday!	假日愉快！	jià-rì yú-kuài

What time is it? 几点了？

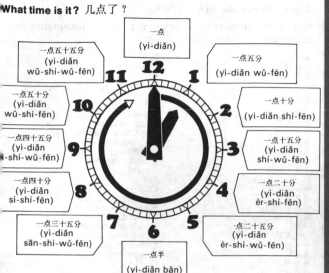

一点
(yì-diǎn)

一点五分
(yì-diǎn wǔ-fēn)

一点十分
(yì-diǎn shí-fēn)

一点十五分
(yì-diǎn shí-wǔ-fēn)

一点二十分
(yì-diǎn èr-shí-fēn)

·点二十五分
(yì-diǎn èr-shí-wǔ-fēn)

一点半
(yì-diǎn bàn)

一点三十五分
(yì-diǎn sān-shí-wǔ-fēn)

一点四十分
(yì-diǎn sì-shí-fēn)

一点四十五分
(yì-diǎn sì-shí-wǔ-fēn)

一点五十分
(yì-diǎn wǔ-shí-fēn)

一点五十五分
(yì-diǎn wǔ-shí-wǔ-fēn)

n everyday conversation, time is expressed as shown above 1 o'clock, 5 past 1, 10 past 1 etc.). However, airline and rain timetables use a 24-hour clock, where the after noon ours are counted from 13 to 24.

The train leaves at ...	列车…发车。	liè-chē ... fā chē
3.04 (1.04 p.m.)	十三点零四分	shí-sān diǎn líng sì fēn
.40 (0.40 a.m.)	零点四十分	líng diǎn sì-shí fēn
n five minutes	再过五分钟	zài guò wǔ fēn-zhōng
n a quarter of an hour	再过一刻钟	zài guò yí-kè-zhōng
alf an hour ago	半小时以前	bàn xiǎo-shí yǐ-qián
bout two hours	大约两小时	dà-yuē liǎng xiǎo-shí
nore than 10 minutes	十多分钟	shí duō fēn-zhōng
ess than 30 seconds	不到三十秒	bú dào sān-shí miǎo
he clock is fast/ low.	这个钟快/慢了	zhè-ge zhōng kuài/ màn le

参照部分

Signs and notices 招贴，指示标记和警告

Here are a number of signs you may see, unfortunately they are rarely accompanied by pīn-yīn.

出口	Exit
收款处	Cash desk
出售	For sale
出租	To let, for hire
大减价	Sales
电梯	Lift (elevator)
休息	Closed
禁止入内	No admittance
禁止摄影	No photos allowed
禁止吸烟	No smoking
禁止游泳	No bathing
客满	Sold out (seats)
无人	Vacant
拉	Pull
冷	Cold
男厕所	Gentlemen (toilet)
请随手关门	Please close the door
请勿打扰	Do not disturb
停电	No electric power
谢绝参观	Visitors not allowed
女厕所	Ladies (toilet)
请按铃	Please ring
请勿触摸	Don't touch
请勿靠近	Keep away
热	Hot
入口	Entrance
太平门	Emergency exit
停止	Stop
推	Push
危险	Danger
问询处	Information office
闲人免进	No entrance
严禁…	… forbidden
已预定	Reserved
有死亡危险	Danger of death
有人	Occupied
私人住宅	Private (house)
油漆未干	Wet paint
待检修	Out of order
免费入场	Admission free
非饮用水	Non-potable water
非工作人员请勿入内	Employees only
候车室	Waiting room
厕所	Toilets

Emergency 紧急情况

By the time the emergency is upon you it's too late to look up the Chinese for "Help!". So have a look at this list beforehand — and, if you want to be on the safe side, learn the expressions shown in capitals.

Call the police	叫警察	jiào jǐng-chá
DANGER	危险	wēi-xiǎn
FIRE	火	huǒ
GAS	煤气	méi-qì
Get a doctor	请医生来	qǐng yī-shēng lái
Go away	走开	zǒu-kāi
HELP	救人啊	jiù rén a
Get help quickly	快找人来	kuài zhǎo rén lái
I'm ill	我病了	wǒ bìng le
I'm lost	我迷路了	wǒ mí lù le
Leave me alone	别管我	bié guǎn wǒ
LOOK OUT	留神	liú shén
POLICE	警察	jǐng-chá
Quick	快	kuài
STOP	站住	zhàn zhù
Stop that man/ woman	拦住那人/女人	lán zhù nà rén/nǚ-rén
STOP THIEF	抓贼	zhuā zéi

Lost 迷路了

Where's the ...?	…在哪儿？	... zài nǎr
consulate	领事馆	lǐng-shì-guǎn
embassy	大使馆	dà-shǐ-guǎn
lost property (lost and found) office	失物招领处	shī-wù zhāo-lǐng-chù
police station	公安局	gōng-ān-jú
I want to report a theft.	我要报一偷窃案。	wǒ yào bào yì tōu-qiè-àn
My ... has been stolen.	我的…被偷了。	wǒ de ... bèi tōu le
handbag	手提包	shǒu-tí-bāo
passport	护照	hù-zhào
wallet	钱包	qián-bāo

CAR ACCIDENTS, see page 75

Kilometres into miles

1 kilometre (km.) = 0.62 miles

km.	10	20	30	40	50	60	70	80	90	100	110	120	130
miles	6	12	19	25	31	37	44	50	56	62	68	75	81

Miles into kilometres

1 mile = 1.609 kilometres (km.)

miles	10	20	30	40	50	60	70	80	90	100
km.	16	32	48	64	80	97	113	129	145	161

Fluid measures

1 litre (l.) = 0.88 imp. quarts = 1.06 U.S. quarts

1 imp. quart = 1.14 l.	1 U.S. quart = 0.95 l.
1 imp. gallon = 4.55 l.	1 U.S. gallon = 3.8 l.

l.	5	10	15	20	25	30	35	40	45	50
imp. gal.	1.1	2.2	3.3	4.4	5.5	6.6	7.7	8.8	9.9	11.0
U.S. gal.	1.3	2.6	3.9	5.2	6.5	7.8	9.1	10.4	11.7	13.0

Weights and measures

1 kilogram or kilo (kg.) = 1000 grams (g.)

100 g. = 3.5 oz.	½ kg. = 1.1 lb.
200 g. = 7.0 oz.	1 kg. = 2.2 lb.

1 oz. = 28.35 g.
1 lb. = 453.60 g.

CLOTHING SIZES, see page 115/YARDS AND INCHES, see page 111

Conversion tables

Centimetres and inches

To change centimetres into inches, multiply by .39.

To change inches into centimetres, multiply by 2.54.

	in.	feet	yards
1 mm	0.039	0.003	0.001
1 cm	0.39	0.03	0.01
1 dm	3.94	0.32	0.10
1 m	39.40	3.28	1.09

	mm	cm	m
1 in.	25.4	2.54	0.025
1 ft.	304.8	30.48	0.304
1 yd.	914.4	91.44	0.914

(32 metres = 35 yards)

Temperature

To convert Centigrade into degrees Fahrenheit, multiply Centigrade by 1.8 and add 32.

To convert degrees Fahrenheit into Centigrade, subtract 32 from Fahrenheit and divide by 1.8.

A very basic grammar

Explaining the basic principles of such an intricate and subtle language as Chinese is not an easy matter. The difference between English and Chinese is nothing like the difference between, say, French and English. The pattern we are used to, that of differences in conjugations and declensions, vocabulary and idioms, is one that is limited to our group of Western languages. As soon as one sets out to compare English and an Oriental language, the difference is much more profound.

Generally speaking, a foreign language not only implies different words and sentence constructions, but also a different way of thinking and reasoning. This is all the more true for China. The country, the people, their customs and above all their language have been almost totally isolated for the whole of their history. The result is an entirely different way of experiencing life.

Most of us consider Chinese to be a forbiddingly difficult language to learn and are usually astonished to meet someone who has made the effort to master this tongue. For the traveller to China, it is not necessary to be fluent, but it will certainly be appreciated by your hosts if you take the time to familiarize yourself with some basic everyday phrases you're likely to need or hear during your visit. For your own appreciation of the new sights and sounds around you, you'll be glad to have acquired at least an inkling of Chinese. And remember, you'll be learning a language spoken by more people than any other, including English.

Mandarin Chinese is spoken by the majority of the people and is the official language of the country. There are nine groups of dialects, six of which are not mutually intelligible including Cantonese and Hakka. Northern, southern and southwestern Mandarin speakers, however, are able to communicate with one another and their language is the official *pǔ tōng huà* (national language); it is this which you'll find featured in this book. Although the dialects differ a great deal in pronunciation, less so in vocabulary, and very little in grammar, written Chinese is always the same.

Nouns and adjectives

There is no definite article (the), singular or plural in Chinese. Thus, the word 书 (*shū*) may mean book, the book, books or the books, depending on the context. Adjectives are generally preceded by the adverb 很 (*hěn* — very) in its positive form. When used predicatively, the verb "to be" (*shì*) can be dropped:

| 我很高兴。 | wǒ hěn gāo-xìng | I am happy. |

Word order

The word order in Chinese sentences is always:

> subject — verb — object

which is also the usual order in English sentences. For example:

我	学	汉语
wǒ	xué	hàn-yǔ
I	learn	Chinese.

Verbs

Chinese verb forms are even more invariable than English ones, with no differences between the singular and plural verb forms at all.

我学	wǒ xué	I learn
你学	nǐ xué	you learn
他/她/它学	tā xué	he/she/it learns
我们学	wǒ-men xué	we learn
你们学	nǐ-men xué	you learn
他们学	tā-men xué	they learn

Although written differently, the characters 他 (*tā* — he), 她 (*tā* — she), 它 (*tā* — it) are all pronounced the same. Note that the form of *tā* meaning "it" is never used at the beginning of a sentence. Personal pronouns (I/me, you, he/him, she/her, etc.) have the same form whether used as subject or object.

Past tense

The suffix 了 *(le)* is placed after the verb to show that the action has been completed:

| 我喝茶。 | wǒ hē chá | I drink tea. |
| 我喝了茶。 | wǒ hē le chá | I drank (have drunk) tea. |

The suffix 过 *(guò)* after a verb indicates the indefinite past, i.e. whether something has or has not happened but without a specific notion of point in time:

| 他去过中国。 | tā qù-guo zhōng-guó | He has been to China. |
| 他没去过中国。 | tā méi qù-guo zhōng-guó | He hasn't been to China. |

Future

The future tense has exactly the same form as the present. To indicate the future nature of the action, an adverb or adverbial phrase must be added:

| 我学汉语。 | wǒ xué hàn-yǔ | I learn Chinese. |
| 我明年学汉语。 | wǒ míng-nián xué hàn-yǔ | I shall learn Chinese next year. |

Questions

Word order in interrogative sentences is the same as in statements, but the word 吗 *(mā)* is added at the end of the sentence:

| 你学汉语。 | nǐ xué hàn-yǔ | You learn Chinese. |
| 你学汉语吗？ | nǐ xué hàn-yǔ ma | Do you learn Chinese? |

A question may feature an interrogative pronoun (e.g.: *shén–me* = what, *shuí* = who, etc.). In this case, the particle *(mā)* 吗 is not added at the end of the sentence:

| 你喝什么？ | nǐ hē shén-me | What do you drink? |
| 谁喝茶？ | shuí hē chá | Who drinks tea? |

A question can also be formed by presenting a choice between a positive and a negative. The particle 不 *(bù)* is inserted between the two propositions:

| 你喝不喝茶？ | nǐ hē bù hē chá | Do you drink tea or not? |

In a question involving a choice between two possibilities, the words 还是 *(hái-shì)* are placed between the two alternatives:

| 你喝茶还是喝咖啡？ | nǐ hē chá hái-shì hē kā-fēi | Do you drink tea or coffee? |

Negatives

不 *(bù)* is placed in front of a verb to indicate negation:

| 我不学汉语。 | wǒ bù xué hàn-yǔ | I do not study Chinese. |

The negative form of 有 *(yǒu — to have)* is 没有 *(méi yǒu)*. *Méi* is also used before the verb to indicate negation in the past tense:

| 我没学汉语。 | wo mei xue han-yu | I didn't learn Chinese. |

Yes and No

There are no specific words in Chinese for yes and no. You simply repeat the verb which was used in the question:

你学汉语吗？	nǐ xué hàn-yǔ ma	Do you learn Chinese?
我学。	wǒ xué	Yes. (I.e.: "I learn".)
我不学。	wǒ bù xué	No. (I.e.: "I don't learn".)

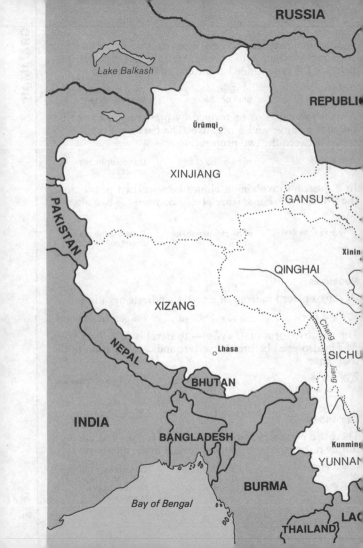

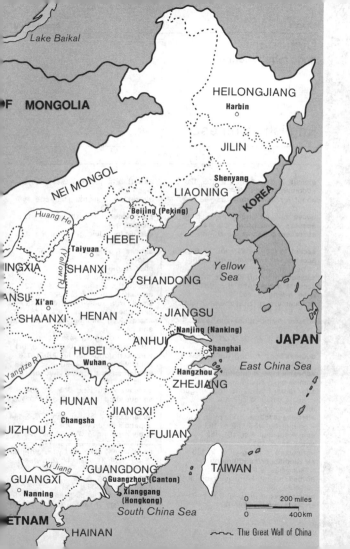

Dictionary
and alphabetical index

English – Chinese

n noun

abacus *n* suàn-pan 算盘 105, 126

abdomen *n* fù-bù 腹部 139

about *(approximately)* dà-yuē 大约 155

above zài...zhī shàng 在...之上 16

abscess *n* huà nóng 化脓 147

absorbent cotton *n* tuō-zhī-mián 脱脂棉 108

accept, to *(payment)* shōu 收 62, 103

accessories *(mechanical)* *n* líng-pèi-jiàn 零配件 125

accident *n* shì-gù 事故 75, 141

account *n* zhàng-hù 帐户 131

ache *n* téng 疼 143

acupuncture *n* (zhā) zhēn-jiǔ (扎) 针灸 81, 139

adaptor *n* duō-lù chā-zuò 多路插座 28, 119

address *n* dì-zhǐ 地址 21, 32, 75, 77, 102

address book *n* tōng-xùn-bù 通讯簿 105

adhesive tape *n* jiāo-tiáo 胶条 105

admission *n* rù chǎng 入场 79, 156

after *(time)* hòu 后 16; *(place)* guò le...zhī hòu 过了...之后 77

afternoon *n* xià-wǔ 下午 153

after-shave lotion *n* xiū miàn hòu xiāng-shuǐ 修面后香水 109

age *n* suì-shu 岁数 151, 152

ago qián 前 151

agriculture *n* nóng-yè 农业 133

air conditioner/conditioning *n* kōng-tiáo 空调 24, 29

airmail *n* háng-kōng (yóu-dì) 航空 (邮递) 135

air mattress *n* qì-rù-zi 气褥子 91

airplane *n* fēi-jī 飞机 65

airport *n* fēi-jī-chǎng 飞机场 20, 21, 65, 73

airport bus *n* jī-chǎng bān-chē 机场班车 20, 65

alarm clock *n* nào-zhōng 闹钟 121

alcohol *n* jiǔ 酒 58

allergic to... duì...guò-mǐn 对...过敏 143, 145

almond *n* xìng-rénr 杏仁儿 57

also yě 也 16

alter, to gǎi 改 116

amber *n* hǔ-pò 琥珀 122

amethyst *n* zǐ-shuǐ-jīng 紫水晶 122

amount *n* shù-é 数额 132

amplifier *n* kuò-yīn-jī 扩音器 119

anaesthetic *n* má-yào 麻药 146, 147

analgesic *n* zhǐ-téng-yào 止疼药 108

and hé 和 16

animal *n* dòng-wù 动物 84

ankle *n* jiǎo-wàn-zi 脚腕子 139, 141

anorak *n* dēng-shān-fú 登山服 116

antibiotic *n* kàng-jūn-sù 抗菌素 145

antidepressant *n* kàng yì-yù yào 抗抑郁药 145

antiques *n* gǔ-dǒng 古董 81, 104

antique shop *n* gǔ-dǒng-diàn 古董店 98

appendicitis *n* lán-wěi-yán 阑尾炎 144

appendix *n* lán-wěi 阑尾 139

apple *n* píng-guǒ 苹果 56, 64, 120

appliance *n* diàn-qì 电器 119

appointment *(to make)* yuē...shí-jiān 约...时间 31, 139, 147; *(business)* yuē...huì-tán 约...会谈 132

apricot *n* xìng 杏 56

April *n* sì-yuè 四月 152

aquarium *n* shuǐ-zú-guǎn 水族馆 79

archaeology *n* kǎo-gǔ-xué 考古学 81

architect *n* jiàn-zhù-shī 建筑师 82
architecture *n* jiàn-zhù-xué 建筑学 81
arm *n* gē-bo 胳膊 139, 141
arrival *n* dào-dá 到达 65
arrive, to dào 到 65, 68, 131
art *n* yì-shù 艺术 81
art gallery *n* huà-diàn 画店 79
arthritis *n* guān-jié-yán 关节炎 143
artist *n* yì-shù-jiā 艺术家 82
ashtray *n* yān-huī-gāng 烟灰缸 28, 37
ask, to wèn 问 77
ask for, to yào 要 26, 61
aspirin *n* ā-sī-pǐ-lín 阿司匹林 108, 145
asthma *n* xiào-chuǎn 哮喘 143
at zài 在 16
at least zuì shǎo 最少 25
attendant *n* fú-wù-yuán 服务员 27
August *n* bā-yuè 八月 152
automatic zì-dòng-de 自动的 122, 124
autumn *n* qiū-tiān 秋天 152

B

baby *n* yīng-ér 婴儿 25, 110
baby food *n* yīng-ér shí-pǐn 婴儿食品 110
babysitter *n* lín-shí bǎo-mǔ 临时保姆 28
back *n* (*body*) bèi 背 139; (*lower part*) yāo 腰 143
back (*rear*) hòu-biān 后边 87
backache *n* yāo-téng 腰疼 143
bacon *n* xián-ròu 咸肉 39
bad huài (de) 坏(的) 14
badminton *n* yǔ-máo-qiú 羽毛球 89
bag *n* dài (zi) 袋(子) 19, 103
baggage *n* xíng-li 行李 19, 65, 71
baggage cart *n* shǒu-tuī-chē 手推车 19, 71
baggage check *n* xíng-li jì-cún-chù 行李寄存处 19, 67, 71
balance (*account*) *n* jié-yú 结余 132
balcony *n* yáng-tái 阳台 24
ball *n* qiú 球 128
ballet *n* bā-léi-wǔ 芭蕾舞 88
ballpoint pen *n* yuán-zhū-bǐ 圆珠笔 105
bamboo zhú (zi de) 竹(子的) 126
banana *n* xiāng-jiāo 香蕉 56, 64
bandage *n* bēng-dài 绷带 108
Band-Aid *n* dài yào-diàn xiàng-pí-gāo 带药垫橡皮膏 108
bangle *n* shǒu-zhuó 手镯 121

bank (*finance*) *n* yín-háng 银行 98, 130, 131
banknote *n* chāo-piào 钞票 131
banquet *n* yàn-huì 宴会 34
bar *n* jiǔ-bā 酒吧 96
barber's *n* lǐ-fà-diàn 理发店 31, 98; (*in hotel*) lǐ-fà-shì 理发室 31
basketball *n* lán-qiú 篮球 89
basketware *n* téng-biān qì-jù 藤编器具 127
bath *n* zǎo-pén 澡盆 24, 26
bathing cap *n* yóu-yǒng-mào 游泳帽 116
bathing suit *n* yóu-yǒng-yī 游泳衣 91, 116
bathrobe *n* yù-yī 浴衣 116
bathroom *n* yù-shì 浴室 27, 28
bath essence *n* xǐ-zǎo-yè 洗澡液 109
bath salts *n* xǐ-zǎo-fěn 洗澡粉 109
bath towel *n* yù-jīn 浴巾 27
battery *n* diàn-chí 电池 119, 121, 125
be, to shì 是 11; (*location*) zài 在 12
beach *n* shā-tān 沙滩 91
bean *n* dòu 豆 51
bean curd *n* dòu-fu 豆腐 51, 52
bean sprout *n* dòu-yár 豆芽儿 51
beard *n* xià hú-zi 下胡子 32
beautiful hǎo kàn (de) 好看 (的) 15
beauty salon *n* měi-róng-shì 美容室 31, 98
bed *n* chuáng (wèi) 床(位) 20, 25, 144, 146
bedpan *n* biàn-pénr 便盆儿 146
beef *n* niú-ròu 牛肉 47, 48
beer *n* pí-jiǔ 啤酒 59
before (*place*) zài...qián-miàn 在…前面 16; (*time*) qián 前 16
begin, to (*film, play*) kāi yǎn 开演 87, 88
behind zài...hòu-miàn 在…后面 16, 77
beige qiǎn kā-fēi-sè (de) 浅咖啡色 (的) 112
bell *n* líng 铃 146
below zài...xià 在…下 16
belt *n* yāo-dài 腰带 117
berth *n* wò-pù 卧铺 69, 82
better hǎo xiē (de) 好些 (的) 15, 26, 101
between zài...zhōng-jiān 在…中间 16
bicycle *n* zì-xíng-chē 自行车 76
bicycle hire/rental *n* (chū) zū zì-xíng-chē (出)租自行车 76

big dà (de) 大(的) 15, 101

bill n zhàng-dān 帐单 32, 62, 102; (banknote) chāo-piào 钞票 131

billion (Am.) n shí yì 十亿 151

binoculars n shuāng-tǒng wàng-yuǎn-jìng 双筒望远镜 123

bird n niǎor 鸟儿 84

birthday n shēng-rì 生日 153, 154

biscuit (Br.) n bǐng-gān 饼干 64

bitter kǔ (de) 苦(的) 61

black hēi-sè (de) 黑色(的) 106, 112

bladder n páng-guāng 膀胱 139

blade n dāo-piàn 刀片 110

blanket n tǎn-zi 毯子 28

bleed, to liú xuè 流血 141, 147

blind (window) n bǎi-yè-chuāng 百叶窗 30

blister n shuǐ-pào 水疱 141

block, to dǔ (le) 堵(了) 29

blood n xuè 血 139, 144

blood pressure n xuè-yā 血压 144

blood transfusion n shū-xuè 输血 146

blouse n nǚ chèn-shān 女衬衫 114

blow-dry n chuī gān dìng xíng 吹干定型 31

blue lán-sè (de) 蓝色(的) 106, 112

blusher n yān-zhi 胭脂 109

boat n chuán 船 74

bobby pin n qiǎ-zi 卡子 110

body n shēn-tǐ 身体 139

boil n jiē-zi 疖子 141

boiled zhǔ (de) 煮(的) 39

boiled water n kāi-shuǐ 开水 28

bond (finance) n gōng-zhài-quàn 公债券 132

bone n gǔ 骨 139

book n shū 书 13, 105

book, to yù-dìng 预订 20, 37

bookshop n shū-diàn 书店 98, 105

boot n xuē-zi靴子 118

borrow, to jiè 借 132

botanical gardens n zhí-wù-yuán 植物园 79

botany n zhí-wù-xué 植物学 81

bottle n píng (zi) 瓶(子) 18, 59, 64

bottle opener n kāi-píng-qì 开瓶器 64, 120

bowel n dà-cháng 大肠 139

box n hé (zi) 盒(子) 64, 120

boxing n quán-jī 拳击 89

boy n nán-háir 男孩儿 111, 128

boyfriend n nán-péng-you 男朋友 93, 95

bra n rǔ-zhào 乳罩 116

bracelet n shǒu-zhuó 手镯 121

braces (suspenders) n bēi-dài 背带 116

brain n nǎo 脑 139

braised gān-shāo 干烧 41

brandy n bái-lán-dì 白兰地 58

bread n miàn-bāo 面包 38, 120

break, to nòng huài 弄坏 119, 123, 147; zhé duàn 折断 141, 142

breakfast n zǎo-fàn 早饭 25, 28, 36, 39

breast n rǔ-fáng 乳房 139

breathe, to hū-xī 呼吸 143, 144

bridge n qiáo 桥 79, 84

briefs n nèi-kù 内裤 116

bring, to ná 拿 14, 59; dài 带 95

brocade n zhì-jǐn-duàn 织锦缎 113

broken huài le 坏了 30, 119; duàn le 断了 141, 142

bronzeware n qīng-tóng zhì-pǐn 青铜制品 104, 127

brooch n xiōng-zhēn 胸针 121

brother (older) n gē-ge 哥哥 93; (younger) dì-di 弟弟 93

brown hè-sè (de) 褐色(的) 112

bruise n qīng-zǐ 青紫 141

brush n shuā (zi) 刷(子) 110

bucket n (xiǎo) tǒng (小)桶 128

buckle n dài-kòu 带扣 117

Buddhist temple n fó-sì 佛寺 81

build, to jiàn 建 82

building n jiàn-zhù 建筑 79, 82

building blocks/bricks n jī-mù 积木 128

bulb n dēng-pào 灯泡 29, 30, 119

burn n shāo-shāng 烧伤 141

burn out, to (bulb) shāo huài (le) 烧坏(了) 29

bus n gōng-gòng qì-chē 公共汽车 20, 72, 73; (airport) jī-chǎng bān-chē 机场班车 20, 65

business n mào-yì 贸易 132

business district n shāng-yè-qū 商业区 80

business trip (to be on) chū chāi 出差 93

bus stop n gōng-gòng qì-chē-zhàn 公共汽车站 72, 73

busy máng 忙 96

but dàn-shì 但是 16

butcher's n ròu-diàn 肉店 98

butter n huáng-yóu 黄油 38, 120

button n niǔ-kòu 纽扣 30, 114, 117

buy, to mǎi 买 12, 68, 105, 132

C

cabin *(ship)* n kè-cāng 客舱 74

cable release n lián-xiàn kuài-mén 连线快门 125

cable *(telegram)* n diàn-bào 电报 135

cake n dàn-gāo 蛋糕 64

cake shop n gāo-diǎn-diàn 糕点店 98

calculator n jì-suàn-qì 计算器 106

calendar n rì-lì 日历 105

call *(phone)* n diàn-huà 电话 137

call, to *(give name)* jiào 叫 12; *(summon)* jiào 叫 75, 157; *(phone)* dǎ diàn-huà 打电话 137

calligraphy n shū-fǎ 书法 81, 104

calm píng-jìng 平静 91

camel n luò-tuo 骆驼 104

camera n zhào-xiàng-jī 照像机 18, 124, 125

camera case n xiàng-jī-hé 像机盒 125

camera shop n zhào-xiàng qì-cái shāng-diàn 照像器材商店 98

can *(of peaches)* n guàn-tou 罐头 120

can *(to be able)* néng 能 13, 14

canal n yùn-hé 运河 84

cancel, to qǔ-xiāo 取消 65

can opener n kāi-guàn-qì 开罐器 64, 120

cap n mào-zi 帽子 116

capital *(finance)* n zī-běn 资本 132

car *(xiǎo-qì) chē* (小汽)车 20, 75

carat n kāi 开 121

carbon paper n fù-xiě-zhǐ 复写纸 106

card *(business)* n míng-piàn 名片 132; *(playing)* pái 牌 93

cardigan n kāi-shēn máo-yī 开身毛衣 116

car hire n zū bāo-chē 租包车 22, 75

carpet n dì-tǎn 地毯 104, 127

car rental n zū bāo-chē 租包车 22

carry, to tí 提 22

cart *(trolley)* n shǒu-tuī-chē 手推车 19, 71

carton *(of cigarettes)* n tiáo 条 126

carving n diāo-kè-pǐn 雕刻品 81

case *(camera, etc)* n hé 盒 121, 125

cash, to duì-xiàn 兑现 131, 135

cash desk n shōu-kuǎn-chù 收款处 103, 156

cashmere n kāi-sī-mǐ 开司米 127

cassette n hé-shì cí-dài 盒式磁带 128; *(video)* lù-xiàng-dài 录像带 119, 124

cassette recorder n hé-shì cí-dài lù-yīn-jī 盒式磁带录音机 119

catalogue n jiǎn-jiè 简介 79

cathedral n dà-jiào-táng 大教堂 80

Catholic tiān-zhǔ-jiào (de) 天主教(的) 82

cave n dòng-xué 洞穴 80

celery n qín-cài 芹菜 51

cemetery n gōng-mù 公墓 80

centre n zhōng-xīn 中心 21, 80

century n shì-jì 世纪 151

certificate n zhèng (míng) 证(明) 17, 146

chain *(jewellery)* n liàn 链 121

chain bracelet n liàn-shǒu-zhuó 链手镯 121

change *(money)* n líng-qián 零钱 131

change, to huàn 换 61; *(train)* huàn chē 换车 68, 69, 73, 123; *(money)* duì-huàn 兑换 19, 20, 130; *(reservation)* gēng-huàn 更换 65

charge *(hire)* n zū-jīn 租金 89, 91; *(telephone)* fèi 费 135, 137

charge, to *(money)* yào (fù) qián 要(付)钱 25, 75, 131

charm bracelet n dài shì-wù liàn-shǒu-zhuó 带饰物链手镯 121

cheap pián-yi 便宜 15, 25, 26, 69, 101

check *(Am.)* n zhī-piào 支票 130, 131, 132; *(restaurant)* zhàng-dān 帐单 62

check, to chá-duì 查对 131; *(luggage)* tuō-yùn 托运 71

check in, to *(airport)* bàn dēng-jī shǒu-xù 办登机手续 65

check out, to jié-zhàng lí-kāi 结帐离开 32

checkup *(jiǎn) chá (shēn) tǐ (检)查(身)体 144

cheers! gān-bēi 干杯 58

chemist's n yào-diàn 药店 98, 107

chemistry n huà-xué 化学 133

cheque n zhī-piào 支票 131, 132

chess set n guó-jì xiàng-qí 国际象棋 128

chest n xiōng-bù 胸部 139, 143

chewing tobacco n kǒu-jiáo yān-cǎo 口嚼烟草 126

chicken n jī 鸡 49, 50

chicken breast n jī-xiōng-pú 鸡胸脯 49

child n ér-tóng 儿童 25, 69, 79; hái-zi 孩子 61, 91, 93, 141

DICTIONARY

词汇表

children's doctor n ér-kē dài-fu 儿科大夫 139

China n zhōng-guó 中国 148

chinaware n cí-qì 瓷器 104, 127

Chinese n hàn-yǔ 汉语 13, 95

Chinese zhōng-shì (de) 中式(的) 39

chocolate n qiǎo-kè-lì 巧克力 64, 120

chop (carved) n yìn-zhāng 印章 121, 127; (uncarved Chinese seal) yìn-zhāng shí-liào 印章石料 121

chopsticks n kuài-zi 筷子 36, 61, 127

Christmas n shèng-dàn-jié 圣诞节 154

chromium n luò 铬 122

church n jiào-táng 教堂 80, 82

cigar n xuě-jiā 雪茄 126

cigarette n xiāng-yān 香烟 18, 95, 126

cigarette case n yān-hé 烟盒 121

cigarette lighter n dǎ-huǒ-jī 打火机 121

cinema n diàn-yǐng-yuàn 电影院 88, 96

circle (theatre) n lóu-shàng 楼上 87

city n chéng-shì 城市 80

classical gǔ-diǎn (de) 古典(的) 128

classical music n gǔ-diǎn yīn-yuè 古典音乐 128

clean gān-jìng 干净 61

clean, to nòng gān-jìng 弄干净 30

cleansing cream n xià-zhuāng miàn-shuāng 下妆面霜 109

clerk n zhí-yuán 职员 27

cliff n shān-yá 山崖 84

clinic n mén-zhěn-bù 门诊部 98

clip n jiā-zi 夹子 121

cloakroom n yī-mào-jiān 衣帽间 87

clock n zhōng 钟 119, 121, 155

cloisonné n jǐng-tài-lán 景泰蓝 81, 104, 127

close, to guān 关 12, 79, 107, 130, 134

closed (sign) xiū-xi 休息 98

cloth n bù-liào 布料 118

clothes n yī-fu 衣服 30, 111

cloud n yún 云 94

coach (bus) n cháng-tú qì-chē 长途汽车 72

coat n dà-yī 大衣 116

coffee n kā-fēi 咖啡 39, 60, 64

coin n yìng-bì 硬币 131

cold lěng 冷 15, 25, 39

cold (illness) n gǎn-mào 感冒 107

cold cuts n shóu-ròu 熟肉 64

collar n yī-lǐng 衣领 114

collar-bone n suǒ-gǔ 锁骨 139

collect call n ràng duì-fāng fù-fèi de diàn-huà 让对方付费的电话 137

colour n yán-sè 颜色 103, 112; (film) cǎi-sè (de) 彩色(的) 124

colour fast bú tuì-sè (de) 不退色(的) 113

colour negative n cǎi-sè dǐ-piàn 彩色底片 124

colour rinse n zhuó sè xǐ fà 着色洗发 31

colour shampoo n rǎn-fà xǐ-fà-gāo 染发洗发膏 110

colour slide n cǎi-sè huàn-dēng-piàn 彩色幻灯片 124

colouring pencil n cǎi-sè qiān-bǐ 彩色铅笔 106

comb n shū-zi 梳子 110

come, to lái 来 92, 95, 138

comedy n xǐ-jù (de) 喜剧(的) 88

commission n shǒu-xù-fèi 手续费 131

commune n gōng-shè 公社 80

company n gōng-sī 公司 136

complain, to yǒu yì-jian 有意见 61

concert n yīn-yuè-huì 音乐会 88

concert hall n yīn-yuè-tīng 音乐厅 80, 88

conductor (orchestra) n zhǐ-huī 指挥 88

confirm, to què-rèn 确认 65

congratulations n zhù-hè 祝贺 154

connection (flight) n lián-chéng háng-bān 联程航班 65

consipated biàn-bì 便秘 142

consulate n lǐng-shì-guǎn 领事馆 156

contact, to lián-xì 联系 131

contact lens n jiǎo-mó jiē-chù-jìng 角膜接触镜 123

contagious chuán-rǎn (de) 传染(的) 144

contain, to hán-yǒu 含有 38

contraceptive n bì-yùn-yào 避孕药 108, 143

contract n hé-tong 合同 132

cookie (Am.) n bǐng-gān 饼干 64

copper n tóng 铜 122

coral n shān-hú 珊瑚 122

corduroy n dēng-xīn-róng 灯芯绒 113

coriander n xiāng-cài 香菜 53

corkscrew n bá-sāi-zuān 拔塞钻 120

corn (Am.) n tián-yù-mǐ 甜玉米 51; (foot) jī-yǎn 鸡眼 108

corner n jiǎo 角 37; (street) lù-kǒu 路口 22, 77

correct *adj* duì 对 11
cost *n* fèi 费 137; *(business)* chéng-běn 成本 133
cost, to yào duō-shao qián 要多少钱 12
cot *n* xiǎo-chuáng 小床 25
cotton *n* mián-bù 棉布 113
cotton wool *n* tuō-zhī-mián 脱脂棉 108
cough *n* ké-sou 咳嗽 108
cough, to ké-sou 咳嗽 107, 143, 144
cough syrup *n* zhǐ-ké táng-jiāng 止咳糖浆 108
counter *n* guì-tái 柜台 135
country *n* guó-jiā 国家 93
countryside *n* nóng-cūn 农村 84
courtyard *n* tíng-yuàn 庭院 80
crab *n* páng-xiè 螃蟹 45
cramp *n* dù-zi jiǎo-tòng 肚子绞痛 143
crayon *n* là-bǐ 腊笔 106
cream *n* nǎi-yóu 奶油 60; *(cosmetic)* xuě-huā-gāo 雪花膏 109
crease resistant kàng zhòu (de) 抗皱(的) 113
credit card *n* xìn-yòng-kǎ 信用卡 32, 62, 102, 131
crepe *n* zhòu-chóu 皱绸 113
crockery *n* táo-cí cān-jù 陶瓷餐具 120
crossroads *n* shí-zì lù-kǒu 十字路口 77
cruise *n* zuò chuán yóu-lǎn 坐船游览 74
crystal *n* shuǐ-jīng 水晶 122
cuff *n* xiù-kǒu 袖口 114
cuff link *n* xiù-kǒu liàn-kòu 袖口链扣 121
cup *n* chá-bēi 茶杯 37
curler *n* juǎn-fà jiā-zi 卷发夹子 110
currency *n* huò-bì 货币 139
currency exchange office *n* wài-huì duì-huàn-chù 外汇兑换处 19, 130
current *(water)* *n* cháo-liú 潮流 91
curtain *n* chuāng-lián 窗帘 29
customs *n* hǎi-guān 海关 17, 102
cut, to *(self)* gē pò 割破 141
cut, to jiǎn 剪 31
cut glass *n* diāo-bō-li 雕玻璃 122
cuticle remover *n* chú pí-xiè jì 除皮屑剂 109
cutlery *n* dāo-chā cān-jù 刀叉餐具 120, 121
cycling qí zì-xíng-chē 骑自行车 89
cymbals *n* bó xiǎo 钹 127
cystitis *n* páng-guāng-yán 膀胱炎 144

D

dairy *n* nǎi-zhì-pǐn diàn 奶制品店 98
dance, to tiào wǔ 跳舞 88, 96
danger *n* wēi-xiǎn 危险 156, 157
dangerous wēi-xiǎn-de 危险的 91
dark àn (de) 暗 (的) 25; *(colour)* shēn-sè (de) 深色 (的) 101, 112, 113
date *(day)* *n* rì-qī 日期 26, 153; *(fruit)* zǎo 枣 56
daughter *n* nǚ-er 女儿 93
day *n* tiān 天 17, 22, 25, 75, 76, 78; rì-qī 日期 153
day off *n* xiū-xi-rì 休息日 153
decade *n* shí nián 十年 151
decaffeinated bú dài kā-fēi-yīn de 不带咖啡因的 39, 60
December *n* shí-èr yuè 十二月 152
decision *n* jué-dìng 决定 25, 102
deck *(ship)* *n* jiǎ-bǎn 甲板 74
deck chair *n* tǎng-yǐ 躺椅 91
declare, to *(customs)* bào guān 报关 18
deep shēn (de) 深 (的) 91
deep-fried jiāo-zhá 焦炸 41
degree *(temperature)* *n* dù 度 142
delay *(transport)* *n* wǎn diǎn 晚点 69
deliver, to sòng 送 102
delivery *n* jì-sòng 寄送 102
denim *n* láo-dòng-bù 劳动布 113
dental clinic *n* yá-kē mén-zhēn-bù 牙科门诊部 98
dentist *n* yá-kē dài-fu 牙科大夫 147
denture *n* jiǎ-yá 假牙 147
deodorant *n* chú tǐ-xiù yè 除体臭液 109
department *(shop)* *n* bù 部 81, 100
department store *n* bǎi-huò shāng-diàn 百货商店 80, 98
departure *n* chū-fā 出发 65
deposit *n* yā-jīn 押金 22, 76
deposit, to *(bank)* cún 存 131
dessert *n* gāo-diǎn tián-shí 糕点甜食 57
develop, to *(film)* chōng-xǐ 冲洗 125
diabetes *n* táng-niào-bìng 糖尿病 143
diabetic táng-niào-bìng (de) 糖尿病(的) 38
dial, to bō 拨 136, 137
diamond *n* jīn-gāng-shí 金钢石 122
diaper *n* zhǐ-niào-bù 纸尿布 110
diarrhoea *n* fù-xiè 腹泻 142
dictionary *n* zì-diǎn 字典 106

diet *(to be on a)* zūn-shǒu tè-bié de shí-pǔ 遵守特别的食谱 38
difficult nán 难 15
dining car n cān-chē 餐车 68, 71
dining room n cān-tīng 餐厅 28
dinner n wǎn-fàn 晚饭 28, 36, 94
direct, to zhǐ 指 77
direction n zhǐ lù 指路 77
director *(cinema)* n dǎo-yǎn 导演 88
directory *(phone)* n diàn-huà-bù 电话簿 136
disabled n cán-fèi-rén 残废人 79
discotheque n dí-sī-kē wǔ-huì 迪斯科舞会 88
discount n zhé-kòu 折扣 132
dish n cài 菜 37, 38, 47, 61
disinfectant n xiāo-dú-yào 消毒药 108
dislocate, to tuō-jiù 脱臼 142
dissatisfied bù mǎn-yì 不满意 103
disturb, to dǎ-rǎo 打扰 28, 156
dizzy tóu-yūn 头晕 142
docks n mǎ-tou 码头 80
doctor n dài-fu 大夫 75, 138, 146
doctor's office n mén-zhěn 门诊 138
dog n gǒu 狗 104
doll n wá-wa 娃娃 128
dollar n měi-yuán 美元 20, 130; *(Hong Kong)* gǎng-bì 港币 130
door n mén 门 156
double bed n shuāng-rén-chuáng 双人床 24
double room n shuāng-rén fáng-jiān 双人房间 20, 24
downstairs lóu xià 楼下 16
downtown n shì-zhōng-xīn 市中心 80
dozen n yì-dá 一打 151
draught beer n sǎn-zhuāng pí-jiǔ 散装啤酒 59
drawing paper n tú-huà-zhǐ 图画纸 106
drawing pin n tú-dīng 图钉 106
dress n lián-yī-qún 连衣裙 114, 116
dressmaker's n cái-feng-diàn 裁缝店 99
dressing gown n yù-yī 浴衣 116
drink n yǐn-liào 饮料 60, 61; *(alcoholic)* jiǔ 酒 58,
drink, to hē 喝 13, 58;
drive, to kāi (chē) 开(车) 22
driver n sī-jī 司机 75
drugstore n yào-diàn 药店 99, 107
drum n gǔ 鼓 127
dry gān 干 31, 59
drycleaner's n gān-xǐ-diàn 干洗店 30

dry shampoo n gān-xìng xǐ-fà-jì 干性洗发剂 110
duck n yā 鸭 49
duckling n chú-yā 雏鸭 49
dull *(pain)* dùn (de) 钝(的) 142
dummy n xiàng-pí nǎi-zuǐr 橡皮奶嘴儿 110
during zài...de shí-hou 在…的时候 16, 152
duty *(customs)* n shuì 税 18
duty-free shop n miǎn-shuì shāng-diàn 免税商店 20
dye *(hair)* n rǎn-fà-jì 染发剂 110

E

each měi 每 125
ear n ěr-duo 耳朵 139
earache n ěr-duo-téng 耳朵疼 143
ear drops n dī ěr yào-shuǐ 滴耳药水 108
early zǎo 早 15
earring n ěr-huán 耳环 121
east dōng 东 77
easy róng-yi 容易 15
eat, to chī 吃 38, 146
ebony n wū-mù 乌木 122
eel n màn-yú 鳗鱼 48
egg n jī-dàn 鸡蛋 39, 43, 64, 120
eggplant n qié-zi 茄子 51
eight bā 八 149
eighteen shí-bā 十八 149
eighth dì bā 第八 151
eighties n bā-shí nián-dài 八十年代 151
eighty bā-shí 八十 150
elastic n sōng-jǐn-dài 松紧带 114
elastic bandage n tán-xìng bēng-dài 弹性绷带 108
Elastoplast n dài yào-diàn xiàng-pí-gāo 带药垫橡皮膏 108
elbow n zhǒu 肘 139
electric(al) diàn (de) 电(的) 119
electrical appliance n diàn-qì 电器 119
electrician's n diàn-qì xiū-lǐ-bù 电器修理部 99
electronic diàn-zǐ (de) 电子(的) 125
electronics n diàn-zǐ 电子 133
elevator n diàn-tī 电梯 28, 100
eleven shí-yī 十一 149
embassy n dà-shǐ-guǎn 大使馆 157
embroidery n cì-xiù 刺绣 127
emerald n lǜ-gāng-yù 绿刚玉 122
emergency n jǐn-jí qíng-kuàng 紧急情况 157

emergency exit n tài-píng-mén 太平门 28, 99, 156

emery board n cuò zhī-jia shā-zhǐ 锉指甲砂纸 109

empty kōng 空 15

enamel n táng-cí 搪瓷 122

end n. mò (wěi) 末 (尾) 153

engineering n gōng-chéng 工程 133

England n yīng-gé-lán 英格兰 148

English yīng-guó (de) 英国 (的) 126

English n yīng-yǔ 英语 13, 106

enjoyable yú-kuài 愉快 32

enlarge, to fàng-dà 放大 125

enough zú-gòu (le) 足够 (了) 15, 68

entrance n rù-kǒu 入口 67, 99, 156

entrance fee n mén-piào 门票 79

envelope n xìn-fēng 信封 28, 106

equipment n qì-cái 器材 18, 89

eraser n xiàng-pí 橡皮 106

estimate (cost) n yù-suàn 预算 133

Europe n ōu-zhōu 欧洲 148

evening n wǎn-shàng 晚上 95, 153

evening dress n wǎn-lǐ-fú 晚礼服 88; (woman) nǚ wǎn-lǐ-fú 女晚礼服 116

every měi 每 151

exchange, to huàn 换 103

exchange rate n duì-huàn-lǜ 兑换率 19, 131

excuse me (sorry) duì bu qǐ 对不起 12, 70; (may I ask) qǐng-wèn 请问 12

exercise book n liàn-xí-běn 练习本 106

exhibition n zhǎn-lǎn-huì 展览会 80

exit n chū-kǒu 出口 67, 156

expect, to děng(dài) 等 (待) 131

expenses n kāi-zhī 开支 132

expensive guì 贵 15, 25, 101

export n chū-kǒu 出口 132

exposure counter n jiāo-piàn jì-shù-qì 胶片计数器 125

express (train) tè-kuài (de) 特快 (的) 66, 68; (mail) kuài-dì 快递 135

extension lead/cord n jiē cháng diàn-xiàn 接长电线 119

external wài(bù de) 外 (部的) 108

eye n yǎn (-jīng) 眼 (睛) 139, 141

eyebrow pencil n huà-méi-bǐ 画眉笔 109

eye drops n yǎn-yào-shuǐ 眼药水 108

eye liner n yǎn-xiàn-bǐ 眼线笔 109

eye shadow n yǎn-yǐng-gāo 眼影膏 109

eye specialist n yǎn-kē dài-fu 眼科大夫 139

F

face n liǎn 脸 139

face powder n liǎn-fěn 脸粉 109

factory n gōng-chǎng 工厂 80, 81

fall (autumn) n qiū(tiān) 秋 (天) 152

fall, to shuāi dǎo 摔倒 141

family n jiā(shǔ) 家 (属) 93, 146

fan n shàn(zi) 扇 (子) 28, 127

far yuǎn 远 15, 77, 100

fare n piào-jià 票价 67, 68, 73; (taxi) chē-fèi 车费 21

farm n nóng-chǎng 农场 84

fast kuài 快 66, 124, 155

fat n zhī-fáng 脂肪 38

father n fù-qin 父亲 93

faucet n shuǐ-lóng-tóu 水龙头 29

fawn n dàn huáng-hè-sè (de) 淡黄褐色 (的) 112

February n èr-yuè 二月 152

fee (doctor) n yī-yào-fèi 医药费 146

feeding bottle n nǎi-píng 奶瓶 110

feel, to (physical state) jué-de 觉得 142

felt n zhān (-zi) 毡 (子) 113

felt-tip pen n ruǎn-xīn-bǐ 软芯笔 106

fever n fā shāo 发烧 142

few hěn shǎo 很少 15; (a) yǒu jǐ-ge 有几个 15, 17

field n nóng-tián 农田 84

fifteen shí-wǔ 十五 149

fifth dì-wǔ 第五 151

fifty wǔ-shí 五十 150

file (nail) n cuò 锉 109

fill in, to tián-xiě 填写 26

filling (tooth) n yá-li de xiāng-bǔ-wù 牙里的镶补物 147

film (cinema) n diàn-yǐng 电影 88; (photography) jiāo-juǎn 胶卷 18, 124, 125

film winder n chán- rào jiāo-juǎn bǐng 缠绕胶卷柄 125

filter n lǜ-sè-jìng 滤色镜 125

filter-tipped dài guò-lǜ-zuǐ de 带过滤嘴的 126

find, to zhǎo 找 13, 28, 77

fine (OK) hěn hǎo 很好 11, 26

fine grain (film) xì-kē-lì de 细颗粒的 124

finger n shǒu-zhǐ 手指 139

fire n huǒ 火 157

first dì-yī 第一 77, 151

first-aid kit n jí-jiù-xiāng 急救箱 120

first name n míng 名 26

fish n yú 鱼 45

fish, to diào yú 钓鱼 90
fishing n diào-yú 钓鱼 90
fishmonger's n yú-diàn 鱼店 99
fitting (tailor) n shì yàng-zi 试样子
114
fitting room n shì-yī-shì 试衣室 115
five wǔ 五 149
fizzy dài qì de 带气的 60
flannel n fǎ-lán-róng 法兰绒 113
flash (photography) n shǎn-guāng-
dēng 闪光灯 125
flash attachment n shǎn-guāng-dēng
jiē-kǒu 闪光灯接口 125
flashlight n shǒu-diàn-tǒng 手电筒
120
flat píng (de) 平(的) 118
flight n háng-bān 航班 65
flight number n háng-bān bān-cì 航
班班次 65
floor n lóu-céng 楼层 27
florist's n huā-diàn 花店 99
flounder n píng-yú 鲆鱼 45
flour n miàn-fěn 面粉 38
flower n huār 花儿 84
flu n liú-gǎn 流感 144
fluid n yè 液 123
flute (Chinese) n dí-zi 笛子 127
fog n wù 雾 94
folding screen n zhé-dié píng-fēng
折叠屏风 104, 127
folk music n mín-jiān yīn-yuè 民间音
乐 128
food n shí-wù 食物 38
food poisoning n shí-wù zhòng-dú
食物中毒 144
foot n jiǎo 脚 139
football n zú-qiú 足球 89
footpath n xiǎo-lù 小路 84
for wèi le 为了 16
forbid n yán-jìn 严禁 156
forecast n yù-bào 预报 94
forehead n qián-é 前额 139
foreign wài (-guó de) 外(国的) 105
forest n sēn-lín 森林 84
forget, to wàng 忘 61
fork n chā-zi 叉子 37, 61
form (document) n biǎo 表 26
fortnight n liǎng-ge xīng-qī 两个星期
153
fortress n yào-sài 要塞 80
forty sì-shí 四十 149
foundation cream n dǐ-céng miàn-
shuāng 底层面霜 109
fountain n quán 泉 80

fountain pen n gāng-bǐ 钢笔 106
four sì 四 149
fourteen shí-sì 十四 149
fourth dì-sì 第四 151
frame (glasses) n jìng-jià 镜架 123
free (vacant) méi rén 没人 15;
(time) yǒu kòng 有空 96
French fǎ-yǔ 法语 113
French bean n biǎn-dòu 扁豆 51
fresh xīn-xiān(de) 新鲜(的) 56, 61
Friday n xīng-qī-wǔ 星期五 30, 153
fried zhá (de) 炸(的) 41
fried egg n jiān-jī-dàn 煎鸡蛋 39
friend n péng-you 朋友 95
Friendship Store n yǒu-yi shāng-diàn
友谊商店 99
from cóng 从 16
frost n shuāng 霜 94
fruit n shuí-guǒ 水果 56
fruit salad n shí-jǐn shuí-guǒ 什锦水
果 56
fruit juice n guǒ-zhī 果汁 38, 39, 60
full mǎn 满 15
fur n máo-pí 毛皮 127
furniture n jiā-jù 家具 81, 127
furrier's n pí-huò-diàn 皮货店 99

G

gabardine n huá-dá-ní 华达呢 113
gallbladder n dǎn-náng 胆囊 139
game n zhì-lì yóu-xì 智力游戏 128;
(food) yě-wèi 野味 49
garden n huā-yuán 花园 84
gardens n yuán-lín 园林 80
garlic n suàn 蒜 51
gas n méi-qì 煤气 157
gastritis n wèi-yán 胃炎 144
gauze n shā-bù 纱布 108
gem n bǎo-shí 宝石 121
general quán-miàn(de) 全面(的) 144
general practitioner n mén-zhěn
dài-fu 门诊大夫
genitals n shēng-zhí-qì 生殖器 139
genuine zhēn de 真的 118
geology n dì-zhì-xué 地质学 81
German dé-yǔ 德语 13
get, to (find) zhǎo 找 11, 138; (call)
jiào 叫 21, 32; (obtain) gǎo 搞 90;
(go) qù 去 100
get off, to xià chē 下车 73
gift n lǐ-wù 礼物 18
gin n jīn-jiǔ 金酒 58
gin and tonic n jīn-jiǔ hé kuí-níng-
shuǐ 金酒和奎宁水 58

ginger n jiāng 姜 51, 53
ginseng n rén-shēn 人参 127
girdle n jiàn-měi něi-kù 健美内裤 16
girl n nǚ-hái'r 女孩儿 111, 128
girlfriend n nǚ-péng-you 女朋友 93, 95
give, to gěi 给 14, 123, 126
gland n fēn-mì-xiàn 分泌腺 139
glass n bēi-zi 杯子 37, 59, 61
glasses n yǎn-jìng 眼镜 123
glove n shǒu-tào 手套 116
glue n jiāo-shuǐ 胶水 106
go, to qù 去 96; (walk) zǒu 走 22, 77
go away, to zǒu kāi 走开 157
gold n jīn 金 18, 121, 122
golden jīn-huáng-sè (de) 金黄色(的) 112
gold-plated dù-jīn (de) 镀金(的) 122
gong n luó 锣 127
good hǎo (de) 好(的) 15, 36, 101
goodbye zài-jiàn 再见 11
goods n huò-pǐn 货品 133
goose n é 鹅 49
go out, to (chū)qù wán'r (出)去玩儿 96
gram n kè 克 120
grape n pú-táo 葡萄 56
grapefruit juice n xī-yòu-zhī 西柚汁 39, 60
gray huī-sè (de) 灰色(的) 112
graze, to (skin) cā pò 擦破 141
greasy duō yóu (de) 多油(的) 110
Great Britain n yīng-guó 英国 148
Great Wall n cháng-chéng 长城 84
green lǜ-sè(de) 绿色(的) 112
green bean n biǎn-dòu 扁豆 51
greengrocer's n shū-cài-diàn 蔬菜店 99
green tea n lǜ-chá 绿茶 38, 60
greeting n wèn-hòu 问候 11, 154
grey huī-sè (de) 灰色(的) 112
grocery n fù-shí-diàn 副食店 99, 120
grotto n xiǎo yán-dòng 小岩洞 80
group n tuán-tǐ 团体 17, 79
guide n xiàng-dǎo 向导 18; (tourist) dǎo-yóu 导游 75, 78, 79
guidebook n lǚ-yóu zhǐ-nán 旅游指南 79, 106
guitar n jí-tā 吉他 127
gum (teeth) n yá-yín 牙龈 147
gymnastics n tǐ-cāo 体操 89, 90
gynaecologist n fù-kē dài-fu 妇科大夫 139

H

haemorrhoids n zhì-chuāng 痔疮 143
hair n tóu-fa 头发 31, 110
hairbrush n fà-shuā 发刷 110
haircut n jiǎn fà 剪发 31
hairdresser's n lǐ-fà-diàn 理发店 99; (hotel) lǐ-fà-shì 理发室 28, 31
hair dryer n diàn chuī-fà-qì 电吹发器 119
hairgrip n qiǎ-zi 卡子 110
hair lotion n hù-fà-yè 护发液 110
hairpin n qiǎ-zi 卡子 110
hair spray n pēn-wù fà-jiāng 喷雾发浆 110
half bàn 半 59, 151
half n yí-bàn 一半 151
half an hour bàn xiǎo-shí 半小时 155
ham n huǒ-tuǐ 火腿 39, 64
hand n shǒu 手 139
handbag n shǒu-tí-bāo 手提包 116, 157
hand cream n rùn-shǒu-shuāng 润手霜 109
handicrafts n shǒu-gōng-yì (pǐn) 手工艺(品) 81, 133
handkerchief n shǒu-juàn'r 手绢儿 116
handmade shǒu-gōng zhì de 手工制的 113
hanger n guà-gōu 挂钩 28
harbour n gǎng-wān 港湾 74, 80
hard yìng (de) 硬(的) 123
hard seating n (train) yìng-zhuò 硬座 69
hard sleeping n (train) yìng-wò 硬卧 69
hardware store n wǔ-jīn shāng-diàn 五金商店 99
hat n lǐ-mào 礼帽 116
hay fever n kū-cǎo-rè 枯草热 107, 143
he tā 他 161
head n tóu (bù) 头(部) 31, 140
headache n tóu-téng 头疼 143
headphones n ěr-jī 耳机 119
health n jiàn-kāng 健康 146
health insurance n jiàn-kāng bǎo-xiǎn 健康保险 146
health insurance form n jiàn-kāng bǎo-xiǎn-dān 健康保险单 146
heart n xīn-zàng 心脏 140
heart attack n xīn-jī gěng-sè 心肌梗塞 143

heating n nuǎn-qì 暖气 24, 29
heavy zhòng (de) 重(的) 15, 101
heel n jiǎo-hòu-gēn 脚后跟 140;
  (shoe) gēn 跟 118
helicopter n zhí-shēng fēi-jī 直升飞机
  76
hello! *(phone)* wéi 喂 137
help! jiù rén a 救人啊 157
help, to bāng-zhù 帮助 14, 22, 106
hem n yī-biān 衣边 114
her tā-de 她的 152
herbal remedies n cǎo-yào 草药 127
here zhèr 这儿 15
high gāo (de) 高(的) 26, 84, 143
high season n wàng-jì 旺季 152
hike, to tú-bù lǚ-xíng 徒步旅行 76
hill n xiǎo shān 小山 84
hip n pì-gu 屁股 140
hire, to zū (yòng) 租(用) 20, 22, 74,
  76, 89, 90, 91, 119
his tā-de 他的 152
history n lì-shǐ 历史 81
hitchhike, to dā chē 搭车 76
hole n dòng 洞 31
holiday n jià-rì 假日 153, 154
holidays n jià (qī) 假(期) 17, 153
home n jiā 家 32, 96
home address n jiā-tíng zhù-zhǐ 家
  庭住址 26
honey n fēng-mì 蜂蜜 39
hoop *(toy)* n tiě-huán 铁环 128
horse n mǎ 马 104
hospital n yī-yuàn 医院 99, 144, 146
hot rè (de) 热(的) 15, 25, 39
hotel n lǚ-guǎn 旅馆 20, 21, 22, 27, 31
hotel reservation n yù-dìng fáng-jiān
  预订房间 20
hot water n rè-shuǐ 热水 24, 29
hot-water bottle n nuǎn-shuǐ-dài 暖
  水袋 28
hour n xiǎo-shí 小时 74, 76, 91, 155
house n fáng-wū 房屋 84
how zěn-me 怎么 12
how far duō yuǎn 多远 12, 77, 84
how long duō cháng shí-jiān 多长时
  间 12, 25; duō-shao shí-jiān 多少
  时间 21, 77
how many duō-shao gè 多少个 12
how much duō-shao 多少 12
hundred yì-bǎi 一百 150
hungry, to be è le 饿了 14, 36
hurry *(to be in a)* hěn jí 很急 22
hurt, to téng 疼 141, 142, 144, 147
husband n zhàng-fu 丈夫 93

I
I wǒ 我 161
ice n bīng 冰 60, 94
ice cream n bīng-qí-lín 冰淇淋 64
ice cube n bīng-kuài 冰块 28
iced tea n bīng-chá 冰茶 60
ill bìng le 病了 142
import n jìn-kǒu 进口 132
important (hěn) zhòng-yào (很)重要 14
imported jìn-kǒu (de) 进口(的) 59, 113
in zài...lǐ 在...里 160
include, to bāo-kuò 包括 25, 62
incorrect bú-duì 不对 11
indigestion n xiāo-huà bù liáng 消化
  不良 143
indoor *(swimming pool)* shì-nèi de
  室内的 90
inexpensive pián-yi de 便宜的 124
infected gǎn-rǎn 感染 142
inflammation ...fā yán ...发炎 144
inflation n tōng-huò péng-zhàng 通
  货膨胀 133
inflation rate n tōng-huò péng-
  zhàng-lù 通货膨胀率 133
influenza n liú-gǎn 流感 144
information office n wèn-xùn-chù 问
  询处 20, 67, 156
injection n zhù-shè 注射 145, 146
injured shòu shāng le 受伤了 141
ink n mò-shuǐ 墨水 106;
  (calligraphy) mò 墨 127
inquiry n wèn-xùn 问讯 68
insect n chóng-zi 虫子 30
insect bite n chóng-yǎo-shāng 虫咬
  伤 107
insect repellent n chú-chóng-jì 除虫
  剂 108
insect spray n chú-chóng pēn-wù-jì
  除虫喷雾剂 108
inside lǐ-biānr 里边儿 16
insurance n bǎo-xiǎn 保险 146
interest *(money)* n lì-xī 利息 132
interested, to be gǎn xìng-qu 感兴趣
  96
interesting yǒu qù (de) 有趣(的) 82
international guó-jì (de) 国际(的) 135
interpreter n kǒu-yì 口译 75, 133
intersection shí-zì lù-kǒu 十字路口
  77
intestine n cháng 肠 140
introduce, to jiè-shào 介绍 92
introduction n jiè-shào 介绍 92, 131
investment n tóu-zī 投资 132
invite, to qǐng 请 94

invoice *n* fā-piào 发票 132
iodine *n* diǎn-jiǔ 碘酒 108
Ireland *n* ài-ěr-lán 爱尔兰 148
Irish ài-ěr-lán (de) 爱尔兰(的) 93
iron *(laundry)* *n* yùn-dǒu 熨斗 119
iron, to yùn 熨 30
ironmonger's *n* wǔ-jīn shāng-diàn 五金商店 99
Italy *n* yì-dà-lì 意大利 148
island *n* dǎo 岛 80, 84
ivory *n* xiàng-yá 象牙 122; *(article)* xiàng-yá zhì-pǐn 象牙制品 81, 104, 127

J

jacket *n* shàng-yī 上衣 114, 116
jade *n* yù 玉 122; *(article)* yù-shí zhì-pǐn 玉石制品 81, 104, 127
jam *n* guǒ-jiàng 果酱 39, 120
jammed qiǎ zhù 卡住 29, 125
jasmine tea *n* mò-lì huā-chá 茉莉花茶 38, 60
January *n* yī-yuè 一月 152
Japan *n* rì-běn 日本 148
jar *n* tǒng 筒 64
jaundice *n* huáng-dǎn 黄疸 144
jaw *n* xià-ba 下巴 140
jazz *n* jué-shì-yuè 爵士乐 128
jeans *n* niú-zǎi-kù 牛仔裤 116
jewel *n* zhū-bǎo shǒu-shì 珠宝首饰 104
jewel box *n* shǒu-shì-xiāng 首饰箱 121
jeweller's *n* zhū-bǎo shǒu-shì-diàn 珠宝首饰店 99, 121
joint *n* guān-jié 关节 140
juice *n* zhī 汁 39, 60
July *n* qī-yuè 七月 152
June *n* liù-yuè 六月 152

K

key *n* yào-shi 钥匙 27
kidney *n* shèn 肾 140
kilo (gram) *n* gōng-jīn 公斤 120
kimono *n* hé-fú 和服 116, 127
kind *(type)* *n* zhǒng 种 142
king-size *(cigarette)* jiā cháng de 加长的 126
kite *n* fēng-zheng 风筝 127
knee *n* xī-gài 膝盖 140
knee-cap *n* xī-gài-gǔ 膝盖骨 140
knife *n* dāo-zi 刀子 37, 61
know, to rèn-shi 认识 21

L

label *n* qiān-tiáo 签条 106
lace *n* gōu-zhī bù-liào 钩织布料 113
lacquerware *n* qī-qì 漆器 81, 104, 127
lake *n* hú 湖 80, 84, 90
lamb *n* yáng-ròu 羊肉 48
lamp *n* (diàn) dēng (电)灯 30, 119, 120
lamp shade *n* dēng-zhào 灯罩 127
landscape *n* fēng-jǐng 风景 92
lantern *n* ān-quán fēng-dēng 安全风灯 127
lapel *n* fān-lǐng 翻领 114
large dà (de) 大(的) 101, 115, 118
last zuì-hòu (de) 最后(的) 68; *(year)* qù 去 151; *(month, week)* shàng-ge 上个 153
late wǎn 晚 15
laugh, to xiào 笑 95
laundry *(place)* *n* xǐ-yī-diàn 洗衣店 30, 99; *(clothes)* gāi xǐ de yī-fu 该洗的衣服 31
laundry service *n* xǐ-yī fú-wù 洗衣服务 24
laxative *n* huǎn-xiè-jì 缓泻剂 108
leap year *n* rùn-nián 闰年 151
learn, to xué 学 165
leather *n* pí-zi 皮子 113, 118
leave, to zǒu 走 32, 95; *(train)* fā chē 发车 69; *(deposit)* jì-cún 寄存 27
left zuǒ (biān) 左(边) 22, 69, 77, 140
left-luggage office *n* xíng-li jì-cún-chù 行李寄存处 19, 67, 71
leg *n* tuǐ 腿 140
lemon *n* níng-méng 柠檬 38, 39, 56, 60, 64
lemonade *n* níng-méng qì-shuǐ 柠檬汽水 60
lemon juice *n* níng-méng-zhī 柠檬汁 60
lend, to jiè 借 132
lens *(glasses)* *n* jìng-piàn 镜片 123; *(camera)* jìng-tóu 镜头 125
lens cap *n* jìng-tóu-gài 镜头盖 125
leotard *n* tǐ-cāo-fú 体操服 116
less shǎo xiē 少些 15
letter *n* xìn 信 29, 134
letter box *n* yóu-tǒng 邮筒 134
letter of credit *n* yín-háng cún-kuǎn zhèng-míng-xìn 银行存款证明信 131
letter telegram *n* yè-xìn-diàn 夜信电 135
library *n* tú-shū-guǎn 图书馆 99

licence *(business)* n xǔ-kě-zhèng 许可证 133

lid n gài 盖 127

lie down, to tǎng xià 躺下 144

life belt n jiù-shēng-yī 救生衣 74

life boat n jiù-shēng-tǐng 救生艇 74

lifeguard n jiù-shēng-yuán 救生员 91

lift n diàn-tī 电梯 28, 100

ligament n rèn-dài 韧带 140

light qīng (de) 轻(的) 15, 101, 128; *(colour)* qiǎn-sè (de) 浅色(的) 101, 112

light n *(electric)* diàn-dēng 电灯 29; *(cigarette)* huǒr 火儿 140

lighter n dǎ-huǒ-jī 打火机 126

lighter fluid n dǎ-huǒ-jī yè-tǐ rán-liào 打火机液体燃料 126

lighter gas n dǎ-huǒ-jī qì-tǐ rán-liào 打火机汽体燃料 126

light meter n cè-guāng-biǎo 测光表 125

lightning n shǎn-diàn 闪电 94

like, to xǐ-huan 喜欢 25, 92, 102, 112; *(want)* xiǎng (yào) 想(要) 14, 24, 62, 96, 103, 113

linen n yà-má-bù 亚麻布 113, 127

lining n chèn-lǐ 衬里 114

lip n zuǐ-chún 嘴唇 140

lipsalve n fáng chún liè yóu-gāo 防唇裂油膏 109

lipstick n kǒu-hóng 口红 109

listen, to tīng 听 128

litre n shēng 升 59

little *(a)* yì-diǎnr 一点儿 13, 15, 31

liver n gān 肝 140

loan n dài-kuǎn 贷款 132

lobster n lóng-xiā 龙虾 45

local n dì-fāng 地方 37

long cháng (de) 长(的) 12, 15, 61, 116, 117

long-distance call n cháng-tú diàn-huà 长途电话 136

long-sighted yuǎn-shì (de) 远视(的) 123

look, to kàn 看 100

look for, to zhǎo 找 14

look out! liú-shén 留神 157

loose *(clothes)* féi 肥 116

lose, to diū 丢 123

loss *(business)* n kuī-sǔn 亏损 132

lost *(object)* diū le de 丢了的 123, 147; *(self)* mí-lù le 迷路了 14

lost and found office n shī-wù zhāo-lǐng-chù 失物招领处 67, 157

lost property office n shī-wù zhāo-lǐng-chù 失物招领处 67, 157

lot *(a)* hěn duō 很多 15

lotion n yè yè 液 110

lotus root n ǒu 藕 51

loud dà-shēng (de) 大声(的) 137

low dī 低 26, 143

lower xià (céng de) 下(层的) 69, 70

low season n dàn-jì 淡季 152

luck n yùn-qi 运气 154

luggage n xíng-li 行李 19, 22, 27, 32, 71

luggage trolley n shǒu-tuī-chē 手推车 19, 71

lump n zhǒng-kuài 肿块 141

lunch n wǔ-fàn 午饭 28, 78, 94

lung n fèi 肺 140

lychees n lì-zhī 荔枝 56

M

machinery n jī-xiè 机械 133

mackerel n qīng-yú 鲭鱼 45

magazine n zá-zhì 杂志 106

mahjong n má-jiàng (pái) 麻将(牌) 127

mail, to jì 寄 29

mailbox n yóu-tǒng 邮筒 134

main zhǔ-yào (de) 主要(的) 100

make, to zhì (zào) 制(造) 113

make-up remover pad n xià zhuāng mián-qiú 下妆棉球 109

man n nán-rén 男人 111

manager n jīng-lǐ 经理 27, 61

mango n máng-guǒ 芒果 56

manicure n xiū shǒu zhī-jia 修手指甲 32

many hěn duō 很多 15

map n dì-tú 地图 77, 106

March n sān-yuè 三月 152

marinaded yān (de) 腌(的) 41

market n nóng-mào shì-chǎng 农贸市场 80, 99

marmalade n jú-zi-jiàng 桔子酱 59

married yǐ-jīng jié-hūn (de) 已经结婚(的) 93

mascara n rǎn jié-máo yóu 染睫毛油 109

mass *(church)* n mí-sā 弥撒 82

massage n àn-mó 按摩 31

match n huǒ-chái 火柴 64, 126; *(sport)* bǐ-sài 比赛 90

match, to xiāng-pèi 相配 112

material *(cloth)* n bù-liào 布料 114

matinée n zǎo-chǎng 早场 87

mattress n rù-zi 褥子 91
mauve zǐ-hóng-sè (de) 紫红色 (的) 112
May n wǔ-yuè 五月 152
may *(can)* néng 能 13
meadow n cǎo-chǎng 草场 84
meal n fàn 饭 62, 145; huǒ-shí 伙食 25
measles n má-zhěn 麻疹 144
measure, to liáng 量 115
meat n ròu 肉 47, 61
mechanical pencil n zì-dòng qiān-bǐ 自动铅笔 106, 121
medical certificate n yī-shēng zhèng-míng 医生证明 146
medicine n yī-xué 医学 81; *(drug)* yào 药 108, 145
medium *(size)* zhōng 中 115
meet, to jiàn miàn 见面 96
memorial *(museum)* n jì-niàn-guǎn 纪念馆 80; *(monument)* jì-niàn-bēi 纪念碑 80
mend, to bǔ 补 30
menu n cài-dān 菜单 37
message n liú-yán 留言 29
method n fāng-fǎ 方法 41
metre n gōng-chǐ 公尺 111, 113
mezzanine *(theatre)* n lóu-shàng 楼上 87
middle zhōng (-jiàn de) 中(间的) 69, 87
mild *(cigarette)* róu-hé de 柔和的 126
mileage n lǐ-chéng (shù) 里程(数) 22
milk n niú-nǎi 牛奶 39, 60, 64, 120
milliard n shí-yì 十亿 151
million n bǎi-wàn 百万 151
mineral water n kuàng-quán-shuǐ 矿泉水 60
mining n kuàng-yè 矿业 133
minister *(religion)* n mù-shī 牧师 82
minute n fēn-zhōng 分钟 69, 155
mirror n jìng-zi 镜子 109, 115, 123
Miss n xiǎo-jie 小姐 11
missing *(to be)* shǎo le 少了 19, 31, 61
mistake n cuò (-wù) 错 (误) 32, 61, 62, 102
moisturizing cream n rùn-fū-shuāng 润肤霜 109
Monday n xīng-qī-yī 星期一 153
money n qián 钱 12; *(foreign currency)* wài-huì 外汇 19, 131
money order n huì-piào 汇票 135

monosodium glutamate n wèi-jīng 味精 38, 53
month n yuè (fèn) 月 (份) 17, 152
monument n jì-niàn-bēi 纪念碑 80
moon n yuè-liàng 月亮 94
moped n xiǎo mó-tuō-chē 小摩托车 76
more duō xiē 多些 15
morning n shàng-wǔ 上午 153; *(early)* zǎo-shàng 早上 32
mortgage n dǐ-yā 抵押 132
mosque n qīng-zhēn-sì 清真寺 80, 82
mosquito net n wén-chàng 蚊帐 28, 120; *(window)* shā-chuāng 沙窗 29
mother n mǔ-qīn 母亲 93
motorbike n mó-tuō-chē 摩托车 76
motorboat n qì-tǐng 汽艇 91
mountain n shān 山 84
mountain pass n shān-kǒu 山口 84
moustache n shàng hú-zi 上胡子 32
mouth n zuǐ 嘴 140
mouth organ n kǒu-qín 口琴 127
mouthwash n shù kǒu yào-shuǐ 漱口药水 108
move, to dòng 动 141
movie n diàn-yǐng 电影 88, 96
movie camera n shè-yǐng-jī 摄影机 124
Mr. n xiān-sheng 先生 11
Mrs. n fū-rén 夫人 11
much hěn duō 很多 15
muscle n jī-ròu 肌肉 140
museum n bó-wù-guǎn 博物馆 80
mushroom n mó-gu 磨菇 51, 53
music n yīn-yuè 音乐 128
musical instrument n yuè-qì 乐器 81, 127
music box n bā-yīn-hé 八音盒 121
must *(have to)* bì-xū 必须 32; yí-dìng 一定 61; *(musn't)* bù néng 不能 38
mustard n jiè-mo 芥末 64
mutton n yáng-ròu 羊肉 47
my wǒ de 我的 18, 20, 27

N

nail *(human)* n zhǐ-jia 指甲 109, 140
nail brush n zhǐ-jia-yóu shuā-zi 指甲油刷子 109
nail clippers n zhǐ-jia-dāo 指甲刀 109
nail file n zhǐ-jia-cuò 指甲锉 109
nail polish n zhǐ-jia-yóu 指甲油 109
nail polish remover n tuì zhǐ-jia-yóu shuǐ 退指甲油水 110

nail scissors n zhǐ-jia jiǎn-dāo 指甲剪刀 110

name (surname) xìng 姓 26; (surname & first name) xìng-míng 姓名 26, 75; jiào 叫 24, 92, 132

napkin n cān-jīn 餐巾 37, 64

nappy n zhǐ-niào-bù 纸尿布 110

National Art Gallery n zhōng-guó měi-shù-guǎn 中国美术馆 81

nationality n guó-jí 国籍 26

natural zì-rán (de) 自然(的) 81

natural history n zì-rán bó-wù 自然博物 81

nauseous ě-xīn (de) 恶心(的) 142

near (zài...fù...) jìn (在...附) 近 16

nearest lí zhèr zuì jìn de 离这儿最近的 73, 98, 100

neat (drink) chún de 纯的 58

neck n bó-zi 脖子 31, 140

necklace n xiàng-liàn 项链 121

need, to xū-yào 需要 30, 90, 133

needle n zhēn 针 28

negative n dǐ-piàn 底片 124, 125

nerve n shén-jīng 神经 140

nervous system n shén-jīng xì-tǒng 神经系统 140

never cóng lái méi-yǒu 从来没有 16

new xīn (de) 新(的) 15, 18

newspaper n bào-zhǐ 报纸 105

newsstand n shòu-bào-tíng 售报亭 20, 67, 105

next xià... 下... 65, 68, 77, 153

next to ...páng-biān 在...旁边儿 16, 77

night n yè (li) 夜(里) 25, 153

nightclub n yè-zǒng-huì 夜总会 88

nightdress n cháng shuì-yī 长睡衣 116

night letter n yè-xìn-diàn 夜信电 135

nine jiǔ 九 149

nineteen shí-jiǔ 十九 149

ninety jiǔ-shí 九十 150

ninth dì-jiǔ 第九 151

no bù (duì/shì) 不(对/是) 11

noisy chǎo 吵 25

nonalcoholic drink n yǐn-liào 饮料 60

nonsmoking jìn-zhǐ xī-yān de 禁止吸烟的 37

noodle n miàn-tiáo 面条; fěn-sī 粉丝 55

noon n zhōng-wǔ 中午 32

normal pǔ-tōng (de) 普通(的) 31

north n běi 北 77

nose n bí-zi 鼻子 140

nosebleed n liú bí-xuè 流鼻血 143

nose drops n dī-bí-yào 滴鼻药 108

not bù 不 11, 16

note (banknote) n chāo-piào 钞票 131

notebook n bǐ-jì-běn 笔记本 106

note paper n xìn-zhǐ 信纸 106

notice n zhāo-tiē 招贴 156

notify, to tōng-zhī 通知 146

November n shí-yī yuè 十一月 152

now xiàn-zài 现在 16

number n hào (-mǎ) 号(码) 27, 65, 136; (numeral) shù-zì 数字 149

nurse n hù-shi 护士 146

O

observatory n tiān-wén-tái 天文台 80

occupied yǒu rén 有人 15, 156

o'clock diǎn 点 37, 70, 76, 155

October n shí yuè 十月 152

oily (hair) chū yóu de 出油的 31; (food) yóu-nì (de) 油腻(的) 61

old jiù (de) 旧(的) 15; (person) nián lǎo 年老 15

old town n lǎo chéng 老城 80

olive n gǎn-lǎn 橄榄 56

on zài...shàng 在...上 16

once yī-cì 一次 151

one yī 一 149

one-way ticket n dān-chéng-piào 单程票 65

on foot zǒu lù 走路 77, 84

only zhǐ 只 13, 16, 108

onyx n gǎo mǎ-nǎo 缟玛瑙 122

open (sign) yíng-yè 营业 98

open, to kāi (mén) 开(门) 12, 15, 108, 134

open-air shì-wài de 室外的 90

opera n gē-jù 歌剧 88

opera house n gē-jù-yuàn 歌剧院 80, 88; (Chinese) xì-yuàn 戏院 80

operation n shǒu-shù 手术 146

operator (telephone) n jiē-xiàn-yuán 接线员 27

opposite zài...duì-miàn 在...对面 77

optician's n yǎn-jìng-diàn 眼镜店 99, 123

or hái shì 还是 16

orange jú-hóng-sè (de) 桔红色(的) 112

orange n gān-zi 柑子 56, 64

orangeade n jú-zi qì-shuǐ 桔子汽水 60

DICTIONARY

orange juice n jú-zi-zhī 桔子汁 39, 60
orchestra n (guǎn-xián) yuè-duì (管弦) 乐队 88; (seats) lóu-xià 楼下 87
order, to (goods) dìng-gòu 订购 102; (meal) diǎn cài 点菜 37, 61
outlet (electric) n chā-zuò 插座 27
outside wài-biānr 外边儿 16
oval tuǒ-yuán (de) 椭圆(的) 101
overalls n gōng-zhuāng-kù 工装裤 116
overdone huǒ tài guò le 火太过了 61
overnight (stay) yí-yè 一夜 25
owe, to gāi fù qián 该付钱 146
oyster n háo 蚝 45

P

pacifier n xiàng-pí nǎi-zuǐr 橡皮奶嘴儿 110
packet n bāo 包 18, 64, 120, 126
paddy field n dào-tián 稻田 84
pagoda n bǎo-tǎ 宝塔 80
pail (toy) n xiǎo-tǒng 小桶 128
pain(ful) téng 疼 142, 143, 145, 146
painkiller n zhǐ-tòng-yào 止痛药 142
paint n yóu-qī 油漆 156
paint, to huà 画 82
paintbox n yóu-huà-xiāng 油画箱 106
painter n huà-jiā 画家 82
painting n huàr 画儿 81
pair n yì-shuāng 一双 116, 118, 151
pajamas n (yí-tào) shuì-yī (一套)睡衣 117
palace n gōng-diàn 宫殿 80
palpitation n xīn-jì 心悸 143
panties n nèi-kù 内裤 116
pants (trousers) n cháng-kù 长裤 116
panty hose n kù-wà 裤袜 116
paper n zhǐ 纸 106
paperback n jiǎn-zhuāng-běn 简装本 106
paperclip n qū-bié-zhēn 曲别针 106
paper napkin n zhǐ cān-jīn 纸餐巾 64, 120
parcel n bāo-guǒ 包裹 134
parents n fù mǔ 父母 93
park n gōng-yuán 公园 80
parka n dēng-shān-fú 登山服 116
party (social gathering) n wǎn-huì 晚会 95
pass (mountain) n shān-kǒu 山口 84

passport n hù-zhào 护照 17, 26, 157
passport number n hù-zhào hào-mǎ 护照号码 26
passport photo n hù-zhào xiàng-piàn 护照像片 124
pastry shop n gāo-diǎn-diàn 糕点店 99
path n xiǎo-lù 小路 84
patient n bìng-rén 病人 146
pattern n yàng-zi 样子 114
pavilion n tíng-zi 亭子 80
pay, to fù (qián) 付(钱) 32, 62, 102, 137, 147
payment n (fù) kuǎn (付)款 132
pea n wān-dòu 豌豆 51
peach n táo-zi 桃子 56
peak n shān-fēng 山峰 84
pear n lí 梨 56
pearl n zhēn-zhū 珍珠 104, 122
pedalo n jiǎo-tà yóu-tǐng 脚踏游艇 91
pedicab n sān-lún-chē 三轮车 75
pedicure n xiū jiǎo zhǐ-jia 修脚指甲 32
pen n gāng-bǐ 钢笔 106
pencil n qiān-bǐ 铅笔 106
pencil sharpener n zhuàn-bǐ-dāo 转笔刀 106
pendant n xuán-shì-wù 悬饰物 121
penicillin n qīng-méi-sù 青霉素 145
penknife n xiǎo-dāo 小刀 120
pensioner n tuì-xiū de (rén) 退休的(人) 79
pepper n hú-jiāo 胡椒 38, 64
per cent n bǎi-fēn zhī 百分之 151
percentage n bǎi-fēn-bǐ 百分比 132
per day yì tiān 一天 22, 89
performance n yǎn-chū 演出 88
perfume n xiāng-shuǐ 香水 110
perhaps yě-xǔ 也许 95
period n shí-qī 时期 104
period (monthly) n (yuè) jīng (月)经 143
period pains n tòng-jīng 痛经 143
perm(anent wave) n tàng fà 烫发 31
permit n xǔ-kě 许可 90
per night yí yè 一夜 25
personal sī-rén (de) 私人(的) 18
per week yì xīng-qī 一星期 25
pewter n xī-là-jí-mǐn 锡镴器皿 122
pheasant n yě-jī 野鸡 49
photo n zhào-piàn 照片 133
photocopy fù-yìn 复印 133
photographer's n zhào-xiàng-guǎn 照像馆 99

photography n shè-yǐng 摄影 124

phrase n duǎn-yǔ 短语 13

pick up, to (person) jiē jiē 接 22, 96

picnic n yě-cān 野餐 62

picture (photo) n xiàng (piàn) 像 (片) 79, 124

piece n jiàn 件 19, 31

pig n zhū 猪 104

pigeon n gē-zi 鸽子 49

pill n piàn 片 145; (contraceptive) bì-yùn-yào 避孕药 143

pillow n zhěn-tou 枕头 28

pimento n là-jiāo 辣椒 51

pin n bié-zhēn 别针 121

pineapple n bō-luó 菠萝 56

pink fěn-hóng-sè (de) 粉红色 (的) 112

pipe n yān-dǒu 烟斗 126

pipe cleaner n qīng-xǐ yān-dǒu qì-jù 清洗烟斗器具 126

pipe tobacco n yān-dǒu yān-cǎo 烟斗烟草 126

place n dì-fang 地方 21, 77

place of birth n jí-guàn 籍贯 26

plane n fēi-jī 飞机 65

planetarium n tiān-wén-guǎn 天文馆 80

plantation n zhòng-zhí-yuán 种植园 84

plaster (cast) n shí-gāo 石膏 142

plate n pán-zi 盘子 37, 61

platform (station) n zhàn-tái 站台 67, 68, 69, 70

platinum n bái-jīn 白金 122

play (theatre) n xì-jù 戏剧 87

play, to (theatre) yǎn 演 87; (music) yǎn-zòu 演奏 88; (tennis) dǎ 打 89; (cards) wánr 玩 93

playing card n pū-kè 扑克 106

please qǐng 请 11

plimsolls n qiú-xié 球鞋 118

plug (electric) n chā-tóu 插头 30, 119

plum n lí-zi 李子 56

pneumonia n fèi-yán 肺炎 144

pocket n yī-dài 衣袋 117

pocket calculator n xiù-zhēn jì-suàn-qì 袖珍计算器 106

pocket watch n huái-biǎo 怀表 121

poison n (yǒu) dú (有) 毒 108

police n jǐng-chá 警察 75, 157

police station n gōng-ān-jú 公安局 99, 157

polish (nail) n zhǐ-jiǎ-yóu 指甲油 109

polo-neck gāo-lǐng (de) 高领 (的) 116

pomegranate n shí-liù 石榴 56

pond n chí-táng 池塘 84

poplin n fǔ-chóu 府绸 113

porcelain n xì cí-qì 细瓷器 81, 104, 127

pork n zhū-ròu 猪肉 47

port n mǎ-tou 码头 59

portable xiù-zhēn (de) 袖珍 (的) 119

porter (hotel) n xíng-li-yuán 行李员 27

post, to jì 寄 29

postage n yóu-fèi 邮费 134

postage stamp n yóu-piào 邮票 29, 134

postcard n míng-xìn-piàn 明信片 106, 134

post office n yóu (-diàn) -jú 邮 (电) 局 99, 134

potato n tǔ-dòu 土豆 51, 64

pottery n táo-qì 陶器 127

poultry n qín-lèi 禽类 49

pound (money) n yīng-bàng 英镑 20, 130

powder compact n xiǎo fěn-hé 小粉盒 121

powder puff n fěn-pū 粉扑 110

prawn n duì-xiā 对虾 45

prefer, to (gèng) xǐ-huan (更) 喜欢 101

preference n xǐ-hào 喜好 101

pregnant huái-yùn (le de) 怀孕 (了的) 143

prescribe, to kāi (yào) 开 (药) 145

present n lǐ-wù 礼物 18

prescription n chǔ-fāng 处方 108, 145

press, to (iron) yùn 熨 30

press stud n àn-kòu 接扣 117

price n jià-qián 价钱 132

priest n shén-fù 神父 82

print (engraving) n bǎn-huàr 版画儿 127

private sī-rén (de) 私人 (的) 24, 78, 156

processing n (photo) chōng-xǐ 冲洗 125

product n chǎn-pǐn 产品 133

profession n zhí-yè 职业 26

professional zhuān-yè (de) 专业 (的) 18

profit n lì-rùn 利润 132

programme n (theatre etc...) jié-mù-dān 节目单 87

propelling pencil n zì-dòng qiān-bǐ 自动铅笔 106, 121

Protestant xīn-jiào (de) 新教(的) 82
prune n méi-zi 梅子 56
public holiday n jià-rì 假日 153
pull, to lā 拉 156
pullover n máo-yī 毛衣 116
pumpkin n nán-guā 南瓜 51
purchase n mǎi jìn de huò-pǐn 买进的货品 132
pure chún (de) 纯(的) 113
purple zǐ-sè (de) 紫色(的) 112
push, to tuī 推 156
pyjamas n (yí-tào) shuì-yī (一套) 睡衣 117

Q

quail n ān-chún 鹌鹑 49
quality n zhì-liàng 质量 101, 103, 113
quantity n shù-liàng 数量 15, 103
quarter n sì-fēn-zhī-yī 四分之一 151
question n wèn-huà 问话 12
quick(ly) kuài 快 75, 157; mǎ-shàng 马上 12
quiet ān-jìng (de) 安静(的) 24, 26
quinine tablets n kuí-níng-piàn 奎宁片 108

R

racket (sport) n qiú-pāi 球拍 89
radio (set) n shōu-yīn-jī 收音机 29, 119
radish (white) n bái luó-bo 白萝卜 51; (red) xiǎo luó-bo 小萝卜 51
railway station n huǒ-chē-zhàn 火车站 21, 67
rain n yǔ 雨 94
rain, to xià yǔ 下雨 94
raincoat n yǔ-yī 雨衣 117
rangefinder n cè-jù-qì 测距器 125
rash n zhěn-zi 疹子 141
raspberry n mù-méi 木莓 56
raw shēng (de) 生(的) 113
razor n tì-xū-dāo 剃须刀 110
razor blade n tì-xū dāo-piàn 剃须刀片 110
reading-lamp n tái-dēng 台灯 28
ready hǎo (le) 好(了) 30, 118, 123, 144
receipt n shōu-jù 收据 67, 102, 103, 146
reception (hotel) n jiē-dài (chù) 接待(处) 24
receptionist n jiē-dài-yuán 接待员 27
recommend, to tuī-jiàn 推荐 88, 139, 147; (food) jiè-shào 介绍 36, 37
record (disc) n chàng-piàn 唱片 128

record player n liú-shēng-jī 留声机 119
rectangular cháng-fāng (de) 长方(的) 101
red hóng-sè (de) 红色(的) 59, 106, 112
reduction n jiǎn jià 减价 25, 74
refill (cartridge) n gāng-bǐ-xīn 钢笔芯 106
refund n tuì kuǎn 退款 103
register, to (luggage) tuō-yùn 托运 71
registered mail n guà-hào 挂号 135
registration (hotel) n dēng-jì 登记 26
registration form (hotel) n dēng-jì-biǎo 登记表 26
religious service n (zuò) lǐ-bài (作) 礼拜 82
rent, to zū yòng 租(用) 20, 22, 74, 76, 89, 90, 91, 119
repair, to xiū-lǐ 修理 30, 118, 119, 121, 125, 147
repeat, to zài shuō yí-biàn 再说一遍 13
report, to bào (-gào) 报(告) 157
represent, to dài-biǎo 代表 132
reservation n yù-dìng 预定 20, 24, 65
reserve, to (yù) dìng (预) 订 20, 37
restaurant n fàn-guǎn 饭馆 36, 67; (hotel) cān-tīng 餐厅 20
return, to (give back) huán 还 76
return ticket n wǎng-fǎn-piào 往返票 65
reverse the charges, to ràng duì-fāng fù-fèi 让对方付费 137
rheumatism n fēng-shī 风湿 143
rib n lèi-gǔ 肋骨 140
ribbon n cǎi-dài 彩带 114; (typewriter) dǎ-zì-jī sè-dài 打字机色带 106
rice n mǐ 米 51; (cooked) (mǐ) fàn (米) 饭 54
right yòu (biān) 右(边) 22, 69, 77; (correct) duì 对 11, 15
ring (on finger) n jiè-zhi 戒指 122
ring, to (doorbell) àn-líng 按铃 156
river n hé 河 74, 80, 84, 90
road n lù 路 84
rock n (yán) shí (岩) 石 81
roll n xiǎo yuán-miàn-bāo 小圆面包 39, 64
room n fáng-jiān 房间 20, 24, 25, 26, 27, 28, 29
room number n fáng-jiān-hào 房间号 27

room service n qīng-sǎo zhěng-lǐ fú-wù 清扫整理服务 24
round yuán (de) 圆 (的) 101
round neck yuán-lǐng (de) 圆领 (的) 116
roundtrip ticket n wǎng-fǎn-piào 往返票 65
rowing boat n yǒu-chuán 游船 74, 91
rubber (material) n xiàng-jiāo 橡胶 118; (eraser) xiàng-pí 橡皮 106
rubber band n xiàng-pí-jīnr 橡皮筋儿 106
rubbings n tà-piàn 拓片 127
ruby n hóng-bǎo-shí 红宝石 122
rucksack n fān-bù bēi-bāo 帆布背包 120
rug n xiǎo dì-tǎn 小地毯 127
ruin n jiù-zhǐ 旧址 80
ruler (for measuring) n chǐ-zi 尺子 106
running water n zì-lái-shuǐ 自来水 24

S

safe (not dangerous) ān-quán 安全 91
safe n bǎo-xiǎn-xiāng 保险箱 27
safety pin n bié-zhēn 别针 110
sailing boat n fān-chuán 帆船 91
sale n mài chū de huò-pǐn 卖出的货品 132
salt n yán 盐 38, 39, 64
salty xián 咸 61
sample n yàng-pǐn 样品 114, 133
sandal n liáng-xié 凉鞋 118
sandwich n sān-míng-zhì 三明治 64
sanitary towel/napkin n fù-nǚ wèi-shēng-jīn 妇女卫生巾 108
sapphire n lán-bǎo-shí 蓝宝石 122
satin n duàn-zi 缎子 113
Saturday n xīng-qī-liù 星期六 153
scald, to tàng shāng 烫伤 141
scalp n tóu-pí 头皮 140
scallop n shàn-bèi 扇贝 45
scarf n wéi-jīn 围巾 117
scarlet xiān hóng-sè (de) 鲜红色 (的) 112
scenic route n fēng-jǐng hǎo de lù 风景好的路 84
scissors n jiǎn-dāo 剪刀 120
scrambled egg n chǎo-jī-dàn 炒鸡蛋 39
screwdriver n gǎi-zhuī 改锥 120
scroll n juàn-zhóu 卷轴 104, 127
sculptor n diāo-sù-jiā 雕塑家 82

sculpture n diāo-sù 雕塑 81
sea n hǎi 海 24, 84, 91
seafood n hǎi-xiān 海鲜 45
seam n jiē-fèng 接缝 114
season n jì (jié) 季 (节) 152
seasoning n tiáo-liào 调料 38, 53
seat n zuò-wèi 座位 69, 70, 87
second dì-èr 第二 77, 151
second n miǎo 秒 155
second class n èr-děng 二等 74
second hand n biǎo-zhēn 秒针 122
second-hand jiù (de) 旧 (的) 105
secretary n mì-shū 秘书 28, 133
see, to kàn 看 13, 25, 81; (meet) jiàn-miàn 见面 96
sell, to mài 卖 100, 132
send, to (goods) fā huò 发货 133; (post) jì 寄 102, 103, 134, 135, 147
sentence n jù (zi) 句 (子) 13
September n jiǔ-yuè 九月 152
serious (injury) (yán) zhòng (de) (严) 重 (的) 141
service n fú-wù 服务 100; (religion) (zuò) lǐ-bài (作) 礼拜 82
serviette n cān-jīn 餐巾 37
setting lotion n lěng-tàng-shuǐ 冷烫水 110
seven qī 七 149
seventeen shí-qī 十七 149
seventh dì-qī 第七 151
seventy qī-shí 七十 150
sew, to féng 缝 30
shade (colour) n sè (diào) 色 (调) 112
shampoo n xǐ-fà-jì 洗发剂 31, 110
shampoo and set n xǐ tóu hé zuò fà 洗头和做发 31
shape n yàng-zi 样子 103
share (finance) n gǔ-fèn 股份 132
shave, to guā liǎn 刮脸 32
shaver n diàn-dòng tì-xū-dāo 电动剃须刀 27, 119
shaving brush n tì xū féi-zào-shuā 剃须肥皂刷 110
shaving soap n tì xū zào-yè 剃须皂液 110
she tā 她 161
ship n lún-chuán 轮船 74
shipment n yì-pī huò 一批货 133
shirt n chèn-shān 衬衫 114, 117
shivery fā-lěng 发冷 142
shoe n xié 鞋 118
shoelace n xié-dài 鞋带 118
shoemaker's n bǔ-xié-diàn 补鞋店 99

shoe polish *n* xié-yóu 鞋油 118
shoe shop *n* xié-diàn 鞋店 99
shop *n* shāng-diàn 商店 99
shopping area *n* shāng-yè-qū 商业区 80, 100
shopping centre *n* shāng-chǎng 商场 99
shop window *n* chú-chuāng 橱窗 100
short duǎn (de) 短 15, 31, 116, 117
shorts *n* duǎn-kù 短裤 117
short-sighted jìn-shi (yǎn de) 近视(眼 的) 123
shoulder *n* jiān-bǎng 肩膀 140
shoulder blade *n* jiān-jiǎ-gǔ 肩胛骨 140
shovel (toy) *n* xiǎo chǎn-zi 小铲子 128
show, to ràng...kàn-kàn 让...看看 14, 124; gěi...kàn-kàn 给...看看 100, 101
shower *n* lín-yù 淋浴 24, 27
shrimp *n* xiā 虾 45, 53
shrink, to suō (xiǎo) 缩（小）113
shut guān (de) 关(的) 15
shutter (camera) *n* kuài-mén 快门 125
sideboards/burns *n* liǎng-cè de hú-zi 两侧的胡子 32
sightseeing *n* yóu-lǎn 游览 78
sign (notice) *n* zhǐ-shì biāo-jì 指示标 记 156
sign, to qiān míng 签名 26, 131
signature *n* qiān-míng 签名 26
silk *n* sī-chóu 丝绸 113, 127
silk factory *n* sī-chóu-chǎng 丝绸厂 81
silk painting *n* juàn-huà 绢画 81
silver (colour) yín-huī-sè (de) 银灰色 (的) 112
silver *n* yín 银 121, 122
silver-plated dù-yín (de) 镀银(的) 122
silverware *n* yín-qì 银器 122
simple jiǎn-dān de 简单的 124
since cóng 从 16
single (not married) méi-yǒu jié-hūn (de) 没有结婚(的) 93
single room *n* dān-rén fáng-jiān 单人 房间 20, 24
single ticket *n* dān-chéng-piào 单程 票 65
sister (older) *n* jiě-jie 姐姐 93; (younger) mèi-mei 妹妹 93
sit, to zuò 坐 95
six liù 六 149

sixteen shí-liù 十六 149
sixth dì-liù 第六 151
sixty liù-shí 六十 150
size (format) *n* xíng-hào 型号 124; (clothes) chǐ-cùn 尺寸 115
skate *n* bīng-xié 冰鞋 90
skating *n* huá bīng 滑冰 89
skating rink *n* huá-bīng-chǎng 滑冰 场 90
skin *n* pí-fū 皮肤 140
skin-diving *n* qián-shuǐ 潜水 91
skirt *n* qún-zi 裙子 114, 117
sky *n* tiān-kōng 天空 94
sleep, to shuì 睡 146
sleeping car *n* wò-pù chē-xiāng 卧铺 车厢 68, 69, 70
sleeping pill *n* ān-mián-yào 安眠药 145
sleeve *n* xiù-zi 袖子 114, 117, 144
slice *n* piàn 片 120
slip *n* chèn-qún 衬裙 117
slipper *n* tuō-xié 拖鞋 118
slow màn (de) 慢(的) 15, 155
slowly màn diānr (de) 慢点儿(的) 13, 22, 137
small xiǎo (de) 小 (的) 15, 25, 61, 101, 115, 118
small change *n* líng-qián 零钱 131
smoke, to xī yān 吸烟 67, 95
snack *n* xiǎo-chī 小吃 62
snap fastener *n* àn-kòu 按扣 117
sneakers *n* qiú-xié 球鞋 118
snow *n* xuě 雪 94
snow, to xià xuě 下雪 94
snuff *n* bí-yān 鼻烟 126
snuff bottle *n* bí-yān-hú 鼻烟壶 104
soap *n* féi-zào 肥皂 28, 110
soccer *n* zú-qiú 足球 89
sock *n* wà-zi 袜子 117
socket (outlet) *n* chā-zuò 插座 27
soft ruǎn (de) 软(的) 123
soft drink *n* bú dài jiǔ-jīng de yǐn-liào 不带酒精的饮料 64
soft-boiled (egg) (zhǔ) nèn de (煮) 嫩的 39
soft seating (train) *n* ruǎn-zuò 软座 69
soft sleeping (train) *n* ruǎn-wò 软卧 69
sole *n* xié-dǐ 鞋底 118; (fish) tǎ-yú 鳎鱼 45
soloist (musician) *n* dú-zòu yǎn-yuán 独奏演员 88
some yì-xiē 一些 15

son n ér-zi 儿子 93

soon hěn kuài jiù 很快就 16

sore throat n sǎng-zi-téng 嗓子疼 143

sorry! duì-bu-qǐ 对不起 12

sort (kind) n zhǒng 种 87

soup n tāng 汤 44

south n nán 南 77

souvenir n jì-niàn-pǐn 纪念品 126

souvenir shop n lǚ-yóu jì-niàn-pǐn shāng-diàn 旅游纪念品商店 99

soy sauce n jiàng-yóu 酱油 38, 53, 64

spade (toy) n xiǎo chǎn-zi 小铲子 128

sparkling (wine) dài qì de 带汽的 59

speak, to shuō 说 13, 137

speaker (loudspeaker) n yáng-shēng-qì 扬声器 119

special tè-bié de 特别的 38

special delivery kuài-dì 快递 135

spectacles n yǎn-jìng 眼镜 123

spectacle case n yǎn-jìng-hé 眼镜盒 123

spice n zuó-liào 作料 53, 127

spicy hòu-wèir de 厚味儿的 38

spinach n bō-cài 菠菜 51

spine n jǐ-zhuī 脊椎 140

spleen n pí pérá 脾 140

sponge n hǎi-mián 海绵 110

spoon n sháo-zi 勺子 37, 61

sport tǐ-yù yùn-dòng 体育运动 89

sporting goods shop n tǐ-yù yòng-pǐn shāng-diàn 体育用品商店 99

sports jacket n yùn-dòng-shān 运动衫 117

sprain, to niǔ-shāng 扭伤 142

spring n chūn (tiān) 春(天) 152; (water) quán 泉 84

spring onion n cōng 葱 51, 53

squab n chú-gē 雏鸽 49

square fāng n 方 101

square n guǎng-chǎng 广场 80

squid n yóu-yú 鱿鱼 45

stadium n tǐ-yù-chǎng 体育场 80

stain n wū-diǎn 污点 30

stainless steel n bú-xiù-gāng 不锈钢 122

stalls (theatre) n lóu-xià 楼下 87

stamp (postage) n yóu-piào 邮票 29, 134

staple n shū-dīng 书钉 106

star n xīng-xing 星星 94

starter (appetizer) n liáng-cài pīn-pánr 凉菜拼盘儿 42

station (rail) n (huǒ-chē) zhàn (火车) 站 21, 67, 70, 73

stationer's n wén-jù-diàn 文具店 99, 105

stationery n wén-jù 文具 105

statistics n tǒng-jì (shù-zì) 统计(数字) 133

statue n diāo-xiàng 雕像 80

stay, to zhù 住 25, 93; tíng-liú 停留 17

steal, to tōu 偷 157

steamed qīng-zhēng (de) 清蒸 41

stiff neck n bó-zi fā yìng 脖子发硬 143

still (mineral water) bú dài qì de 不带汽的 60

sting, to zhē 蜇 141

stir-fried bào-chǎo (de) 爆炒(的) 41

stitch, to féng (bǔ) 缝(补) 30, 118

stocking n cháng-wà 长袜 117

stomach n wèi 胃 140

stomach ache n wèi téng 胃疼 143

stools n dà-biàn 大便 144

stop! zhàn zhù 站住 157

stop, to tíng (xià) 停(下) 22, 68, 70, 72

stop thief! zhuā zéi 抓贼 157

store (shop) n shāng-diàn 商店 98

straight (drink) chún de 纯的 58

straight ahead yì-zhí 一直 22, 77

strange qí-guài 奇怪 82

strawberry n cǎo-méi 草莓 56

street n jiē (dào) 街(道) 26, 77

streetcar n diàn-chē 电车 72

street map n jiāo-tōng-tú 交通图 21

string n shéng-zi 绳子 106

strong lì-hai (de) 厉害(的) 145; (cigarette) yǒu jìn de 有劲的 126

student n xué-sheng 学生 17, 20, 79, 93

student hostel n zhuān-mén jiē-dài xué-sheng de lǚ-guǎn 专门接待学生的旅馆 20

study, to xué (xí) 学(习) 93

sturdy jiē-shi (de) 结实(的) 101

subway (rail) n dì-tiě 地铁 73

suede n fān-máo-pí 翻毛皮 113, 118

sugar n táng 糖 38, 64

sugar cane n gān-zhe 甘蔗 56

suit n yí-tào xī-fú 一套西服 117

suitcase n xiāng-zi 箱子 19

summer n xià (tiān) 夏(天) 152

Summer Palace n yí-hé-yuán 颐和园 81

sun n tài-yáng 太阳 94

sunburn *n* shài-shāng 晒伤 107
Sunday *n* xīng-qī-tiān 星期天 79, 153; xīng-qī-rì 星期日 153
sunglasses *n* mò-jìng 墨镜 123
sunshade *(beach)* *n* zhē-yáng-sǎn 遮阳伞 91
sunstroke *n* zhòng-shǔ 中暑 143
sun-tan cream *n* shài-hēi-gāo 晒黑膏 110
sun-tan oil *n* shài-hēi-yóu 晒黑油 110
supermarket *n* zì-xuǎn shāng-chǎng 自选商场 99
supervisor *n* fù-zé-rén 负责人 27
suppository *n* shuān-jì 检剂 108
surgery *(consulting room)* *n* wài-kē mén-zhěn 外科门诊 138
suspenders *(Am.)* *n* bēi-dài 背带 117
swallow, to tūn-fú 吞服 145
swamp *n* zhǎo-zé 沼泽 84
sweater *n* máo-yī 毛衣 117
sweatshirt *n* cháng-xiù yùn-dòng-shān 长袖运动衫 117
sweet *(food)* tián (de) 甜(的) 59, 61
sweet pepper *n* shì-zi-jiāo 柿子椒 51
swell, to zhǒng 肿 141
swelling *n* (hóng) zhǒng (红)肿 141
swim, to yóu-yǒng 游泳 90
swimming *n* yóu-yǒng 游泳 89, 91
swimming pool *n* yóu-yǒng-chí 游泳池 90
swimming trunks *n* yóu-yǒng-kù 游泳裤 117
swimsuit *n* yóu-yǒng-yī 游泳衣 117
switch *n* kāi-guān 开关 30
switchboard operator *n* jiē-xiàn-yuán 接线员 27
swollen zhǒng le 肿了 141
synagogue *n* yóu-tài jiào-táng 犹太教堂 82
synthetic rén-zào (de) 人造(的) 113
system *n* xì-tǒng 系统 140

T
table *n* zhuō-zi 桌子 37
tablet *n* piàn 片 108
table-tennis *n* bīng-bāng-qiú 乒乓球 89, 90
tailor's *n* cái-feng-diàn 裁缝店 99
take, to *(carry)* bān 搬 19
take away, to dài-zǒu 带走 102
take off, to qǐ-fēi 起飞 65
talcum powder *n* shuāng-shēn-fěn 爽身粉 110
tangerine *n* jú-zi 桔子 56

Taoist temple *n* dào-guàn 道观 81
tap *(water)* *n* shuǐ-lóng-tóu 水龙头 29
tape recorder *n* cí-dài lù-yīn-jī 磁带录音机 119
tax *n* shuì 税 133
taxi *n* chū-zū qì-chē 出租汽车 20, 21, 32, 67
taxi booking-office *n* chū-zū qì-chē-zhàn 出租汽车站 20
tea *n* chá 茶 39, 60, 64, 127
tea cup *n* chá-bēi 茶杯 127
tea pot *n* chá-hú 茶壶 127
team *n* duì 队 90
teaspoon *n* tāng-chí 汤匙 145
telegram *n* diàn-bào 电报 135
telephone *n* diàn-huà 电话 29, 136
telephone, to dǎ diàn-huà 打电话 136
telephone directory *n* diàn-huà-bù 电话簿 136
telephone number *n* diàn-huà hào-mǎ 电话号码 96, 136, 137
telephoto lens *n* wàng-yuǎn jìng-tóu 望远镜头 125
television *(set)* *n* diàn-shì-jī 电视机 29, 119
telex *n* diàn-chuán 电传 135
telex, to fā diàn-chuán 发电传 131
tell, to gào-su 告诉 14, 73, 77, 137
temperature *n* wēn (dù) 温(度) 90; *(body)* tǐ-wēn 体温 142, 144
Temple of Heaven *n* tiān-tán 天坛 81
ten shí 十 148
tendon *n* jī-jiàn 肌腱 140
tennis *n* wǎng-qiú 网球 89
tennis court *n* wǎng-qiú-chǎng 网球场 89
tenth dì-shí 第十 151
term *(word)* *n* shù-yǔ 术语 132
terminus *n* zhōng-diǎn-zhàn 终点站 72
tetanus *n* pò-shāng-fēng 破伤风 142
textile *n* fǎng-zhī 纺织 133
Thailand *n* tài-guó 泰国 148
thank you xiè-xie 谢谢 10, 11
that nà 那 12, 100
theatre *n* jù-cháng 剧场 80, 87
theft *n* tōu-qiè (-àn) 偷窃(案) 157
then *(before)* rán-hòu 然后 16
there nàr 那儿 15
thermometer *n* tǐ-wēn-biǎo 体温表 108, 146
they tā-mén 他们 161
thick hòu (de) 厚(的) 113
thief *n* zéi 贼 157

DICTIONARY

thigh n dà-tuǐ 大腿 140
thin báo (de) 薄(的) 113
think, to jué-de 觉得 93, 94
third dì-sān 第三 151
third sān-fēn-zhī-yī 三分之一 151
third class n sān-děng 三等 74
thirsty, to be kě le 渴了 14, 36
thirteen shí-sān 十三 149
thirty sān-shí 三十 149
this zhè 这 12, 100
thousand yì-qiān 一千 150
thread n xiàn 线 28
three sān 三 149
throat n sǎng-zi 嗓子 140
throat lozenge n hóu-lóng hán-piàn 喉咙含片 108
through jīng-guò 经过 16
through train n zhí-dá liè-chē 直达列车 69
thumb n mǔ-zhǐ 拇指 140
thumbtack n tú-dīng 图钉 106
thunder n léi 雷 94
thunderstorm n bào-fēng-yǔ 暴风雨 94
Thursday n xīng-qī-sì 星期四 153
ticket n piào 票 87, 90; (plane) jī-piào 机票 65; (bus, train) chē-piào 车票 69
ticket office n shòu-piào-chù 售票处 20, 67
tide n cháo 潮 91
tie n lǐng-dài 领带 117
tie clip n lǐng-dài jiā-zi 领带夹子 122
tie pin n lǐng-dài bié-zhēn 领带别针 122
tight (clothes) jǐn 紧 116
tights n kù-wà 裤袜 117
time n shí-jiān 时间 68; (clock) diǎn 点 155; (occasion) cì 次 145
timetable (train) n liè-chē shí-kè-biǎo 列车时刻表 68
tin (can) n guàn-tou 罐头 120
tin opener n kāi-guàn-qì 开罐器 64, 120
tinted zhuó-sè (de) 着色(的) 123
tired lèi le 累了 14
tissue (handkerchief) n zhǐ-shǒu-juànr 纸手绢 110
to xiàng 向 16
toast n kǎo miàn-bāo-piàn 烤面包片 39
tobacco n yān-cǎo 烟草 126
today jīn-tiān 今天 153
toe n jiǎo-zhǐ 脚趾 140

toilet (lavatory) n cè-suǒ 厕所 24, 28, 29, 38, 67
toilet paper n wèi-shēng-zhǐ 卫生纸 110
toiletry n guàn-xǐ wèi-shēng yòng-pǐn 盥洗卫生用品 109
toilet water n shuǎng-shēn xiāng-shuǐ 爽身香水 110
tomato n xī-hóng-shì 西红柿 51, 64, 120
tomb n líng-mù 陵墓 80
tomorrow míng-tiān 明天 30, 76, 94, 153
tongue n shé-tou 舌头 140
tonic water n kuí-níng-shuǐ 奎宁水 60
tonight jīn-wǎn 今晚 30, 87, 96
tonsil n biǎn-táo-xiàn 扁桃腺 140
too tài 太 15, 25, 101, 118; (also) yě 也 16
tooth n yá 牙 147
toothache n yá-téng 牙疼 147
toothbrush n yá-shuā 牙刷 110
toothpaste n yá-gāo 牙膏 110
toothpick n yá-qiān 牙签 38
top n dǐng (bù) 顶(部) 32
topaz n huáng-yù 黄玉 122
torch (flashlight) n shǒu-diàn-tǒng 手电筒 120
touch, to chù-mō 触摸 156
tour n yóu-lǎn lù-xiàn 游览路线 78
towards xiàng 向 76
towel n máo-jīn 毛巾 27
towelling n máo-jīn-bù 毛巾布 113
tower n tǎ 塔 80
town n chéng 城 20; shì 市 76
town centre n shì-zhōng-xīn 市中心 21
toy n wán-jù 玩具 127, 128
toy shop n wán-jù-diàn 玩具店 99
tracksuit n yí-tào yùn-dòng-shān 一套运动衫 117
traffic light n hóng-lǜ-dēng 红绿灯 77
train n liè-chē 列车 68, 69, 70, 73
tram (streetcar) n diàn-chē 电车 72
tranquillizer n zhèn-jìng-yào 镇静药 145
transfer (bank) n zhuǎn-zhàng 转账 132
transformer n biàn-yā-qì 变压器 119
translate, to fān-yì 翻译 13
translator n fān-yì 翻译 133
transport n jiāo-tōng 交通 76
travel, to lǚ-xíng 旅行 92

词汇表

travel agency n lǚ-xíng-shè 旅行社 99

travel guide n lǚ-yóu zhǐ-nán 旅游指南 106

traveller's cheque n lǚ-xíng zhī-piào 旅行支票 20, 62, 102, 130

travelling bag n lǚ-xíng-dài 旅行袋 19

travel sickness n yùn-chē 晕车 107

treatment n zhì-liáo 治疗 145

tree n shù 树 84

trim, to xiū-jiǎn 修剪 32

trip n lǚ-xíng 旅行 154

trolley n shǒu-tuī-chē 手推车 19, 71

trousers n cháng-kù 长裤 117

try, to shì 试 115

T-shirt n zhēn-zhī chèn-shān 针织衬衫 117

tube n tǒng 筒 110

Tuesday n xīng-qī-èr 星期二 153

turkey n huǒ-jī 火鸡 49

turn, to (change direction) guǎi (wān) 拐(弯) 22, 77

turquoise qīng-lǜ-sè (de) 青绿色(的) 112

turquoise n lǜ-sōng-shí 绿松石 122

turtle-neck gāo-lǐng (de) 高领(的) 116

tweezers n niè-zi 镊子 110

twelve shí-èr 十二 149

twenty èr-shí 二十 149

twice liǎng cì 两次 151

twin beds n liǎng-zhāng dān-rén-chuáng 两张单人床 24

two èr 二 149

typewriter n dǎ-zì-jī 打字机 20

typewriter ribbon n dǎ-zì-jī sè-dài 打字机色带 106

typing paper n dǎ-zì-zhǐ 打字纸 106

U

ugly nán-kàn 难看 15

ulcer n wèi-kuì-yáng 胃溃疡 143

umbrella n yǔ-sǎn 雨伞 117; (beach) zhē-yáng-sǎn 遮阳伞 91

unconscious hūn guo qu le 昏过去了 141

under zài...xià miàn 在…下面 16

underdone (meat) méi shóu 没熟 61

underground (rail) n dì-tiě 地铁 73

underpants n nán-nèi-kù 男内裤 117

undershirt n bèi-xīn 背心 117

understand, to dǒng 懂 13

undress, to tuō (yī) 脱(衣) 144

United States n měi-guó 美国 148

university n dà-xué 大学 80

until (zhí) dào (直)到 16

upper shàng (céng de) 上(层的) 69

upset stomach n fǎn-wèi 反胃 107

upstairs lóu-shàng 楼上 16

urgent jǐn-jí (de) 紧急(的) 14

urine n niào 尿 144

use, to yòng 用 135

usual (tōng) cháng de (通)常的 145

V

vacancy n kōng fáng-jiān 空房间 24

vacant méi rén 没人 15

vacation n jià-qī 假期 153

vaccinate, to zhù-shè yù-fáng yì-miáo 注射预防疫苗 142

vaccination n yù-fáng zhù-shè 预防注射 17

vacuum flask n nuǎn-shuǐ-píng 暖水瓶 120

valley n shān-gǔ 山谷 84

value n jià-zhí 价值 132

vegetable n shū-cài 蔬菜 51, 52

vegetable store n shū-cài-diàn 蔬菜店 99

vegetarian sù (de) 素(的) 38

vein n jìng-mài 静脉 140

velvet n tiān-é-róng 天鹅绒 113

venereal disease n xìng-bìng 性病 144

vermouth n wèi-měi-sī 味美思 58

very hěn 很 16

vest n bèi-xīn 背心 117; (Am.) xī-fú kǎn-jiān 西服坎肩 117

veterinarian n shòu-yī 兽医 99

video camera n shè-xiàng-jī 摄像机 124

video cassette n lù-xiàng-dài 录像带 119, 124

video recorder n lù-xiàng-jī 录像机 119

Vietnam n yuè-nán 越南 148

view n hǎo-kàn de fēng-jǐng 好看的风景 24, 26

village n cūn-zhuāng 村庄 84

vinegar n cù 醋 38

vineyard n pú-tao-yuán 葡萄园 84

visa n qiān-zhèng 签证 17

visiting hours n tàn-shì shí-jiān 探视时间 146

V-neck jī-xīn-lǐng (de) 鸡心领(的) 117

vodka n fú-tè-jiā 伏特加 58

volleyball n pái-qiú 排球 89

voltage n diàn-yā 电压 28

vomit, to ǒu-tù 呕吐 142

DICTIONARY

词汇表

W

waist n yāo 腰 114
waistcoat n xī-fú kǎn-jiān 西服坎肩 117
wait, to děng 等 22, 95, 108
waiter n fú-wù-yuán 服务员 37
waiting room (station) n hòu-chē-shì 候车室 67; (airport) hòu-jī-shì 候机室 65
waitress n fú-wù-yuán 服务员 37
wake, to jiào-xǐng 叫醒 27, 70
Wales n wēi-ěr-shì 威尔士 148
wallet n qián-bāo 钱包 157
walnut n hé-tao 核桃 56
want, to (xiǎng-) yào (想)要 20, 101, 112, 123
warm rè (de) 热(的) 94
wash, to xǐ 洗 30
washbasin n shuǐ-chí-zi 水池子 29
watch n biǎo 表 121, 122
watchmaker's n zhōng-biǎo-diàn 钟表店 99, 121
watchstrap n biǎo-dài 表带 122
water n shuǐ 水 24, 34, 90
waterfall n pù-bù 瀑布 84
water flask n shuǐ-hú 水壶 120
watermelon n xī-guā 西瓜 56
water ski n huá-shuǐ-bǎn 滑水板 91
wave n làng 浪 91
way (road) n lù 路 77
weather n tiān-qì 天气 94
weather forecast n tiān-qì yù-bào 天气预报 94
wedding ring n jié-hūn jiè-zhǐ 结婚戒指 122
Wednesday n xīng-qī-sān 星期三 153
week n xīng-qī 星期 17, 22, 25, 153
weekend n zhōu-mò 周末 153
well (healthy) hěn hǎo 很好 11
west n xī 西 77
Western xī (fāng de) 西(方的) 108
Western-style xī (shì de) 西(式的) 39
what shén-me 什么 12
when (date) jǐ hào 几号 12; (time) jǐ diǎn 几点 12
where nǎr 哪儿 12
which nǎ-ge 哪个 12
whisky n wēi-shì-jì 威士忌 18, 58
white bái-sè (de) 白色(的) 112
who shéi 谁 12
why wèi-shén-me 为什么 12
wick n dēng-xīn 灯芯 126
wide kuān (de) 宽(的) 101

wide-angle lens n guǎng-jiǎo jìng-tóu 广角镜头 125
wife n qī-zi 妻子 93
wig n jiǎ-fà 假发 110
wild boar n yě-zhū 野猪 49
wind n fēng 风 94
window n chuāng-hù 窗户 29, 37; (shop) chú-chuāng 橱窗 111
wine n pú-tao-jiǔ 葡萄酒 64
winter n dōng (tiān) 冬(天) 152
with (thing) yǒu 有 16; (person) gēn...yi-qǐ 跟……一起 16
withdraw, to (bank) qǔ 取 131
without méi-yǒu 没有 16
woman n fù-nǚ 妇女 163
wood (forest) n shù-lín 树林 84
wool n chún-máo 纯毛 113
word n cí 词 13
work n gōng-zuò 工作 93
working day n gōng-zuò-rì 工作日 153
worse gèng huài le 更坏了 15
wound n shāng-kǒu 伤口 141
wrap, to bāo 包 103
wrapping paper n bāo-zhuāng-zhǐ 包装纸 106
wrist n shǒu-wàn 手腕 140
wristwatch n shǒu-biǎo 手表 122
write, to xiě 写 13, 101, 132
writing pad n pāi-zhǐ-bù 拍纸簿 106
writing paper n xìn-zhǐ 信纸 28
wrong cuò (de) 错(的) 15

X

X-ray (photo) n x guāng piān-zi X光片子 142

Y

year n nián 年 151
yellow huáng-sè (de) 黄色(的) 112
yes duì 对, shì 是 11
yesterday zuó-tiān 昨天 153
yoghurt n suān-nǎi 酸奶 39, 64
you nǐ 你; (pl) nǐ-mén 你们 161
young nián-qīng (de) 年轻(的) 15

Z

zero líng 零 149
zip (per) n lā-suǒ 拉锁 117
zoo n dòng-wù-yuán 动物园 73, 80
zoology n dòng-wù-xué 动物学 81

汉语索引